Negotiating Cultures and Identities

Negotiating Cultures
and Identities
Life History Issues, Methods,
and Readings

John L. Caughey

University of Nebraska Press
Lincoln

Portions of Part 1 of this book have been previously
published in different form. Parts of Chapter 2
appeared as "How to Teach Self Ethnography," in
Strategies for Teaching Anthropology, ed. Patricia C. Rice
and David W. McCurdy, 174–80 (Upper Saddle River
NJ: Prentice Hall, 2002). Parts of Chapter 4
appeared as "Gina as Steven: The Social and Cultural
Dimensions of a Media Relationship," *Visual Anthropology Review* 10, no. 1 (1994): 126–35. Copyright
1994 by the American Anthropological Association.
Reprinted from *Visual Anthropology Review* by permission of the University of California Press.

Typeset in Quadraat fonts by Bob Reitz. Book design
by R. Eckersley.

Library of Congress Cataloging-in-Publication Data
Caughey, John L., 1941–
Negotiating cultures and identities: life history
issues, methods, and readings / John L. Caughey.
p.   cm.
Includes bibliographical references and index.
ISBN-13: 978-0-8032-6466-3 (pbk.: alk. paper)
ISBN-10: 0-8032-6466-6 (pbk.: alk. paper)
1. Ethnology—Methodology.   I. Title.
GN345.C39   2006
305.80072—dc22
2006008013

To my teachers and students

Contents

Exercises

Preface

Meeting a stranger, we may wonder: Who is this person before us, what is her life like, how does she feel, think about, and experience her world? This book is about seeking to answer such questions culturally. It is about understanding others and ourselves though exploring how we negotiate the multiplicity of cultural meanings at play in our lives. Studies of culture are usually oriented toward groups, institutions, or societies. They typically lose much of their power to explain individual lives through reliance on generalizations about the allegedly shared cultural orientations of sets of people in a specific group or community. However, the cultural dimensions of any life are always intricate and complex, and much can be learned by shifting our attention from groups to individuals. To do so we need to suspend the psychological theories so favored in this society and seek to understand American lives culturally, that is, to engage in life history research or ethnography that is centered on individual people.

I believe we can learn interesting and important things about individuals and cultures by talking with people about their lives and observing them in action. Many of the useful complications that postmodern thinking has introduced into ethnographic work are incorporated into the approach developed here, but there is also a definite "realist" tinge to this presentation. When we venture out of the library and engage with individuals whose lives are different from our own, interesting, important, and, I believe, accurate cultural understandings can result. I also think that attention to race, gender, ethnicity, class, disability, and sexual orientation can be significantly advanced by careful ethnographic investigation of how the cultural dimensions of these always culturally constructed and culturally variable *concepts* are actually experienced by particular individuals in particular social contexts.

Intended to result in a double (two-person) cultural biography, the method proposed here requires that you, the researcher, conduct a cultural investigation of another person and, simultaneously, a cultural investigation of yourself. This book is a how-to guide to self-ethnography as well as to the ethnographic study of another person. The comparison between one's own life and someone else's sheds important light on the cultural dimensions of both lives as well as on the cultural nature of the issues with which all individual humans struggle.

The book is divided into two sections. Part One explores issues and methods in conducting life history research. In the Introduction I provide an account of a bicultural Asian American woman and the implications her experiences have for the study of other American lives. In Chapter 1, I explain the general approach to life history that I will be developing, offer two more examples of individuals who operate with multiple cultural traditions, explore the nature and contents of cultural traditions, and consider the kinds of relationships we develop with our traditions. In Chapter 2, I describe the steps involved in carrying out an ethnographic investigation of the cultural dimensions of one's own life and that of another person. Here I discuss ways to adapt ethnographic interviewing and participant observation to the study of individual lives. I also review ethical issues, note taking, and interpretation. In Chapter 3, I discuss identity and role analysis, the importance of the misunderstandings and "rich points" that emerge in the encounter between researcher and participant, and the use of identification as a method in life history. In Chapter 4, I show how individuals must deal with conflicts among the values of their various traditions and I explore the strategies we employ to mediate these conflicts, including the use of media consumption, dreams, and interior dialogues. In Chapter 5, I discuss the issues involved in representing individual lives and offer strategies for writing a double life history portrait. I pay special attention throughout to the ways in which contemporary Americans negotiate multiple cultural traditions. Part Two contains a brief introduction and nine life histories. Written by students as well as professional ethnographers, these accounts explore how individual Americans handle their complex cultural situations. These life histories illustrate many of the issues raised in Part One and provide a variety of models for conducting and writing life history portraits. The book concludes with an annotated bibliography of suggestions for further reading.

The approach I present here is suitable for use in upper-level undergraduate or lower-level graduate courses in Life History, Ethnography, American Studies, Anthropology, Sociology, Women's Studies, and other forms of culture studies, especially those that require students to carry out interviews or engage in participant observation. I have developed this approach in undergraduate and graduate fieldwork courses on life history in American Studies and Anthropology and also in classes on other topics where an interview project was one of several assignments. A fieldwork assignment is helpful when addressing cultural topics such as immigration, consumerism, media studies, religion, material culture studies, ethnic studies, women's studies, and disability studies, since classroom work can be supplemented by asking students to interview someone whose life is pertinent to the subject of study. In most cases it is not feasible to ask students to investigate a community or institution, but it is often quite practical and very illuminating to ask them to interview a single individual. I hope this book will also be helpful to those who want to conduct life history research on their own, outside an academic setting. But I have found that pursuing this type of work in a class or other working group is particularly beneficial because we learn so much from discussing research methods, questions, problems, and experiences with others who are similarly engaged.

Acknowledgments

For help in thinking about individuals and their cultures I would like to thank, first, the people with whom I have done life history. This includes members of the Old Order Mennonite community in Pennsylvania, islanders of Chuuk in Micronesia, Sufis in the Margalla Hills of Pakistan, and several staff members and clients on the psychiatric ward of Philadelphia General Hospital. I would especially like to thank, Gina and Claire, the psychotherapists with whom I engaged in life history research in Washington DC. I am also grateful to my anthropology teachers, especially Ruben Reina, who taught the fieldwork course that I took in 1967 when I was a graduate student at the University of Pennsylvania, and Ward Goodenough, Tony Wallace, Olga Linnares, Igor Kopytoff, and A. I. Hallowell, all of whom helped me think about culture and life history. Many field-working colleagues have influenced me through their writings or conversations, and here I would like to especially thank Michael Agar, Erve Chambers, Jay Mechling, Rich Horwitz, Sandi Patton-Imani, Jenny Thompson, Elizabeth Clark-Lewis, Melissa Landsman, Joshua Woodfork, Susan Leonardi, Janice Radway, and Sharon O'Brien. I would also like to thank my colleagues in the Life Writing Project, a working group at the University of Maryland, as well as the College of Arts and Humanities and The Consortium on Race, Gender, and Ethnicity, which provided grants to this writing group. I would also like to thank my wife, Patricia, and my daughter, Ananda, for their patience with this project. Finally, I am especially indebted to students in my classes on life history and ethnography at the University of Maryland, who have taught me so much about the method, interest, and meaning of this kind of research.

PART ONE

Issues and Methods in Life History

Introduction

SALMA'S STORIES

Because this book is about the cultural study of individuals, I want to begin with the description of a particular life. Much of the traditional and even contemporary discussion of individuals in cultural studies still involves the assumption that individuals know, think, feel, speak, and act with *one* culture, the culture of the community or society to which they belong. While sometimes useful, such a perspective seriously obscures the issues that we will investigate in this book.

Consider Salma. When I met her several years ago, she was a twenty-one-year-old student at the University of Maryland. Born in Pakistan, tall and graceful, she "looked South Asian" and was a Pakistani citizen. But she also had spent more than half her life in the United States. Her father's work in banking led the family to move back and forth regularly between Karachi and Washington DC.

Salma was fluent in American English, and much of her secondary and high school education took place at American public schools in a middle-class suburb of Washington. A senior when I met her, she wore trendy American clothes, including skirts and shorts, and was very hip to the ways of American college students. But she also regularly returned to Pakistan. There she spoke fluent Urdu, donned the *shalwar kameez* and jewelry of young Pakistani women, played out the nuances of etiquette rituals, and slipped easily out of American individualism into the warm communal embrace of her extended and extensive Pakistani family. She dreamed of being successful in terms of both cultures. For example, although she knew it was out of the question, one of her daydreams was to win an Olympic gold medal in track for Pakistan.

At the time I knew her, Salma had serious concern about her real options for the future. As graduation approached, she had to make a choice. As a communications major she thought she might take up a career in local television. With her degree and internship experience, the idea of making her way as a single career woman in Washington seemed exciting, attractive, and quite practically possible. But it was a hard choice.

The alternative, which also appealed to her, involved a return "home" to Pakistan as her parents wished. There, as is the custom, they would complete the arranged marriage that they and her wider family wished to make for her with a distant cousin she had met but once. There she would reconnect with her many close family members but live in the home of her husband's extended family. His conservative Muslim family would never approve of her making a career in the disreputable world of media.

What is Salma's culture? The question is absurd. Obviously, she knows and is fluent in the ways of two very different cultures. When in the United States she can operate fluently with American concepts, rules, values, and customary ways of behaving. On visiting Karachi she can switch fluently into a traditional Pakistani mode of speaking, acting, and feeling.

And *where* are Salma's cultures? In one sense, of course, they are located on opposite sides of the world in the two different societies where each prevails. When Salma is in one place she encounters the culture of that society and engages, adjusts, and blends in with it. But the situation is not this simple. When she steps into her Pakistani family home in the Washington suburbs she usually speaks Urdu rather than English and operates in a Pakistani daughter's role with her parents. They cope well with life in the United States but are much less "Americanized" than she. In a sense Pakistani culture prevails in her home, as it does in the Massachusetts Avenue Muslim mosque and other zones of the Washington Pakistani immigrant community. Occasionally, too, while in Pakistan, Salma may switch to an American mode, as in attending a function at the U.S. embassy, reading an American novel, or receiving a long-distance phone call from one of her American friends.

As these example show, Salma does not leave Pakistani culture behind in Karachi when she returns to the United States. Both cultures are "out there" but also exist within her mind, her consciousness, and her heart. Mentally and emotionally she can switch from one language and culture to another, but being bicultural means she carries the knowledge, symbolism, and imagery of both cultures with her in her mind. And while she usually chooses to operate with the appropriate mode in the appropriate place, her subjective sense of what is going on, the problems she copes with, and how she feels about them is complexly affected by both Pakistani and American cultural meaning systems and by her conscious awareness of the differences. For example, her concern about the materialistic, "anti-spiritual" aspects of American society reflects, in part, her Muslim, Pakistani perspectives. Similarly, her discomfort with the treatment of women in Pakistan reflects, in part, her experience with contemporary American gender expectations and feminist values. Her encounter with American racism, including her sense of being a "woman of color" here, both overlaps and contrasts with the "colorism" she knows in South Asia. Her very sense of her identity is complicated by the problems of having to think of herself in terms of two different and contradictory systems of self-conception, including evaluations of alternative futures such as "career woman" in Washington or *biivi* (wife) in Pakistan. "Which way of life should I choose?" she wonders.

To some Americans it will seem obvious that Salma should choose the United States. But to many Pakistanis, including most of her family, it is equally obvious that the other choice is correct. "Halfies" – those who have bicultural experiences similar to Salma's – can appreciate the dilemma. As another woman told me, "It makes sense to us [Americans] that she would choose to stay here; it fits our values. But I know enough about the other side to see how this could be a real dilemma." We can guess that Salma's biculturalism will help her, in certain ways, in whichever society she chooses. We can also imagine that the necessity of choosing and the presence, in her mind, of the alternative values will cause her difficulties when things are not going well along the cultural path she chooses.

In a general way Salma's personal problem is representative of those of other South Asians I know who are coping with this kind of bicultural dilemma. Many choose life in the West. Others return to India or Pakistan to embrace South Asian ways in opposition to what they see as the flaws of American culture. Others, like Salma's parents, seek to negotiate both cultures. But generalization at this level loses touch with the complexity of individual experience. The different ways particular people make and live these three choices vary drastically. If we want to understand the South Asian bicultural dilemma better, we need to attend closely to the intricacies of individual experience and then work back up toward generalization.

In some ways, Salma's problems also point to the dilemmas of other kinds of people who are classified as "bicultural," "hybrids," "meztizos," or "halfies." This set of individuals has recently received considerable scholarly and popular attention as better awareness of the complexities of cultural life in the contemporary global society has begun to take hold.[1] This attention is useful in that it is helping to break the traditional assumption that we can understand a person by knowing his or her culture. Unfortunately, conceptualizations of biculturalism have often been simplistic or highly abstract because they have not been sufficiently grounded in careful life history research with real individuals.

Salma's cultural situation cannot be adequately grasped by an approach based on the assumption that she is a halfie who knows two monolithic cultures, Pakistani and American. Salma's dilemma, like that of other bicultural individuals, is much more complex. Salma does not know one single huge Pakistani culture; rather, she is familiar with and caught in a complex relationship with specific particular traditions of upper-class southern, urban Pakistani culture as well as a special ambivalent relationship to the Shia Sufi version of Islam. Similarly, her American culture actually involves a complex set of relationships to a variety of American traditions, including East Coast, urban, upper-middle-class school experience; a complex relationship with various American media; including an interest in feminist film criticism; and a knowledgeable, participatory interest in American sports; including track and field. An adequate examination of Salma's cultural situation requires a detailed inquiry into the specific relationships she has with particular versions of the unique complex of American and Pakistani traditions with which she thinks, talks, and acts.

Such an approach is necessary in investigating more extreme forms of biculturalism and multiculturalism generally. But such an approach, I will argue here, is also necessary to the investigation of any American life, whether or not the person has ever left the United States. To advance work on "the individual and culture" we need to address the complexities of the individual's relationship with multiple cultures. To be sure, some individuals have a much more radical set of contrasting cultures than others, but every contemporary individual is influenced by a variety of different and competing cultural traditions. How we negotiate these multiple cultures is a basic issue that life history needs to address.

CHAPTER ONE

Individuals and Their Cultures

With Salma's experience in mind, let's consider how we might explore the relationships between an individual and his or her cultural traditions. As we think about this issue I will assume that you are beginning your own investigation of another individual's life, so I will orient this discussion to helping you develop strategies for interviewing the person with whom you are working. But first, some background. Questions about individuals and their multiple cultural traditions may seem important to a life history project, but they have been oddly neglected in culture studies generally and in ethnography in particular. Ethnography involves a cultural description, or a cultural portrait, based on interviews and participant observation, but the subject portrayed is typically a group, a community, a scene, an institution, or a society. The operative pronoun in ethnography is not "he" or "she" but "they," as in ethnographic formulations such as the following: "The Northern Mapangu tribe conduct ritual sacrifices because *they* believe these appease the gods."

Of course, such an approach is a useful and informative mode of generalization for many purposes. Ethnography of this kind has helped us understand a great deal about the very different ways people of particular communities perceive themselves and their worlds, and it has deepened our knowledge of how cultures work at the community level. If we think of culture as a system of meaning, an interpretive framework, a language-concept system that a particular set of people uses to interpret experience and act in the world, then ethnography has usually focused on the ways in which a set of people who "share" a given frame of reference view themselves and their world and how this frame of reference influences their behavior. A key aspect of such work is overcoming one's own ethnocentrism in order to try and understand the concepts and values guiding other people's thoughts and actions. In constructing a description of the culture of the group, ethnographers typically meld differences and alternatives among individuals to construct a generalization that represents how members of this group typically think and act, even though there are inevitably considerable differences among the individuals who make up the group.[1]

Despite its importance, this approach is a kind of statistical fiction that overlooks variation and difference for the sake of generalization. It obscures the multiculturalism of most societies, communities, institutions, and families. While it is now generally understood that it is dangerous to generalize about Western civilization or American culture, the tendency still is to assume that this variation is group-specific cultural variation; that is, we think of the United States as a multicultural society because we understand that it is made up of sets of people like Chinese Americans, African Americans, WASPs (white Anglo-Saxon Protestants), Italian Americans, Chicanos, and Old Order Mennonites, each of which has its own distinctive culture. At a more sophisticated level we might appreciate that any such group actually contains systematic subgroup differentiation, that there are different kinds of Chicano groups and that men and women in Old Order Mennonite culture have different perspectives because they learn somewhat different values. For many purposes it is useful to explore this kind of variation, but it, too, remains at the level of generalization about groupings of people, about "they," about the culture that people supposedly share. Once again, this orientation obscures the enormous complexities of any given individual's particular beliefs and values.[2]

The Life History Research Tradition

For these reasons it is sometimes useful and important to shift our ethnographic perspective and take up the task of constructing a cultural portrait of a particular individual. In anthropology and sociology, such fieldwork has long been done through the tradition of life history research.[3] Studies in this field have significantly inspired and oriented the approach I will present here, but there are three characteristics of traditional life history that I want to modify.

First, there has been a strong tendency to focus on individuals who are understood to be "representative" of a particular group or culture. This line of thinking flows from the assumption that the value of a life history is in showing the typical life of someone in a particular group. But it is also valuable to explore how cultures work at the individual level and how people manage their cultural conditioning. Given this orientation, there is no reason to focus on a representative person. In fact, any two supposedly typical individuals are likely to seem quite different when we shift our focus to the level of the individual case. Also, we are likely to be just as interested in – and to learn as much or more about cultures and individuals from – people who are unusual, atypical, rebellious, or deviant. In choosing your "informant," "subject," or "research participant" – that is, the person you will interview – don't look for someone typical; look for someone interesting.[4]

A second characteristic of much life history research is its unfortunate tendency to shift from cultural to psychological modes of interpretation. This switch occurs partly because of the strong psychocultural orientation in life history research and partly because of the pervasiveness of psychological explanations in the cultures that influence us as researchers. But if we are interested in cultural analysis there is no reason to lapse into psychological explanation just because we are considering individuals instead of groups. There are ways psychology may enter our work, as will be discussed below, but here we are interested in exploring cultural approaches to understanding individual lives. Don't try to psychoanalyze the person you're working with; try to understand this life culturally instead. For this reason it may sometimes be useful to borrow the term "person-centered ethnography" to describe the kind of work we are conducting.[5]

A third characteristic of traditional life history is the assumption that the individual has one single culture. Such an approach weakens the potential power of cultural interpretations of individuals. As discussed earlier, it would be absurd to ask, "What is Salma's culture?" This woman is clearly multicultural; she knows and thinks with a variety of very different cultural traditions drawn from Pakistan and the United States. While hers may be an extreme case, most people in this society have important similarities to Salma even if they have never left the country. That is, if we take culture to be a frame of reference characteristic of a group or set of people, then most of us know and think with a variety of different cultures or cultural traditions. As an introduction to the problem of individual multiculturalism and the issues of person-centered ethnography, let's consider two case studies drawn from my life history research with American psychotherapists in Washington DC.

Gina's Cultures

Gina, a clinical social worker, is a forty-eight-year-old divorced white woman and single mother who lives in a northern Virginia suburb not far from Washington. In its broad outlines, her life as a single mother and career professional is similar to that of millions of other Americans, but in seeking to culturally understand how Gina thinks, feels, and behaves it is hardly sufficient to say that she is a person with American culture.

To construct a more effective cultural portrait we might begin by observing that Gina did not grow up in the affluent upper-middle-class suburb she now lives in but rather in an Italian American working-class community in New Jersey. The culture of this community contrasts strongly with that of her current neighborhood. While she was growing up in New Jersey, "family" did not refer to the nuclear family of husband, wife, and children or to the blended/divorced family variations so prevalent in her suburb; rather, it referred to a wider extended-family grouping, an emotionally close-knit and supportive kin group of aunts, uncles, and thirty-two cousins. In this community women hardly ever pursued careers; they were expected to stay at home as wives and mothers, and, following the conservative Catholic moral code, divorce was strongly disapproved of and virtually unknown.

Gina knows this cultural tradition as fluently as she does the northern Virginia upper-middle-class system, in which careers and divorces are quite in style. She slips back into Italian American culture and operates within it again easily when she returns to New Jersey for family visits. From the point of view of knowing the cultures of these communities, it is not that she knows one or the other. She is not working class or upper middle class; she is both. She knows both cultures.

Each culture influences Gina's particular relationship to the other. Although she is fluent in the northern Virginia culture, she is also in critical tension with it. She is not a true believer in all of its values; she breaks its rules, and she is not seen as "typical" by some of its members. For example, she deplores the lack of support that neighbors give each other and views many of the people in her neighborhood as emotionally repressed. Conversely, she is proud of her Italian American heritage and identifies with many of its values, including her version of the code of looking after family. However, she is critical of the conservative views on women that prevail in this New Jersey community, yet she feels vulnerable to her aunts' disapproval of her career and divorce. Her engagement with each culture complicates her relationship with the other.

Gina's life in both communities is further complicated by two other cultural traditions. The conservative Italian American Catholicism that prevailed there and that was powerfully represented by the church, mass, confession, and the priests dominated her upbringing in New Jersey. Gina is now in critical tension with this version of Catholicism, which she refers to as "old Catholicism." She is particularly critical of what she considers the false views of humans as "lowly sinners" and what she sees as the restrictive ideals of self-sacrifice for women.

Gina still defines herself as Catholic, but she identifies with liberal American Catholicism and ideals of liberation theology and social justice. She reads more liberal Catholic writings such as those of Matthew Fox and Thomas Merton, which make connections with Eastern philosophy. This mix of traditions is located partly in her reading but also in the women's prayer group she attends on a weekly basis. While she is in tension with old Catholicism, she is very conscious of its influence on her. As she says, "It's in my bones." In depressive moods she sometimes wonders if she will be "punished for my rebellion and breaking away."

Gina also thinks and operates with two more or less distinctive psychological traditions. The first is her American clinical social work tradition. She completed her Master of Social Work degree in the mid-1980s. The version of social work that she learned involves a complex system of concepts about negative psychological states, such as "obsessive," "depressive," "narcissistic," and "MPD," and their supposed origins in certain social situations that evoke negative first-family dynamics – dynamics she is trained to alleviate through complex techniques in individual and group therapy.

Gina is a dedicated and successful practitioner of this system, and she plays the role of therapist to a variety of clients who come to the office not far from her home. Partly because of referrals associated with her earlier work as a rape and domestic violence counselor, she deals particularly with clients who are victims of abuse and violence. The way she plays her role as therapist is affected by her other cultural traditions. For example, she understands her practice partly through the religious perspective of her liberal Catholic tradition and thinks of her work as a kind of religious calling or "service." Her relationships with her clients are also affected, she knows, by her Italian American heritage. She tends to treat them as "family" and will seek to help them outside the office situation in ways that go beyond those considered customary in social work. Conversely, she uses ways of thinking from her social work tradition to critique aspects of the Italian American tradition, such as referring to her conservative father as a "sociopath."

A second therapeutic tradition with which Gina operates involves a radical, eclectic psychotherapeutic approach associated with a psychological institute in Washington DC where she goes for postgraduate training. This system involves a blend of Western psychological traditions (object relations, existential psychology, Jungian psychology) with Asian psychological traditions (Taoist, Sufi, and Hindu traditions). Finally, Gina is also a student of tae kwon do, a form of the martial arts. She encountered this tradition when she sought to enroll her son in a martial arts school, thinking it would be good discipline for him. He failed to take any interest, but she was hooked. She attends class regularly, has advanced to the level of white belt, and as she puts it, "I love the fighting."

What is Gina's culture? The question seems as absurd as asking about Salma's culture. In each case a better question is, What are her cultures? Gina thinks, feels, and acts with at least eight distinctive cultural traditions. Knowing her cultures as well as the social situations within which she employs them, we can construct a more effective cultural explanation of her life. Most of what she says and does clearly reflects her engagement in one or another of these traditions, and the roles she plays in any particular world are usually significantly affected by several of her cultural traditions. An adequate cultural understanding of Gina requires attention to multiple cultural influences.

Claire's Cultures

The patterns that characterize Gina's life as a white, American, middle-age female therapist are similar to and yet different from the cultural situations of other therapists, white middle-class women, and Washington-area residents. Let's consider the parallel case of Claire. Studies emphasizing "the" culture of sets of people would lump these two women together. A life history perspective calls for examining each life individually and assumes that this complex effort is a legitimate and worthwhile form of case study. Only when we have a series of carefully detailed life histories can we develop an adequate comparative analysis of how similarly located individuals are actually similar and different in their cultural orientations.

Instead of suppressing difference to create fictional sameness, we are interested in the cultural complexity of individual experience.

Like Gina, Claire knows (1) a version of East Coast middle-class American culture and (2) an associated tradition of psychotherapy (psychology). Like Gina, she is involved with a variety of additional cultural traditions, and here parallels but also significant differences emerge. One of Claire's base traditions is (3) working-class Jewish culture, which she learned growing up in Virginia where her parents were shopkeepers. Her relationship with (4) Judaism is of some significance, but she is much more oriented toward another spiritual-religious tradition, (5) an imported version of Tibetan Buddhism. She regards this as her primary orienting tradition, and she regularly meditates and attends a local Tibetan Buddhist temple. Claire is also involved in (6) a rather macho militaristic exercise program, "The Sergeant's Program," and is a member of (7) The Forum, a social change organization (formerly EST). Finally, she is also extremely involved with (8) opera. Musically talented, as a teenager and young adult she trained extensively to be an opera singer. Now, as an adult, she continues to take voice lessons on her own, and the tradition continues to be aesthetically important to her. As we shall see below, opera also influences how she thinks about and performs other cultural traditions, including psychotherapy.

What is Claire's culture? Again, as with Salma and Gina, Claire's situation strongly suggests that it is productive to conceive of the individual as operating with an extensive set of differing and often partially contradictory cultural traditions.[6] You may want to investigate numerous issues in trying to understand the particular life you will be investigating, but it is likely that all of them will be illuminated by considering how the various cultural traditions the person works with impinge on the issue in question.

Cultural Traditions

The anthropological definition of culture usually points to a large-scale, organized worldview or belief system, including a set of guidelines for how to behave in the world. With some variable degree of accuracy, such a system is assumed to characterize a given society or community and to be widely and partially shared by at least many of its members. Even in relatively traditional, relatively homogeneous tribal cultures it has been recognized, however, that this is a generalized construction that oversimplifies the internal diversity and resistance that actually exists in individual belief and behavior. For example, when I studied the Pacific Island society of Chuuk, I learned that the society included a variety of special knowledge systems, such as curing, navigation, and sorcery. An adequate portrait of one individual required an investigation of what version of what cultural traditions the person knew and how he or she balanced and employed these systems within the wider context of Chuukese society.

To understand individuals in complex, multicultural, contemporary societies, the concept of cultural tradition seems essential.[7] Like the concept of culture, that of cultural tradition or cultural model points to a system of meaning that includes its own vocabulary and beliefs and its own set of rules for acting in the world. But it is a smaller-scale system, one among many ways of thinking and acting that individuals encounter. Like the traditional concept of culture, cultural tradition is itself a concept and something that ethnographers and other people may attribute to someone else or to themselves. While it is a scholarly concept, it seems to have a certain subjective validity. When we interview our research participants we find that they naturally talk about their lives in terms of their engagement with different social situations – with Italian American customs, tae kwon do, opera, Tibetan Buddhism, or clinical social work. They also recognize that values and customary behavior shift as they enter different social worlds where one or another of these systems prevails. People's descriptions of their everyday lives helps lead us toward identification of their various cultural traditions.

So, given this orientation to life history, a basic step in your research will involve establishing the particular cultural traditions with which the person you are studying is engaged. Here it will be useful to briefly outline some of the kinds of traditions you are likely to encounter in working with a research participant in the United States.

Kinds of Cultural Traditions

Large National/Societal Cultures

Most people living in the United States know a particular version of one or more large national cultural traditions. Like many other nation-states or large societal units, the United States can be understood to have a widely shared – if hugely complex, internally differentiated, and steadily evolving – "mainstream culture" that can be plausibly differentiated from the national culture of other societies like France or Japan. The language, assumptions, values, and customs of such a national tradition are likely to prevail in such large institutional structures as public educational institutions, the legal system, the military, economic systems, and the mass media. Most people are forced to encounter, learn, and cope with some version of the widespread American system by their presence in the United States. Scholars working at this level of analysis typically have no problem identifying general beliefs and values that seem to characterize such systems in comparison to other societal cultures. In this country, for example, particularly American values such as materialism, occupational achievement and success, individualism, romantic love, and the nuclear family are widely prevalent. Gina knows that she knows mainstream American culture, and she easily identifies what she sees as the characteristics of middle-class WASP Americans. Knowing this culture, of course, does not mean accepting it, and given her working-class and Italian American orientations, Gina is in considerable tension with the prevailing "mainstream" values of the community in which she lives. Salma knows a similar version of this culture, which is why her parents are concerned that she has become "Americanized." Having been raised in Pakistan, they know that their daughter has been deeply affected by the dominant culture of American society, with its American English language, individualistic style, emphasis on career for women, and faith in romantic love as a basis for marriage. Salma, too, can talk astutely of American cultural characteristics because she can compare it with a version of the mainstream upper-middle-class Islamic, extended-family-oriented culture that prevails through much of urban Pakistan.

The nature and description of large national/societal cultures is a huge problem, but it is one that we do not need to solve. What we are interested in is getting some sense of what version of which national culture or cultures the individuals whom we are studying seem to possess and how they relate to them. As we have seen, for example, Salma is quite fluent in two national cultures. Given her knowledge of Pakistani culture, she is both more aware and more critical of the mainstream American tradition than many of those who are more deeply mired in it.

Regional Cultures

Despite the strength of forces toward homogenization, in the United States, as in Pakistan, there is still widespread regional variation in the dominant culture. Again, our task is not to describe these regional cultures at the societal level but to consider which version or versions of American regional cultures our subject has been exposed to and how he or she relates to them. Gina, for example, knows an East Coast, suburban, professional, northern Virginia version of early-twenty-first-century American mainstream culture, a complex that is significantly different from what she would be dealing with in suburban Alabama or rural Montana. This culture includes a high-pressure "beltway" version of occupational achievement and power, a ready acceptance of divorce, and considerable faith in psychotherapy. Gina accepts aspects of this regional culture, such as faith in psychotherapy, and she is skeptical of other aspects, such as "obsessive" WASP emphasis on achievement and success.

Racial-Ethnic Cultures

Many Americans are strongly oriented toward one or another ethnic culture, such as Gina's Italian American culture, Claire's Jewish American tradition, or Salma's South Asian tradition. Sometimes these traditions are more, sometimes less important to a given individual. Often people know and identify with more than one ethnic tradition. Typically an American ethnic tradition is associated with a particular race. Again, people may know more than one such tradition and, as through adoption, may know a tradition that does not fit their stereotypical racial classification, as with an individual who is Jewish and black. Race itself, a highly charged and significant aspect of American society, is conceptualized very differently through different cultural traditions, as we will discuss below. A key issue for your life history will be exploring how your subject defines his or her racial and ethnic identities through different cultural traditions.

Class Traditions

Sometimes class is measured by income, but for our purposes it is better understood as a complex of different cultural traditions. A question you will want to ask is, With which version of which class traditions is the individual you are studying involved? As with Gina and Claire, people may be fluent in two or more very different class cultures.

Religious and Spiritual Traditions

Despite the supposedly secular orientation of American society, a majority of Americans are importantly oriented toward one or more spiritual or religious traditions. Like Claire, who is both Jewish and Tibetan Buddhist, many people know more than one such tradition.

Family Traditions

To an important degree, nuclear families, households, and extended families develop their own version of American family cultures. When the husband is Canadian and the wife Filipina, the children may be enculturated in two very different family traditions.

Educational Traditions

Schools have their own social segments which often have their own cultural traditions, such as the preppies, jocks, and skateboarders of American high school or the sorority and fraternity cultures of American colleges. To double-major in English and biology is to know two very different academic frames of reference. The educational traditions a person experiences may have a significant influence on later life, as with the case of a lawyer who was a Women's Studies major.

Occupational Traditions

Each occupation has its own complex cultural traditions, and these are usually quite intricate. Gina's version of clinical social work is influenced by particular psychological traditions, by her work in rape and domestic violence counseling, and by her studies of radical therapy and Asian psychotherapy. Given her earlier training and experience as an English teacher, she also has a special interest in "bibliotherapy."

Political Traditions

Some people are significantly influenced by allegiance to political traditions ranging from those of the Republican or Democratic parties to those of the Green Party, radical feminism, or some combination of several such traditions. Sometimes a youthful allegiance is completely rejected, or it may continue to exert a significant influence as a person shifts to other political orientations as he or she moves through different life stages.

Philosophical Traditions

Some secular individuals may be oriented by a philosophical system like existentialism, American pragmatism, or some version of Eastern philosophy.

Psychological Traditions

One of the conspicuous features of American society is the popularity of various psychological theories. These systems prevail in psychological institutions, but they leak out into the wider society in such a way that ordinary individuals untrained in psychology are importantly oriented in their understandings of self and others by Freudian or Jungian psychoanalysis, by attachment theory or Gestalt psychotherapy, or by ideas about post-traumatic stress syndrome or the characteristics of adult children of alcoholics. Again, people are often oriented by several such systems. From the perspective developed here, such systems are best understood as cultural belief systems. What does it mean that the person you are interviewing is oriented to Jungian psychology or believes that he or she is an adult child of an alcoholic? What aspects of identity does he or she draw from this belief system, and how does it influence or relate to other belief systems?

Military Traditions

The occupational cultures of the U.S. Army, Navy, Marine Corps, and Air Force have had important effects not only on current members of the armed service but on many people who grew up in military bases as "army brats" or served temporarily in the military.

Sports Traditions

All professional and amateur sports, including standard American variants such as football and more minor or esoteric forms like rugby, paintball, or karate, have their own complex cultures. To what extent is your subject invested in some sport as a weekend player or fan?

Musical Traditions

For Claire, opera was once a possible occupation, and it continues to exert a significant influence. A successful businessman I know followed the Grateful Dead well into middle age. Musical traditions ranging from reggae to hip hop to country and western can be a minor or major source of meaning.

Media Traditions

Most people in the United States have several ongoing media involvements, ranging from minor escapes to major obsessions. Connections to favorite TV programs, popular novels, detective or romance fiction, or films and videos may involve intense identification or other forms of imaginal connection with particular media figures. Sometimes these connections are based in face-to-face or virtual groups such as fan clubs, reading groups, or chat rooms.

Artistic Traditions

Painting, sculpture, pottery, and other artistic traditions, professional or amateur, are often major forms of meaning. They typically include their own esoteric vocabulary, beliefs, and ritualized forms of "how-to-do-it" knowledge. An individual may engage with one or more such tradition in solitude or in a studio or class world.

Clubs and Other Voluntary Associations

Groups such as boys and girls clubs, sports teams, volunteer fire departments, Veterans of Foreign Wars posts, self-help groups, amateur theater, and other leisure and lifestyle groups are often significant forms of meaning and engaging social worlds. Are any such social worlds important to your subject?

This list could be developed further or broken down into much more detail, but it points to the numerous kinds of cultural traditions and associated social worlds you will want to be alert for when you begin interviewing your research participant.

The Contents of Cultural Traditions

Cultural traditions can be explored in a variety of ways, but in getting a feel for how a particular tradition influences your research partner it will often be helpful to consider three characteristics. First, cultural traditions may be understood as routinized ways of thinking that orient us to ourselves, other people, and the world; they are language concept systems that answer the implicit questions, What's going on? Who am I here? and How should I relate to these people? Here we need to consider the tradition's basic vocabulary, the meaning system's key terms – for example, words for identities, roles, and situations within this world – and how these help us uncover the basic assumptions, values, and beliefs at play. Second, in addition to basic terms, beliefs, or formulations, the language of a tradition is also likely to be embodied in various standard stories or kinds of stories involving characteristic action plots and stock characters. Third, we are likely to find that a given tradition includes a variety of scripts or guidelines for how to behave.

For example, Gina's martial arts tradition, tae kwon do, involves beliefs about the utility of this system of fighting for both self-defense and self-discipline as well as ideas about its history (in Korea) and its place within the larger world of American-based forms of the martial arts. It also includes its own special vocabulary for kinds of forms or throws and for different "belts," both as objects and as markers for identities within the system (for example, "I'm a white belt, he's a black belt"). Similarly, the tradition includes basic origin stories about the history of the tradition and stories that a teacher or other experienced members tell about significant events that involved the use of tae kwon do in fighting situations or in developing character in previously undisciplined individuals. Finally, of course, the tradition includes scripts for how to act;

recipes for particular forms of kicking, blocking, and throwing; rules about how to behave toward the master; etiquette within the teaching studio; and rules about using the power of this system only as a last resort for self-defense.

To learn this or any other cultural tradition is to internalize some version of such beliefs, concepts, stories, and scripts. In order for us to learn about a research partner's tradition, it is sometimes useful to go to official outside sources, such as a website on tae kwon do or a scholarly account of Italian American culture. However, it is usually best to ask your research partner to tell you about the tradition with attention to the beliefs and language and practices used within it. In this way you will get a sense of the tradition and this person's view of the tradition. You will also begin to learn about how he or she *relates* to the tradition.

Relationship to a Cultural Tradition

Recognizing that your research participant knows a given cultural tradition will be just the beginning of your investigation. You will also want to systematically explore how the person relates to each of his or her major traditions. What version of the tradition does the person know, how was it acquired, and how well does he or she know and play it? How important is it relative to other traditions, and what is the individual's current orientation to the tradition?[8] Is he or she a "true believer" who totally and uncritically accepts its tenets and assumptions, as Gina seems to be with tae kwon do? In speaking about the tradition, Gina seems to accept much of its philosophy and practice, but she also has her own particular relation to it in that she is a relative beginner, she is interested in its power, and she connects it particularly with therapy. In other cases, the person, perhaps like Gina with her "old Catholicism," may be in a position of rebellion, rejection, or resistance in relation to a tradition, seeking to break free of its hold but still influenced by it. Or is the person, like Claire with her Tibetan Buddhism, in some critical tension with the tradition, accepting some aspects but rejecting or modifying others? This kind of critical, selective, or negotiated relationship with a tradition is one that we will encounter often and will need to investigate carefully in our interviews. We will also want to explore how the individual's relationship to a given tradition is affected by the combination of additional traditions with which he or she operates.

As we have already seen, for example, Gina's activities as a clinical social worker are significantly affected by her Catholic and Italian American traditions. Finally, we will want to consider how successfully the individual negotiates the contradictions and dilemmas that flow from involvement with multiple cultural traditions.

CHAPTER TWO

Methods in Life History Research

In her classic description of fieldwork, anthropologist Barbara Myerhoff compares ethnography in another society with research at home. The contrasts she sets up are helpful in thinking about the issues of our life history project. As she points out, people of an unfamiliar culture often seem "strange" to us. From our own cultural perspectives, their ways of speaking and acting seem odd, just as ours do to them. The ethnographic effort, then, is to overcome this ethnocentric judgment by seeking to make the point of view of the other intelligible and to understand the other culture from within.

> The anthropologist engages in peculiar work. He or she tries to understand a different culture to the point of finding it to be intelligible, regardless of how strange it seems in comparison with one's own background. This is accomplished by attempting to experience the new culture from within, living in it for a time as a member, all the while maintaining sufficient detachment to observe and analyze it with some objectivity. This peculiar posture – being inside and outside at the same time – is called participant observation. It is a fruitful paradox, one that has allowed anthropologists to find sense and purpose within a society's seemingly illogical and arbitrary customs and beliefs. This assumption of the natives' viewpoint, so to speak, is a means of knowing others through oneself, a professional technique that can be mastered fairly easily in the study of very different peoples. Working with one's own society, and more specifically, those of one's own ethnic and familial heritage, is perilous, and much more difficult. Yet it has a certain validity and value not available in other circumstances.[1]

In our life history work we try to see things from the point (or points) of view of the person we are interviewing. To know the other through oneself is an act of conceptual empathy and culturally informed imagination. While we may quibble with Myerhoff's suggestion that this effort is relatively "easy," she has clearly identified the direction in which we need to go in seeking to grasp the logic of another person's cultural meaning.

Myerhoff contrasts this kind of research with ethnography at home, with people of one's own ethnic and familial heritage, including oneself.

This she considers much more difficult. Why? Because it is hard to grasp the cultural dimensions of one's own world precisely because this world seems so natural. Familiar patterns are hidden because we take them for granted. Everything we think, feel, say, and do is permeated by our cultural conditioning, but it is not easy to recognize this. We need to defamiliarize that which is familiar. We need to make our own ways strange and a problem for investigation. But how can we do this?

The best device for accomplishing this work is comparison. Just as our own cultural conditioning helps us to see the patterns of other cultures, so experience elsewhere helps us to apprehend the subjective ruts of our own thinking. This is the major rationale for the double or dialogic orientation of our life history project. Working with someone whose cultural traditions contrast with ours will help us find patterns in both systems.

Myerhoff suggests that working with one's own culture may be not only difficult but also "perilous." Subjecting one's own cultural beliefs and values to ethnographic scrutiny may bring to light prejudices, vanities, contradictions, wounds, and hypocrisies that are painful to look at. There is also the problem of relativization that goes along with discovering the cultural constructedness of that which we believe, value, and trust as true. Faith in a religious tradition can be challenged by learning and recognizing the appeal and possible validity of a scientific tradition or a very different religion. Learning about a cultural tradition different from our own highlights the arbitrary, constructed nature of our own beliefs.

After suggesting that work on one's own culture is perilous, Myerhoff goes on to suggest that it has "a certain validity and value not available in other circumstances." It seems fundamentally valuable to probe the cultural dimensions of our lives for the purpose of self-understanding as well as to know others better. If this life history project works well, it can help you to better understand the mysterious, complex, and powerful ways in which cultures work for and on all of us.

Selecting a Research Participant

Choosing an appropriate person to interview is crucial to the success of your project. How do you select a good research participant? There will be two participants in this project, but one of them you already have, because one of them is you. The next step is to find someone whose life, in its similarities to and differences from your own, helps you see the cultural dimensions of both of your lives better. So, starting from who you are culturally, who would make an interesting research participant?

The logic of the project sets up certain parameters. From a cultural studies perspective, you want someone with a background different from your own. However, if that person were totally different from you – say, if he or she didn't not speak your language – you'd have more problems than you want to take on here. On the other hand, there is also a problem if he or she is too much like you. It's not that there "wouldn't be anything to learn," as one student suggested, but rather that it would be hard to discern what there is to learn because of the lack of contrast. The best relationship is one with some common cultural ground and many cultural contrasts.

Ordinarily, when we meet strangers who are culturally different from us, we find some common ground to talk about because it is more comfortable than addressing differences. For our purposes it is useful to have some common interests and then to venture off into the contrasts. For example, if you are both students at the same university but your participant was raised in Mumbai, India, and you in Cleveland, Ohio, the common ground will help you connect with each other, but the differences will help reveal the distinctive patterns of each of your lives.

Some suitable combination of similarities and differences would characterize your relations with hundreds of different possible life history partners. How do you narrow the choices? One person might be more appealing to you because he or she has pursued a philosophical or career direction of interest to you or experienced a world you are concerned about. One of my students was curious to know more about Eastern philosophies and mystical religions, so an immigrant from Tibet and an Anglo devotee of a local Zen Buddhist temple were intriguing possibilities. A student considering a career in law chose to interview a local criminal defense lawyer. A woman curious about her family's diluted ethnic traditions sought out a recent immigrant from Scotland. A woman disturbed by the sight of so many homeless people as she commuted to work decided to interview a woman of that world.

These interests helped to orient each of these projects, but they did not determine the outcomes. The Anglo woman knows more than Zen Buddhism, the criminal lawyer knows many other worlds besides law, and the homeless woman knows much more than the "culture of homelessness." Reflecting on your interests in possible informants can also be revealing of your own cultural orientations and concerns. For example, the young woman's interest in Eastern philosophies reflected dissatisfaction with her own Western religious tradition and an earlier sympathetic response to exposure to certain countercultural and New Age traditions.

Exercise 1: Selecting a Research Participant

Make a list of three kinds of people or specific individuals you might like to interview. Imagine what it might be like to work with them. What are the likely cultural connections and contrasts between yourself and each of them? Why do they seem interesting to you? Consider what cultural influences might have led to your choices. Consider each person's likely availability and schedule. Depending on the project, you may want to have at least four hour-long interviews – and several more, if at all possible. Consider the person's reflectiveness, storytelling abilities, and apparent interest and enthusiasm for the project. Given all this, who might be the best choice?

Another consideration in choosing a research participant involves degrees of risk and danger. Undergraduate students in my class occasionally think it would be "cool" to interview someone from the Ku Klux Klan or the American Nazi Party, a drug dealer, or a member of a motorcycle gang. It would partly depend on the student's prior connection with these worlds, but in most cases I would not approve such a proposal. As with other kinds of excursions into unfamiliar social worlds, it is important to recognize the possible misunderstandings and physical hazards involved. You should also consider conceptual and emotional risk. In ethnography, entering other conceptual worlds can be perilous. Moving out of your familiar cultural framework and social routine is a kind of philosophical adventure that takes us into interesting but potentially dangerous spaces with different meanings and values. In veering toward another way of thinking, you put your own meanings and values at risk. This is one reason why "culture shock" is listed as a form of mental disturbance in the American Psychiatric Association's *Diagnostic and Statistical Manual of Mental Disorders*. To some degree, risk is all to the good. It stretches us and can make the project more interesting and valuable; beyond a certain level, however, working across cultural boundaries can become counterproductive. It is likely that some research participants would push too many of our own buttons. For example, a Japanese American woman in one of my classes wanted to interview a Japanese American who had been interned in the World War II relocation camps in this country. Her parents had had that experience, but they refused to talk to her about it. When she succeeded in interviewing a man who had been confined in one of the camps, what she learned was so painful that it seriously disturbed and depressed her.

Exercise 2: Problematic Research Participants
Consider several kinds of people who would not be good research partners for you. Can you identify cultural dimensions of these anxieties and sensitivities? Does pinpointing these dimensions help to clarify some of your own cultural orientations?

Still another consideration in selecting a research participant involves the degree to which you may already have a culturally defined role relationship with a potential subject. I have known a few ethnographers who have conducted successful interviews with a close family member, a spouse, a boy- or girlfriend, or a boss if there were good cultural contrasts. But the kind of relationship you want to develop with your research participant requires pushing past the constraints of ordinary culturally constituted roles. If you already have a highly structured relationship, that relationship is likely to impede rather than facilitate the work you want to do.

Asking a Research Participant

Once you've found someone you would like to work with, how do you actually ask the person for help? It is important to be open about what you are proposing, and your own interest is likely to be your best approach. Most people respond positively to a respectful request when they know it is for something that is important to you. You should state that this request for help is part of a university class assignment or research project so that the person understands the context. This explanation also gives the interview request a kind a legitimacy that might be lacking if the project were presented as only some whim of your own.

You should tell the person how much time you will need for the interviews. Once people get involved, they usually get interested and are typically happy to meet longer than the minimum initially agreed on, but you need to start with what you see as a minimum. Approaching someone you don't know and asking for an interview usually creates some anxiety. But remember, the worst that's likely to happen is that the person will politely decline, and all you have to do is ask someone else. Most people are willing to participate in this kind of project. So when the answer is "yes," have your schedule in front of you and be ready to set up the first appointment.

Preparing for the First Interview

Once you have your research participant lined up, there is much to do in preparing for the first interview. As you think about the interview, make notes. These thoughts will be an important initial part of the material that will make up your ethnographic record (see below). Given your own interests and the person you have selected, you will have certain special areas you intend to explore. However, you will want to place these concerns within a wider cultural portrait of this person. It will be useful to begin broadly, to try and get a general feeling for the cultural traditions your subject works with before focusing on a particular theme.

It is good to begin with an open-ended question that invites the person to talk about his or her life at some length from his or her own perspective. Try to think of an initial question that isn't threatening, one that will evoke something about the person's self-understanding and provide openings to explore the life further. It is often productive to ask, "If you were going to tell the story of your life, what would be the chapters of your life so far?"

Since most people already think of their life as having different phases, this question taps into the person's subjective organization of his or her personal history and readily lends itself to follow-up questions about what life was like in each phase, such as "So what was it like growing up in . . . ?" And from there you can go on to ask about the particular cultural traditions the person encountered in that phase of life; for example, "So, during the year you were sent to Hebrew school. What was it like? How did you respond? Did Judaism become important to you then?" To give the person a chance to think before the first interview, you may want to let him or her know that you would like to begin this way.

Self-Ethnography

Before the first interview, you have another task: to start exploring your own cultural traditions. Since a major purpose of this project is to set up a productive interview situation that helps us to understand the cultural dimensions of two lives – yours as well as your research partner's – it is important to begin work on analyzing your own cultural traditions. A good way to start is to do Exercise 3.

Exercise 3: The Chapters of a Life

Ask yourself, "If I were going to write my autobiography, what would be the chapters of my life so far?" Go back in memory into each phase and write a paragraph of what life was like then for you. Carefully reflect on each phase and consider what cultural traditions you encountered in each one. How were they presented to you, by whom, and in what contexts? How much did your learn of the tradition, and how did you respond to it? On a separate page, list the cultural traditions you have identified. Then consider what relationship you currently have to each one. Are you a complete believer, or are you in some critical tension with the tradition?

It is always appropriate to ask ourselves the questions we plan to ask our research partner. Not only does this practice give us a sense of how it feels to try and answer the question, but it also gives us examples we can share with the person to show that we are thinking about these matters together. The goal is to explore cultural influences together, not to treat the other person as an object of study. Asking yourself these questions is also useful as an introduction to our excursion in self-ethnography. It helps us to begin the process of exploring our own cultural traditions and our particular relationships with them.

The Theory of Self-Ethnography

In anthropology, the classic ethnography was typically imagined as something like this: An ethnographer with culture A interviewed a person with culture B. The interviews would generate "texts," or answers to questions, which the ethnographer would then interpret. The ethnographer would further organize and analyze this material and write it up for an audience back home in culture A.

Part of the logic of this approach was the idea that an ethnographer with culture A could be "objective" about culture B. That is, the ethnographer's enculturation in culture A would allow him or her to see culture B more clearly; the ethnographer would not be burdened by the biases and problems involved in trying to understand culture A, since he or she knew it already. It was assumed that the job was to understand cultures other than one's own, to culturally understand someone else, not ourselves. In this life history project we are trying to construct an ethnographic approach that includes some of this classic model but goes beyond it as well.

The most rigid and conservative forms of classic ethnography explicitly rejected introspection. "Anthropological techniques exclude introspection," wrote Jacques Maquet.[2] Such statements reflect a number of outmoded assumptions, including the idea that ethnography is only an objective study of someone else's culture. Even where the major focus is on another culture, it is now recognized that the culture the ethnographer brings to the encounter affects what happens. It is considered important, then, that the ethnographer should be aware of his or her culture in order to avoid blunders and misinterpretations that reflect his or her own cultural perspectives.

Such admonitions are, however, often little thought through. Just how can a person be instantly "aware" of his or her culture? Do we really believe that through a mere shift of attention one can do a rapid-fire ethnographic survey of the complex cultural dimensions of one's own thinking? The process is much more challenging than this. After trying for several days to identify her cultural traditions, a graduate student in anthropology wrote, "After a lot of struggle I was able to piece together a list of my cultural traditions or at least what I think they are."

Why is this process difficult? There seem to be several reasons. First, an exploration of anyone's cultural traditions, including our own, is a complex process because some aspects of culture are so familiar that they are hard to see, while others are below the surface of awareness. Also, an account of our own traditions is always a construct or interpretation that cannot match the complexity of our experience. Self-ethnography is also difficult because it is unfamiliar. We may know that culture influences much of what we think, feel, and do, but we do not ordinarily focus on this. Even those of us in anthropology or other fields of cultural study rarely set out to systematically explore our own cultural influences. To put it another way, studying the ways our cultures influence us is not usually part of our culture.

Although excursions in self-ethnography are challenging, they can clearly get at many important influences and dramatically increase our awareness of our own cultural traditions. However, as we shall see, self-ethnography, like all ethnography, requires careful, step-by-step analysis in an introspective mode.

But what about introspection? Isn't "looking inward" at one's cultural experience – as opposed to "looking out" at the cultural experience of another – a dubious method? If so, then most ethnography suffers from this problem. When we ask our subjects to answer questions about their experiences (for example, "What was your life like during that phase? How did Judaism affect you at that time?"), we are asking them to introspect. So, to reflect analytically on one's own cultural experience ("How did Judaism affect me at the time?") involves only a minor variation from standard procedure. We are merely asking ourselves to do the same thing we ask our research partners to do.

While most anthropologists now routinely call for specification of one's own cultural location in ethnographic reports, there is still some uneasiness with this. This unease reflects the still-prevalent assumption that ethnography in the United States should be about cultures other than those of the ethnographer, as well as the idea that it is a "narcissistic indulgence" to focus ethnographic attention on oneself. While granting that narcissistic indulgence is not what we are striving for, a careful analysis of one's own culture is entirely legitimate. Whether or not we are insiders in one or more of the cultures of our research participants, our interest in individuals and cultures in the United States makes our own cultural experience a legitimate topic of study. One of the reasons for valuing the life history project is that it helps to culturally illuminate our own lives as well as the lives of our subjects.

As you prepare for your interview, keep asking yourself the questions you might ask your research partner, keep working on your list of your own cultural traditions, and consider how the interview process may help you increase your awareness of your relationship with each of these traditions, including how they affect your anticipations about how the interview will develop. For example, if you are from the South and your research participant is from the North, what concerns flow through your mind about meeting up with this "Yankee"? Where do these cultural stereotypes come from, and what do you think about them? You should also consider how the research participant might be thinking about you and the concerns he or she might have about this project.

Ethics in Life History Research

Before you start your interviews you need to consider the ethics of life history research in relation to the special characteristics of your project. Like other research with living human subjects, ethnographic research is governed by rules established by professional associations, such as the American Anthropological Association, and by the Code of Federal Regulations of the Department of Health and Human Services as administered by the Institutional Review Board and Human Subjects Review Committee at your college or university. You need to familiarize yourself with these rules and obtain any needed permissions. The following guidelines are particularly important. First, you need to be careful about interview and participant-observation research that explores what are defined as sensitive areas of a subject's life, such as substance abuse, sexual activity, or illegal conduct. We need to be careful in asking questions about these areas and in protecting any records we make about our subject's responses. If such information were publicly or officially linked to the person, the individual might, for example, be fired from a job or put at risk of criminal or civil liability. In life history projects you are not usually seeking to uncover sensitive material, but it often comes out as we learn more about another person. The accepted ethical solution is to avoid using personal names or any other identifiers that link the subject and the information. That is, we do not want to provide information such as a job title or an organization address that would allow outsiders to know whom you are writing about. Care with identifiers applies not only to the final paper, article, or book you might write but also to field notes and tapes. If your field notes and tapes include sensitive material, you should not put the person's name on them in case you accidentally leave the notes in a public place where others might find them. It is advisable to have your research participant sign a release form that explicitly states how you will deal with issues of identification.[3]

Considerations of ethics go beyond these minimal rules. It is important to be alert to any possible harm or embarrassment you might cause your informant. This person has voluntarily agreed to help you, and you are obligated to be respectful and considerate of his or her privacy, well-being, feelings, and points of view. Even though you are conscientious about ethics, you might sometimes feel ambivalent about what you are doing and worry that there are aspects of "betrayal" involved in getting close to the person you are working with in order to "study" him or her. Carefully consider any discomfort you feel. If you are uncomfortable with any aspect of what you are doing, use self-ethnography to explore ways in which you might deal with this issue better, such as by modifying your approach. You may also want to discuss the issue with your research partner, your adviser, or a member of the Human Subjects Review Committee.

One major source of ethical angst has to do with the unequal power between investigator and subject. One way of shifting this inequality is to make the research as collaborative as possible by understanding and dealing with the person you are working with as a co-investigator or teacher rather than as a subject. Balance is also facilitated by making the project partly an exercise in self-ethnography in which you ask yourself the same questions you are asking your research participant and subject the answers to the same kind of analysis. Self-ethnography helps you ask better questions and facilitates rapport by turning interviews partly into an exchange of notes, but it also helps to resolve the ethical dilemmas of life history research. It sensitizes you to the nature of the questions, helps show you where you may want to be especially careful, and helps alert you to material you may want to leave out of your notes. Self-ethnography balances the relationship between you and the person you are working with.[4]

Exercise 4: Interview Ethics

If you were being interviewed by an ethnographer for a project similar to the one you are conducting, what considerations would you want to be given about sensitive aspects of your own life? What aspects of your life would you want to remain off the record? What are the cultural bases of these concerns? Now, shifting perspective, what do you see as the possible special concerns and risks for the person you are interviewing? How might your project be harmful or embarrassing to him or her? What steps do you need to take to avoid such problems?

Doing Interviews

Good life history requires careful, in-depth interviewing. Try to find a mutually convenient location that is quiet, comfortable, and conducive to private, one-on-one conversation. As long as they are reasonably quiet, restaurants, diners, and cafés are good places, and the sharing of coffee or food tends to be helpful to the interview process. If you are invited to your research participant's apartment or home, that will be even better.

Begin the first interview by chatting a bit rather than starting with formal questions. Small talk helps people relax and defuses apprehension. But soon you will want to shift into the interview mode. "So, I'd like to begin our interview today by asking about your life so far." Have your tape recorder with you, pull it out, and ask if it is alright to tape record the interview. Explain that you "really want to get down what you're saying accurately." You can add here that "If there is anything you want off the record, just let me know and I'll be glad to turn off the tape recorder." In case your research partner doesn't want to be taped, have a notebook ready.

As discussed earlier, it is usually appropriate to begin with the "chapters of a life" question. Relax, try to connect with the person, listen carefully, and seek to get into what he or she is saying and how he or she is seeing things. Express interest and, especially with the first interview, be ready to follow the person's lead. If your research partner seems uncertain, gently help him or her along ("Could you tell me more about what that was like?") or move on to the next phase ("I'd like to hear more about this, maybe next time, but so I can get an overview of your life, could you tell me about what happened after that year?"). While it is helpful to consult field manuals on interviewing, there is no rigid formula. In the end you have to find your own way of interviewing, one that fits with the particular project, your personal style, how your relationship with your research participant develops, and the mood that each of you happens to be in that day. Look for a style that feels comfortable to both of you and that allows you to pursue your own interests while giving the person freedom to express thoughts you might not have brought out if you had assumed more control. Michael Agar has likened the progression of an interview to a funnel: be open and nondirective at first, trying to take in a lot, but then gradually sharpen the focus by asking about the topics or themes you want to pursue.

One of the best questions is, "Could you give me an example?" or "Do you have a story about that?" People often give general answers to interview questions, but if they are asked for an example they often provide detailed stories that illustrate, illuminate, and complicate what they are saying. These stories are often crucial for your research. It often helps if you tell a story from your own life to evoke this level of discussion and to explain what you are asking about. This also helps improve rapport and shows that the research participant is not the only one revealing information. Finally, be patient and listen. When you ask a question, don't jump in with a comment or clarification if the person doesn't reply immediately. Give him or her a chance to think and reflect.

By the end of the first or second interview, if you have an overall picture of the person's life, you will have made a good start.[5]

Interviewing on Cultural Traditions

Whatever topic you are pursuing, as you interview further it will be important to delve more deeply into your research partner's cultural traditions. In learning about the chapters of his or her life, you will have learned about some of the traditions he or she works with – occupational traditions, racial-ethnic traditions, media traditions, religious traditions, and the like. Now you will want to explore significant traditions further. Here are some kinds of questions that may be useful.

Begin by asking the person to give you a general description of the tradition: "I was interested in what you said about how important Tibetan Buddhism has become to you. I'm not at all familiar with this; could you tell me about Tibetan Buddhism? What is it like as a spiritual tradition?" The answer will be valuable in giving you the person's general sense of the tradition and will likely raise questions about specific beliefs (such as reincarnation) or particular practices (such as meditation) that you can delve into further: "I was interested in what you said about the practice of group meditation at the Temple. Could you tell me more about this? It sounds like there are different types of mediation. What do people call these different types? It helps if I know how people talk about these things, so please give me the names of the different rituals, the names people use at the Temple."

Such questions will help you learn something about the basic vocabulary or key terms of the tradition and some of the general beliefs involved. Such questions will also lead you to the important scripts or ways of doing things. Here, ask specifically about how one does some of the particular customary activities that seem important or that you are particularly interested in: "What exactly is the sequence of steps you go through in your meditation practice? What are these supposed to accomplish?" Ask also about stories: "I think you said that the teacher gives talks at the beginning of the gathering. What kinds of stories does she tell? Could you give me an example?" Ask also about less official, informal stories: "And afterwards, when people are just informally talking, do the members talk about their experiences with Tibetan Buddhism, like how it might have helped them? What kinds of stories do they tell? Could you give me an example?" Then you might go on to ask about what your research partner thinks such stories mean and why people tell them. All these questions will add to your sense of the tradition as your research partner understands it – and will provide material to ask more about.

Along the way or subsequently, you will want to explore how your research partner *relates* to the tradition. Again, some information or at least hints of this will likely have come out in his or her general description, and you will want to use these as entry points: "I was interested in what you said about your own attraction to the meditative side of Tibetan Buddhism. Is this what is most important to you?" Then you might want to follow with questions like these: "Are there other aspects that you are not so interested in or disagree with? How important is this tradition outside your experience at the Temple? How does it affect your social work practice? Could you give me an example?"

But before starting these interviews, ask yourself the same kinds of questions.

Exercise 5: Asking about Cultural Traditions

Take one of your own cultural traditions that is pertinent to your life history project and interview yourself about it. Ask yourself the following kinds of questions, write down your responses, and think about what they mean: How would you briefly describe the major beliefs, values, and general characteristics of this cultural tradition? What are key terms in the basic vocabulary of the tradition? What are some of the key scripts or recipes for behaving? What are some standard official and informal stories? Why do people tell these stories? What stories do you tell, and what do they mean? How do you relate to this tradition? What is especially important to you? What are you in critical tension with? How does your relation to the tradition compare with that of other people you know who are involved in it? How might you adapt these questions in interviewing your research participant?

Doing this exercise should help illuminate a tradition of importance that you bring to the project and will help you in conversing with your research partner about his or her traditions.

Participant Observation

You can write a good life history using interviews alone, but your portrait will be richer if you engage in participant observation. While usually applied to the ethnographic study of groups, this technique is also valuable in the study of individuals. It involves getting a sense of what a person's life is like by following your research participant though his or her social worlds where particular cultural traditions prevail. As people get comfortable with what you are doing, they will usually allow you to accompany them as they go from one social situation to another.

It is important to keep notes about such visits. Although isolated observations can be useful, you should aim to write accounts or vignettes of your subject in action in particular social settings. In his or her workplace, you will get a good sense of how your research participant relates to his or her occupational tradition. Be alert, too, for the ways his or her other traditions may be present here. What does this workspace and its decorations tell you about the person's various cultural systems? For example, in her office, an Indian immigrant social worker has not only standard social worker texts and references but also a statue of a Hindu goddess, reproductions of abstract expressionist paintings, family photos, and several books by Carl Jung. The items in this setting materially represent this woman's engagement with Hindu mysticism, her biracial family, Western art, and archetypal psychology.

Next, who were the characters in a particular scene? What were they wearing? How do their clothing and jewelry represent particular cultural traditions? What action took place, and what gestures, movements, and tasks were performed? What words were spoken? What was the dialogue? Selecting from what you observed, can you write a storylike description that conveys the way different cultures were manifested in the scene?

Exercise 6: Questions for Participant Observation
Before engaging in participant observation in your subject's worlds, try observing some scenes in your own worlds that might help you draw contrasts with those of your research participant. Take your workspace or room at home, even a drawer in your desk, and describe it with an eye to how the material culture reflects your orientation to your cultural traditions. Write a brief, storylike scene of an event that took place at home or at work that illustrates your use of multiple cultural traditions in action. How might you apply this approach in observing your research partner's worlds?

Consider using visual materials in your interviews and observational work. Ask your research partner why he or she likes that painting on the wall. It is also often helpful to conduct interviews using a person's family photographs, some of which may show the person in different social worlds. You may also find it useful to photograph your subject in action and to get photographs of you and your research partner together. This obviously poses identification issues, so you will need to get permission to take and use photographs. Sometimes it is helpful to photograph a person's material surroundings even if a portrait of the person is not suitable.[6]

Carry a pocket notebook when you are doing observational work with your research participant. Often you can make notes in the midst of a scene. People who know you are there to work will usually be tolerant of this practice. In other situations, such as a family dinner, it is not appropriate to take notes, but you can write up your observations soon afterward and elaborate on them later. These observational notes provide firsthand evidence of scenes you will hear about in interviews, furnish important data for your analysis, and generate material for interview questions that you might never have thought to ask if you had not been in the scene. Finally, when you write your life history, some of these observations can be used as documentary illustrations of your generalizations. As with interviews, you will want to check with your subject about whether certain observations should be considered off the record.[7]

The Ethnographic Record in Life History

Much of what you are learning in your cultural study of your subject and yourself will exist only in your thoughts and memory. A lot of it, however, will be on paper or computer disks; as you proceed, many pages of interview transcripts and observational notes will accumulate. Both the ongoing research and the eventual writing will be improved if you develop and maintain an organized and efficient way of storing and retrieving your fieldwork notes.

As discussed earlier, it is best to tape-record interviews, since this is the only reliable way to get a verbatim record of what people have to say. Given current technology, you will need to transcribe the tapes. To really analyze interviews, you must have the material before you in written form on the page or computer screen. Transcribing is tedious work, and some ethnographers prefer to simply type as fast as possible and then read and analyze later. Alternatively, you may want to reflect on the material while you are transcribing, making notes to yourself on the side. Whether you do this during transcription or afterward, such analysis is a crucial step in your study. First, reviewing your transcripts helps you improve your methods. Listen to how you are asking questions. Are you phrasing them clearly, giving people time to answer, and encouraging elaborations? It may be useful to make notes on your methods to help you do better the next time. Reviewing your interviews also works as a reencounter with your research partner. Here you can listen more carefully and reflectively to what he or she says. You can study a given statement by replaying it again and again. What does it seem to mean? Is it an important clue to how the subject thinks with one of his or her meaning systems? Watch also for your reactions. How did you react to this at the time? How are you reacting now? Does your reaction suggest anything interesting about your own cultural traditions? While it is best to transcribe the tapes of each interview in their entirety, as you proceed you may find that you can skip some portions.

You will also want to type out expanded versions of the notes you take as a participant observer. Even if the session was mainly an interview, type out whatever observations you wish to make, including, perhaps, what you and the other person said after the tape recorder was turned off. Review these notes and add your reflections and reactions.

After several interviews and observations, you will have many pages of interviews and observations. How can you organize this ethnographic record? Whether you keep the material on computer disk or as a hard copy, the best way to organize it is some system of files that facilitates ongoing research and makes the task of writing easier. The system should allow you to locate and access particular statements or observations on given issues or themes that, absent some ordering system, will otherwise be "lost" to you in the sheer volume of accumulated records.[8]

Here is a suggestion for organizing your material in a series of nine files:

1. File for each visit. It is usually preferable to keep one copy of all the material from a given visit in one place. This arrangement preserves the structure of each visit and allows you to see the context in which any given

statement or observation was made. Make a separate computer file or manila folder with the date and a brief title, such as "1/13/04 Interview with Gina at Anthony's Café: Therapy and Family." Within this file will be your interview transcripts and visit notes ordered in numbered pages. Outline the material and make this index/outline the first page of the file. This one-page outline should list the topics discussed and observations made keyed to the file page number on which the material exists. This outline will help you to access material, either by hand or by computer sort, on any topic you want to review.

2. *File on overall biography of research partner.* Keep this file, which draws on and copies material from various sessions, as an overview of the person's life. At the front of the file place a one-page chronological outline of the person's biography keyed to the chapters of his or her personal history.

3. *File on overall biography of your life.* Keep a file on yourself similar to the one on your subject. Organize it with an eye to the contrasts between the two biographies.

4. *Set of files listing the subject's cultural traditions.* Each tradition may have its own file or subfile with copies of transcript pages or observational notes from the various visits that are pertinent to this system. Also include the subject's interview statements and your own notes assessing his or her relationship with each tradition. The first page of each file should be a summary outline of your sense of the person's relationship with this tradition.

5. *Set of files on your cultural traditions.* This file should parallel the one you are keeping on your research participant. Keep here your working notes on your cultural traditions and your relationship to them.

6. *File on the relationships among the subject's different cultural traditions.* Develop here a map of the way your research partner's traditions connect with each other. Does one tradition seem to have priority? How does the person balance contradictory systems? How is each tradition influenced by the others? Again, this file should include copies of interview pages or observational notes plus your analyses of these notes.

7. *File on the relationships among your cultural traditions.* This file should parallel the one above on your subject. It should include a map of the connections and mutual influences of your cultural traditions.

8. *File of outlines on how you might write up your life history paper.* Even early on in this project, it is important to consider how you might put the ma-

terial you have gathered together into a life history paper or article. How will you start? Will you develop the material chronologically or by topic? What will be your theme? Where might a particularly good scene go in relationship to your other material? How will you deal with the contrast between yourself and your subject? We will address these issues in detail in Chapter 5, but it is helpful to keep thinking about ways you might write up your material as you proceed. Thinking about these issues will sharpen your sense of your material, push you to see connections and themes, and suggest areas you need to ask more about. It will help you write the kind of paper you are beginning to imagine.

9. *File on questions to ask and observations to make.* As you review and analyze your material or find memories popping up in your own mind, questions will occur to you. Often they slip away again if you don't write them down. If you make a note of these questions and file them here, you will find that it helps you prepare for the next interview.

Analyzing Field Notes

A crucial step in life history work is analyzing and interpreting the material you are collecting and filing. The orientation of your project will affect how you do this, but a major part of your work will involve identifying and seeking to understand points of view. This kind of life history involves the process of seeking to move through and past your own points of view in order to enter into the thought processes of your research partner, and then moving back to reflect freshly on your own patterns of thinking.

Analyzing transcripts and observations should be an ongoing part of your research. Try to keep refining your understanding as you go along. As discussed above, reflect on each interview soon after it is completed, but also regularly spend some time with all the materials you have gathered, not just the recently completed interview. Earlier notes will become more revealing as you learn more from recent interviews and observations. Read notes carefully for clues to the points of view of your research participant and yourself: What is this person expressing about point of view in this record of what he or she says and does?

Sometimes people will tell you directly about point of view; for example, "My ethnic heritage is the center of my life" or "It has caused me much conflict and pain; I feel very ambivalent about my ethnic heritage." These direct statements will be key quotes for your files, but even here you will want to attend carefully to the specific words, tone, and examples your research participant uses. Such direct, orienting quotes provide the basis for asking further questions that will increase your understanding.

People may also express points of view indirectly in what they say or in the stories they tell about their experiences. Try to read such statements or stories for a sense of how the person feels and thinks about life. Pay particular attention to the words and phrases he or she uses. Can you identify key terms within these quotes? Language is not only the medium we talk with but also the medium we think with. Language structures people's sense of themselves and their worlds. Often it is useful to repeat key quotes to yourself and to try and imagine, given what you already know about the person, what it would mean to say this. Try the quote on, like an actor reading a part, to "get into" the person's way of thinking.

Look for key terms within each of the frames of reference you are uncovering. When I was working with an Old Order Mennonite community, for example, I noticed how people often used the term "plain" in a way that was unfamiliar to me. To say that something was plain turned out to be a positive value judgment, meaning simple, straightforward, not ostentatious or showy. When a term is unfamiliar, ask about contrasting terms. To understand the Mennonite sense of "plain," it is important to explore its opposite, "fancy," which is a negative judgment. Be aware, too, that people may use familiar terms, such as "family," "leadership," or "success," differently from how you expect.

As you go over your records, make notes to yourself and file them. For example, if a quote tells you something about the person's religion, make a note for your file on the person's cultural traditions. If a quote suggests a further question you need to ask about the relationship of religion to family, toss a note into your question file. Consider also how this statement contrasts with the way you think. How does your evaluation of your religious traditions parallel and contrast with your research participant's statement? Can you think of stories or examples in your life that provide a sharp contrast? Put such notes and reflections in the files on your own cultural traditions, and make a note in the file of your life history paper outlines as to how you might use this story in an appropriate section of your paper. Does all this suggest further questions that you need to ask?

As you get ready for your next interview, review your questions file and prepare a list of topics to explore. Briefly review the files in general, including especially your files on the person's cultural traditions and your outlines of how you might write up your project. Such preparation will focus your attention for whatever you will encounter on your next visit.

The Meaning of the Life History Method

Once you have reviewed the nuts and bolts of life history research and actually begun trying it, you will probably find that there is much that is interesting, powerful, and valuable about this kind of work. The relationship you develop with your research participant is unlike other social relationships and carries several interesting and elusive kinds of meaning. If the work goes well, you will think more creatively about several issues. Your sense of the limits, virtues, and challenges of life history will become clearer as you actually do it. Systematically moving beyond the barriers of your own customary points of view into another person's thought world is a fascinating and enlightening process. Moving back again, your own ways of thinking and feeling become defamiliarized, noticeable, and open to new scrutiny and reflection.

You are likely to view the general issue you are focusing on in your project – whether that is immigration, gender, race, religion, or disability – more clearly as you see how it relates to the actual complexities of the two cases of yourself and the other person. You will expand your awareness of the challenges people face in struggling with their circumstances and cultural traditions in trying to make and live a meaningful life. You will also see how cultural traditions profoundly affect our constructions of identity.

CHAPTER THREE

Individual Identities, Multiple Cultures

Cultures are systems of meaning that allow us to make sense of the world "out there." But cultures also enable and constrain us in our attempts to understand who we are. An important part of life history involves exploring how you and the person you are interviewing construct and enact your identities. Just what kind of a person does each of us understand ourselves to be, and how did we arrive at that understanding? You will get at self-conceptualization partly by the way a person handles social relationships and selects clothing and other aspects of dress. But the most important material will be the ways in which a person constructs a self-presentation through stories and self-descriptions.

Be alert to how people "language" their identities through what they say about the chapters of their life, but also listen to how self-descriptive statements come through in all kinds of matters you discuss. Another way of getting at identity is to directly ask your research participant how he or she would explain who he or she is. But before doing this, try it on yourself.

Exercise 7: Who Am I?
Ask yourself "Who am I?" or "What kind of a person am I?" Write down at least ten words or phrases in response to this question.

I am _____

I am a _____

I am a person who _____

I am not a _____

Here are some answers I have been given by students in my classes:

a unique individual	whatever I want to be
an American Jew	middle class
afraid of death	gay
Caucasian	Korean, but Westernized
a John Wayne fan	loves shopping
264-xx-xxxx	not sure who I am

overweight	opposed to homosexuality
not Princess Diana	an ABC (American-born Chinese)
bisexual	not what I would have been if born in Russia

These answers show how people draw from the set of concepts that happens to be available to them and suggest the relative, culturally constructed nature of our social identities. Another common set of answers focuses on personal characteristics, personality, or personal identity:

fat, I hate my body	independent
a failure	aggressive
neat	moody
responsible	shy
generous	depressed
a loner	adult child of an alcoholic

By using such terms we may think we are understanding ourselves in personal, psychological terms, but such self-constructions are highly cultural. They are standardized conceptualizations based on applying terms and concepts for personality and character made available to us by our current cultures. If you or I had been enculturated in Mumbai, India, rather than in the United States, our repertoire of concepts for answering the "Who am I?" question would be organized by Hindi or Maharati words and phrases from particular Indian frames of reference, and we might describe ourselves as Jain, Goan, or Brahmin.

The meanings of identity terms exist in complex relationships of contrast with other, linked terms. Such terms usually vary drastically or subtly from one culture to another. Even seemingly similar concepts will have different shades of meaning. Thus what Indians think it means to be *aurat* (woman) contrasts with related terms like *admi* (man). But what it means to be *aurat* is not the same as being a "woman" in contemporary mainstream America. And what it means to be a *hijva* (a castrated male who wears a sari and enacts certain special female roles) is beyond the realm of American identity concepts. Moreover, many identity terms are highly evaluative. For example, all cultures have ideas about being handsome, beautiful, or attractive, but the definitional criteria vary considerably over time and space. How these criteria affect a person's sense of self-worth depends on the current, local, aesthetic tradition.

45

Cultures contain not only different repertoires of words for self-description but also differing theories of the self and its structure, functioning, and continuity. In Indian Hindu culture, reincarnation is widely accepted, and it is believed that one's being is born again and again. Many secular Americans see death as the absolute end of one's life. These contrasting theories affect the basis for self-understanding. Similar cultural differences characterize many psychological processes. Are dreams meaningless forms of cognitive garbage dumping, significant messages from unconscious levels of personality, or subtle indications from the spiritual world? Our attempts to understand both our interior experience and our sense of ourselves as particular kinds of people are filtered through evaluative ways of thinking provided by our cultures. A goal of life history is to try and understand something of how this works for the two people with whom you are concerned.

Cultural Traditions and Identities

While it can be useful to consider broad cultural contrasts such as those between the United States and India, if we want to get a better sense of the complexity of culture and identity we need to shift our attention to cultural traditions. Each broad societal culture has its own self-conception system, and people who learn two such traditions know two different ways of understanding themselves. Indians in the United States may be versed in theories of karma and also work with Western psychology. Such people have to negotiate multiple constructions of self and identity. And so does everyone else. Not only does each broad societal culture have its own network of concepts about identity and the self, but so too does virtually every cultural tradition. To recognize individual Americans as multicultural requires us to consider the ways in which they operate with multiple and often contradictory senses of identity.

Consider Gina. In answering the "Who am I?" question she brings up a variety of terms and phrases that are linked to her different cultural traditions, including her sense of ethnic identity: "My Italianness is the driving force of my life." Although she feels proud to be Italian, she resists some aspects of the Italian American tradition, such as judgments expressed by her aunts that she is a "failure" for having been divorced. While identifying as Catholic, she struggles to resist the traditional Catholic perspective through which she sometimes sees herself as "sinful." When she thinks about herself in terms of her occupational tradition, she sees herself as a psychotherapist, and on good days, as a very effective therapist.

Shifting to personal terms, Gina describes herself as thoughtful – "I'm very thoughtful, blah! It kills me . . ." – partly because of her orientation to Italian and religious codes that emphasize "always doing for others." At times, drawing on her psychological traditions, she applies terms like "depressive" to herself as she ponders the effects of her own first family and her harsh treatment by her father. When she shifts to the tae kwon do tradition, she describes herself as "a white belt" who "loves fighting" and is "really good with my fists." What is Gina's identity? She has many senses of self, but they are neither random nor a chaotic pastiche. Her various senses of self are directly linked to the concepts of the several cultural traditions she thinks with.

Similarly, you will need to explore how your research participant's and your own self-understandings are linked to your various cultural traditions. This will include consideration of how each of your identities is defined by dimensions of difference.

Race, Gender, Class, Ethnicity, Sexual Orientation, and Disability

Analytic categories such as race, gender, class, ethnicity, disability, nationhood, and sexual orientation are important in understanding many aspects of American society partly because they help reveal lines of power, inequality, and oppression. For example, they help explain the underlying dynamics of work in the United States, including who is privileged, who is underpaid, and who is excluded. Analysis based on these structural categories has often focused on large social patterns such as differential pay for similar kinds of work. How do these categories apply in the study of individual lives?[1]

In answering the "Who am I?" question, Americans often use categorizations that mark them off as different from an assumed reference set of others. Many U.S. citizens do not note the fundamental fact that they are "American" unless they are living abroad or currently caught up in an international situation that emphasizes nationality. Similarly, cultural categorizations referring to race, gender, ethnicity, and class are often used, whether with pride or not, by people who identify themselves as different from an assumed mainstream white, male, heterosexual, WASP, middle-class typicality. Americans are more likely to identify themselves as black rather than white, as a woman rather than as a man, and as gay or lesbian rather than as heterosexual. Consider how you and your subject use categories of difference in answering self-conception questions and what this means about your social locations in contemporary America. In following this direction, you will also need to explore how these categories relate to the multiple cultural traditions out of which you and the other person construct your identities.

Categories of difference are cultural constructs that are defined in very different ways within different meaning systems. At the societal cultural level, "race" and "class" are not even present as categories (or social realities) in some societies. Similarly, since caste is not a category in mainstream America, it is not usually available or used in efforts at self-description except by individuals, such as those with South Asian backgrounds, who are influenced by cultures where it is an issue. Furthermore, where present, race, gender, and sexual orientation are defined in very different ways. Individuals who move across societal boundaries are often caught between disjunctive category systems. A Pacific islander who came to the United States considered himself superior at home to the outlying islanders, who were traditionally seen as unsophisticated and backward. Living in Florida, he was subjected to several racist incidents in which he was treated as inferior, such as by being denied entry to a "white" barbershop because of his relatively dark skin color. "But I am not an African American," he vainly protested.

Just as the general cultures of different societies conceptualize race, class, and gender in very different ways, so too do the varied cultural traditions present in American society. We are all entangled in a variety of different ways of understanding these categories. The cultures of different racial-ethnic groups do not define these terms the same way. Different class traditions conceptualize class differently, different ethnic traditions view gender differently, different religious and political traditions conceptualize race differently, and so on. Dominant American societal cultural traditions have traditionally privileged white, male, middle-class, heterosexual, non-disabled persons. Furthermore, the ideological systems within the dominant culture often obscure the degree to which this occurs by using explanatory systems that blame those who are excluded for their personal failure to attain the positions from which they are socially excluded. Conversely, a variety of countertraditions of liberation and resistance have arisen that have sought to redefine the situation in ways that raise the status of those who have been excluded. For example, within deaf culture deaf people are valorized, while "hearies" (hearing people) are conceptualized as inferior.

As the readings in Part Two of this book illustrate, most Americans are familiar with and affected by a variety of conflicting ways of thinking about difference in relation to their identities, social situations, and social relationships. For example, as Joshua Woodfork shows in Reading 6, the "biracial" professor he interviewed is often defined as "African American," as if this term somehow encompassed his personhood. In fact, he is also conceptualized by himself and others as "half white," "German," "a professor," a "baseball fan," "a therapist," and an "opera fan." Thus his own sense of himself is differentiated far beyond the racial-ethnic label. However, given the peculiar salience of race in the United States, his other identities are often affected by the fact that he is seen as an African American professor, opera fan, and therapist. Similarly, sexual orientation exists in complex relationships to other cultural traditions, including those of religion. Another young man interviewed by Woodfork currently identifies as "gay" but expects to marry and become "straight" later because his family's religious tradition, that of the Jehovah's Witnesses, disapproves of homosexuality.[2]

Exercise 8: Categories of Difference

Consider the set of cultural traditions you were entangled in while growing up. How were race, class, ethnicity, gender, sexual orientation, and disability generally conceptualized in each tradition? What labels were used, and how did the perspectives involved overlap and contrast? Think of several specific incidents in which some of these concepts were manifested in conversation or action, and analyze the incidents. How were you involved, how did you feel, how did you react, how did the incident affect you, and what did you learn? How do you now conceptualize difference in terms of your cultural traditions? To what extent do you accept the orientations of these traditions? Do you seek to modify and resist them? How do you handle the contrasts among the traditions you think with?

Given what you know so far, how do you think your research participant conceptualizes race, class, ethnicity, gender, sexual orientation, and disability? How do the traditions the person thinks with construct these categories, and how do you think the person accepts, modifies, or rejects these conceptualizations? How might this affect other identities and relationships, including the ways the person relates to you? What questions would help you explore this further?

Social Worlds, Roles, and Dramas

Answers to the "Who am I?" question also include terms for social roles. Here are some examples:

a good wife	Eric's girlfriend
a lifeguard	a waitress
a professor	a psychotherapist
massage therapist	Katharine's niece
a maid	a World War II reenactor

Another important aspect of life history involves an exploration of the social situations a person regularly passes through and the ways he or she or plays the roles that these social worlds require. Many of the different cultural traditions we think with are embodied in particular, concrete social institutions. When Claire goes to the ashram, the Tibetan Buddhist cultural tradition prevails and she is a "disciple"; when she goes to work, the therapeutic tradition dominates and she becomes a "therapist"; when she goes home, she steps into an American middle-class family system; and so forth. The cultural structuring and power dynamics of each of such worlds typically require us to play a social role that matches the role of others in these worlds. At work Claire plays "therapist" to people who act as her "clients." When she goes home, she plays American "mother" to her son and daughter. To be fluent in a cultural tradition is, in part, to know the expectations and obligations of the roles in the social worlds where that tradition prevails.

Knowing what is expected of Claire as a therapist, a Tibetan Buddhist, and a mother is very important, but we also need to know *how* she actually plays these roles in the particular social dramas with which she is involved. Role theory abstracts and generalizes about "the" role of the therapist or mother. This is useful, and it has a certain reality for individual as well as group analysis. People in any institution generalize about patterns and rules of role play; for example, "Doctors are supposed to do x," "Most nurses do y," and "Orderlies generally do z." But an individual who occupies any such role doesn't play it in the same way as the next person. Attention to variation in strategy, skill, and style, in conformity and resistance, and in desire and motivation is crucial for life history research.

Role theory has long recognized that people have to switch from one role to another as they move from one social world to another. A woman who is a lieutenant in the police force and a mother at home needs to make a rather drastic shift as she changes social worlds. It has been less sufficiently recognized that we also need to understand how a person carries cultural traditions from one world into another and how this affects the personal playing of social roles, the individual experience of social worlds, and the switching back and forth among them.

For example, Claire and Gina both play the role of therapist in the same sector of the Washington DC suburbs, and each had several years of postgraduate training at the same psychological institute. However, Gina plays therapist very differently from how Claire enacts the "same" role. Some of these variations may have to do with personalities, but others are connected to their differing cultural traditions.

Gina and Claire both "know" that the roles of therapist and client are governed by legal rules, professional ethics, and customary practice, and to a degree they follow these norms. However, Claire is more conservative in her handling of the relationship. She is very careful about holding to the fifty-minute time limit on therapy sessions, and she never gets involved with clients outside the office. Gina is much less formal about timing and regularly gets heavily involved in her clients' lives outside the therapy session. She goes with clients to court, twelve-step programs, family homes, hospitals, restaurants, and grave sites. Much of this variation between Gina and Claire stems from the ways they have developed their practice in relation to the cultural traditions they think with. Gina explicitly brings her version of her Italian American ethnic tradition into the role. Although she is aware that some other therapists see what she is doing as excessive or even unethical, much of her sense of what to do with clients comes from her ideas about rightness: "I guess I am depending on that gut sense of mine about 'What is the right thing to do here?' not 'What does the book say?'" Many of her ideas about rightness come directly out of "the code" of relations in Italian American culture. Growing up in an extended family culture, "you always find someone to intervene for you, affirm you, stick up for you. . . . [My clients] don't have that." She directly extends her sense of "family" to clients, and for her this means going out of her way to help them any way she can. This includes a strong, protective, "fighter" dimension, Consider this example:

> There is this young woman that I work with, and she got fired from her job unjustly. She was working as a hostess at [a local restaurant] and she went to work when she had the flu. She was really very sick, and the jerkball boss fired her because she wasn't up to speed and that was just *outrageous*. [The young woman was upset but would not do anything.] So I called the manager [laughs] as "Mrs. Magilicutty" who was in charge of the neighborhood women's group, and we were in there last weekend and we saw this waitress and she was the best and we would like to line up a year's worth of parties [at the restaurant] and we want her to be the hostess. And the man said, "Uh, oh, well she no longer works here." And I said, "Oh, why is that?" and he made excuses and said, "We have other people." But I said, "Oh, no! I watched her and she was a *natural!*" Well, she [the client] was tickled pink, you know, because we just kind of called him on his shit. . . . I mean he was stuttering and he tried to talk me into letting someone else do it and I said [coldly], "No. I don't think so," and we just made life miserable for him. . . . No, she wouldn't go back, it was just to torture him. Which I thought was a pretty healthy model for my client [laughs].

Hardly what is to be found in "the book" of the clinical social worker's role expectations, this kind of action on Gina's part is totally consistent with how she is an "advocate" or "champion" who goes "out for justice" for her clients.

Exercise 9: Social Roles

Make a list of the social worlds you move through on a daily, weekly, or monthly basis. List the cultural labels for the roles you are expected to play in each world and the complementary roles of the people with whom you interact. Identify some of the legal and customary expectations and obligations that govern particular role relationships. How do issues of power and social control play out here? What role violations are people concerned with, and how are they enforced? How is the way you play these roles similar to and different from how they are typically played? Consider a story or incident of role violation or resistance. What does this story "say" about how you play your role? How is your style of role play related to cultural traditions other than those that officially prevail in a particular social world?

Now reconsider these questions for your research partner. What are the general roles the person plays, and how does he or she play them in comparison to others? What questions might you ask in order to get stories and incidents that illustrate the person's style? Consider asking, also, about accompanying the person through some of his or her social worlds.

Participant Observation in the Study of Roles

As people get a sense of what you are trying to do with your life history research, they will usually understand that it is useful for you to accompany them to the places they regularly go. When I was working with Gina I wanted to visit her home, office, therapy group, and tae kwon do club, and she willingly assented. As you go with your research participant through his or her various social worlds, try to get a feeling for what life is like in each location. Make specific observations with an eye to writing scenes that illustrate how your subject enacts roles. It was important to interview Gina about her therapy group, the martial arts center, and family life at home, and it was a powerful addition to go with her into these worlds. Note how effectively this method is used by Douglas Harper, Barbara Myerhoff, and Jenny Thompson in the readings in Part Two, and consider how you might adapt some of their techniques in your research.

Once again, an interesting problem in writing descriptions of scenes and social roles is the issue of point of view. Does a given vignette convey your point of view or that of your subject? If you, as author, construct a storylike event from what you observed of your subject, it may include some of his or her meaning, but it is inevitably going to represent your point of view because you selected what to say about what you observed. Your take on the scene from your frames of reference will be useful to tell the reader something about how you saw things, and it can serve as a vehicle to bring the reader into the scene, but it is best if such descriptions can then be supplemented by scenes that convey the subject's point of view. How can that be accomplished?

One method is to develop scenes based on the stories your research partner tells you. During an interview, when your research participant offers a general statement and you ask for an example, the person is likely to come up with storylike scenes, often with dialogue, that convey his or her point of view. Often, especially if it was a quick or abbreviated account, it is useful to ask more questions to fill in details such as additional dialogue, action, gesture, facial expression, and setting which help to convey the subject's point of view.

Also try taking a scene where you were both present and write the contrast between your point of view and that of your research participant. For example, if you were at the research participant's office, the objects of the setting (for example, a picture on the wall), the feel of the office, and the quality of a brief conversation with a co-worker will have made an impression on you that your description will convey. But now you can go back over the same scene in an interview with your participant. What does that painting on the wall mean to him or her? What to him or her is the feel of the office? What did he or she think about that interaction with the co-worker? Techniques like this will enable you to get at how a scene looks to your subject and to develop a contrast between the participant's points of view and your own.

The Ethnographic Encounter

There is one additional, new social situation that is crucial to your study. This is the life history scene you and your research participant are beginning to construct and to regularly move in and out of together. This scene, like any other, is also structured by role relationships, here that of "ethnographer" and "research participant" within the cultural tradition of life history. The cultural biographies you will write about yourself and the other person will be created out of what takes place in this encounter. This relationship is your "data," your "experiment," the very medium out of which your interpretation will be developed. So you want to learn how to understand and play the relationship creatively in your research, and simultaneously you want to observe, record, study, and analyze its cultural nature. A key section within the story you tell will be your description of the encounter between you and your participant.

Anthropologist Michael Agar has offered an important way of thinking about the informant-ethnographer relationship and a guide to understanding and using it creatively. Focusing on how the encounter typically involves an ethnographer operating with one cultural tradition and an informant operating with an alien tradition, Agar stresses the importance of what he variously calls "breakdowns" or "rich points." These are situations in which the informant says or does something that doesn't "make sense" to the ethnographer, violates the ethnographer's expectations, or causes the ethnographer to be surprised or puzzled. As Agar shows, these moments can be a crucial point of entry into understanding an unfamiliar cultural tradition.[3]

In ordinary social situations we typically gloss over breakdowns or lose the opportunity to learn by simply disagreeing. When I was doing research in Micronesia years ago, I was talking with an elderly Chuukese man in company with another American. We were discussing creatures that lived in the lagoon, and after discussing various kinds of fish the man noted that "Of course, sharks are people." The other American said, "No they aren't," and asserted that although some sharks carry young in the womb, rather than laying eggs, it is only porpoises and whales that are mammals like us. Later, I went back to the man and asked him further about what he meant. It turned out that in one Chuukese cultural tradition, sharks are conceptualized as humans. The cursed descendants of an incestuous relationship between a man and a woman of a nearby island, sharks are considered a form of human being. As such they are believed susceptible to the magic used against ordinary people.

Going back to Agar's point, we can see that by ignoring or disagreeing with the Chuukese man, I would have missed an opportunity to learn an aspect of his worldview. When something doesn't "make sense," that means it doesn't fit with our frame of reference, but it may well make sense in a cultural tradition we are trying to understand. As Agar suggests, we should be alert to statements that suggest or imply a different way of constructing things and use them to learn about the alternative logic. But breakdowns and rich points are also illuminating in our ethnographic effort to better understand our own frames of reference. Our surprise at a different point of view often clearly reveals an assumption of ours that we might not have noticed without the breakdown bringing it to our attention.

In this regard, the idea of breakdowns and rich points can usefully be extended to anything that catches our attention about what our research partner says or does. What we find moving or fascinating, that which bothers, shocks, or disturbs us is based on the ways of thinking about the world we have been enculturated to use. These reactions point us outward to the alternative ways of seeing, evaluating, and acting, and they also point back inward to the assumptions and patterns of our own cultural conditioning.

Exercise 10: Breakdowns and Rich Points

Think back on your encounters with your research participant so far. Has he or she said or done things that did not make sense to you? Might you be able to find here a clue to something significant about the way he or she sees or thinks or acts in the world? Similarly, ask yourself what has pleased, surprised, bothered, or concerned you about what your informant has said. Can you find the cultural basis of your reaction, and does this help you to see something about how you make sense of things? Can you explain breakdowns that occur as involving a difference between one or more of his or her cultural traditions and one or more of yours?

Agar speaks of an ethnographer with one cultural tradition meeting an informant who operates with a single, different cultural tradition. However, as we have seen, the ethnographic relationship actually involves two people who carry in mind a variety of different cultural traditions. The ethnographic encounter is likely to involve the meeting, meshing, and sometimes clashing of a dozen or more cultural frames of reference.

Consider the following list. On the left side are several of the major cultural traditions of my research partner, Claire. On the other side are several of my cultural traditions. This kind of diagram allows us to ask a variety of questions that may help us understand cultural correspondences and breakdowns in the ethnographic encounter.

Claire's Traditions	John's Traditions
East Coast white U.S. culture	East Coast white U.S. culture
(critical relationship)	(critical relationship)
middle class/working class	middle class
psychology	anthropology
Judaism	Presbyterian (lapsed)
Tibetan Buddhism	Eastern philosophy
opera (major interest)	blues/rock (minor interest)

We can notice first where there are points of convergence. Both Claire and I are familiar with middle-class white American culture, both of us are middle-aged, and both of us are involved in a critical relationship with the dominant culture that stems back to our coming of age in the 1960s. My understanding of opera is minimal, and one of our breakdowns involved my initial failure to see the complexity and depth of her involvement in opera, including its association with her therapeutic tradition. We are both interested in Eastern philosophy, and this helped us to connect and aided my understanding of how she integrates her version of Buddhism with psychotherapy. On the other hand, once, when speaking from her Jewish frame of reference, Claire said, "I don't trust WASPs." I experienced a breakdown. As a WASP I realized that I do not construct WASPs as untrustworthy, and I also wondered if she distrusted me. Working on the breakdown led me to understand her point of view and experience better, including the anti-Semitic prejudice that she as a Jewish woman had experienced in Washington DC.

Exercise 11: Contrasts and Convergence in Cultural Traditions
Construct a list of cultural traditions similar to the one above putting your research partner's cultural traditions on one side and yours on the other. List them in ways that show areas of convergence and divergence. Use the idea of breakdowns to consider the relationships among different traditions on the chart, that is, to explore the ways in which your forms of thinking mesh with or diverge from those of your research participant. This perspective may help you culturally understand your relationship with your participant better, and it should help you conceptualize breakdowns that have occurred or will occur. Consider not only obviously matching traditions but also connections between seemingly unrelated systems.

Identities and Identification

As we learn more about how our research partners play their personal and social identities, we will begin to get a feel for how they react to certain situations. One way of furthering this understanding is to deliberately try to imagine what it might be like to be in their shoes in their situations.

We often half-consciously identify with others. In watching a film we may identify with particular characters, projecting our subjectivity onto them and vicariously feeling how they experience a situation in the story – how they are smitten by this person, shamed by another, led to feel sorry for someone else, and how they then decide to take one course of action instead of another. Similarly, as a friend tells us a story, we feel his or her initial anxiety and frustration and then elation and relief almost as if it were happening to us. This capacity for identification is deliberately cultivated in acting school, where students are given exercises to help them identify with – or "become" – the characters they will portray onstage. In life history work it is also useful to cultivate our capacity for identification. It is true, of course, that there are complications and limitations, and that we can never completely feel what someone else feels ("It's a girl – a guy, a white, an Italian, an Asian – thing, you wouldn't understand"), but we can take such understanding as is possible to a higher level via deliberate attempts to identify with our research participants. The basic method is to consciously try and imagine what it is like to be the other person, with his or her cultural background and cultural traditions, assuming one of his or her social identities and encountering a particular social situation. The point, of course, is not to think about how *you* would respond to a given situation – given your cultural traditions – but how he or she might respond, given his or her traditions.[4]

Consider, for example, the story that Gina told about her waitress-client that I quoted earlier in this chapter. Given what we know about Gina, it's not hard to put ourselves in her shoes and feel how outraged she was by the manager's unfair treatment of Gina's client. Knowing what I know about her cultural traditions, I can imagine how "natural" it would be for me as her – though it would not be for Claire – to take the aggressive, out-for-justice reaction she took. Doing so helps me feel my way into her world. It helps me deepen my understanding of what she has told me and brings me into a better position to go further, to go back to other situations she has told me about and to ask additional questions to carry my understanding further.

Exercise 12: Identification in Life History Research

Consider a recent experience of your own, one that you might tell as a kind of story. Go back into your memory of the experience, adopt the social role you had, and reenter the situation. Recall what it looked and felt like to you then, how you saw what was before you, and how you thought to yourself, using the words and phrases you did, in deciding what to do. Consider how the mix of cultural traditions you brought to the experience influenced your thoughts, feelings, and reactions.

Now try this exercise in relation to your research partner. Begin by taking a story she told you and try to imaginatively reenter the situation as her, with her cultural traditions. Try to feel what this must have been like for her, how it felt and looked from her point of view. Imagine being her, saying the words she said in telling the story. Take the dialogue she reported and use it as a script; say these words as if you were her. Notice what this is like and what you have learned by doing this.

Now consider some situation your research partner encounters that you have not yet discussed together. Try to put yourself through it as she might experience it. To what extent do you feel you can do this? Often we imagine several possibilities. What questions arise? Some questions may arise because we are not sure which of a person's ways of thinking might kick in. Make a note about the possibilities you imagine.

In your next interview ask your research participant about this situation. Ask her to go back into the situation, to recall what it was like, how she saw it, how she thought to herself about it. Interview her about this based on your own effort at identification. What clarifications emerge? Whether your identification was on or off target, the effort at identification and the questions and subjective feel it provides should help you get closer to finding out what you can about your research participant's cultural ways of orienting and acting in the world.

Because it carries the satisfaction of gaining some mutual understanding across cultural boundaries, across the ignorance and ethnocentric misunderstandings that often separate us, a successful ethnographic relationship can be peculiarly satisfying and meaningful. This theme is evident in several of the readings in Part Two. By reflecting carefully on your experience with your research participant, you may learn important things about the complex ways that identities and social relationships are influenced by multiple cultural values.

CHAPTER FOUR

Negotiating Conflicting Cultures
and Competing Values

During your life history research, it is good to step back from time to time and organize the material you have gathered with an eye to how you might write it up. Perhaps you have gone into your project with a general question in mind, such as a South Asian immigrant's adjustment to the United States, or how someone in a special occupational niche balances work and family demands. Perhaps a question like this emerged as you reflected on your own life in contrast with that of your research participant. In either case, you need to explore how the material you have gathered speaks to the ways you and your participant experience and handle the issue under consideration. In doing so you will also want to consider how both of these individuals manage and negotiate their multiple cultural traditions and how this affects their handling of the theme you are exploring.

Outlining Your Project

Outlines provide an overall map of the material obtained, and writing them out helps you discover, organize, and structure the theme you want to work with. How can you introduce, develop, illustrate, and conclude a story of how this theme works for your two subjects given the multiple cultural traditions each of you works with?

As your outline develops, think back over the materials you already have for each section of the paper. Look at your notes, reading for quotes, scenes, stories, and examples. Study each example carefully. How does it speak to the questions you have? Does it fit with what you already think you know? If not, what does it tell you that you need to consider? Where could a quote go in the outline so that it speaks most effectively to your theme? Where could all your best quotes, stories, and scenes be placed? Asking these questions will help you see what more you need to get to fill in or complete the outline of the theme you are concerned with and how the various cultural traditions and values work out in relation to it.

Competing Values

As we have seen, contemporary Americans juggle a variety of different cultural traditions such as work traditions, religious traditions, ethnic traditions, and psychological traditions. Typically, at least some of these traditions do not fit well together because they include such different values, that is, very different ideas about what makes life worthwhile and what is important, desirable, and undesirable.

A primary function of culture is to offer people a plausible and convincing worldview and an ordered set of ideas about what is good and bad. Cultures tell us what is important, how to choose, how to feel, and how to act. Humans are not born with this kind of cognitive orientation to life; we have to learn it through culture. Each culture offers a way of creating order out of chaos, but there are many different ways of making sense of the world and lots of different values to choose from. Any given system is one arbitrary way of ordering things. Another function of culture is to make us ethnocentric, to convince us that the way we learned is the way things are and that other ways – the worldviews of people in other groups – are misguided, confused, or deluded.

The difficulty in learning and thinking with multiple cultural traditions is that the answers they provide to questions about what is important are not only different but often contradictory as well. To think with several cultures is to be caught among contradictory systems of meaning.

How do individuals negotiate different systems of meaning? How do conflicting values work at the level of individual experience? What strategies do the two individuals you are studying use to handle cultural contradictions?

Mainstream Cultural Conflicts

Every large-scale cultural system contains at least some contradictions. Mainstream America tells us to be individualistic, but it also tells us to conform and "fit in." It tells us, through mass-media advertisements and holiday rituals, that eating is gratifying and satisfying, but it also tells us that we should "be thin." It tells us not only to work hard but also to "keep priorities straight" and spend lots of time with our families. These contradictions are culturally recognized as difficult, and "confusion," "stress," and even "psychiatric problems" are attributed to them. Sometimes it is useful to directly ask yourself and your participant, "What kinds of value conflicts do you experience, and how do you deal with them?" Given the complexities of this area, it is also useful to try and generate pertinent material indirectly.

Doing Future Autobiography

One way to get at values is to ask people about their hopes and fears for the future. As usual, try this on yourself first and then ask your research partner.

Exercise 13: Goals for the Future
Imagine yourself ten years in the future. What kinds of situations would you like to be in? What for you would be a very good future? What for you would be a bad future? Try to imagine what such a future would be like. Outline or write out a one- or two-page description of each scenario. Make a note about how you think your research participant might answer this question. Now try asking him or her.

To analyze what our answers to questions about the future reveal about our values, we need to consider the relationship between individual values and cultural values. Although we often think of values as "personal," the individual's meanings and purposes are always closely connected to the values that characterize the cultures to which he or she has been exposed. A person may construct a cultural value in original and innovative ways, or may even resist a value strongly and seek out alternative values, but in doing so the person is usually influenced by some other cultural (or countercultural) tradition. Through agreement or opposition, an individual's sense of values is always closely related to the cultural traditions he or she has encountered and engaged with, including those of national/societal cultures.

Consider the results of the preceding exercise. By asking people to describe a good or bad future, you obtain a revealing reflection of the values they hold. Despite variation in age, gender, ethnic affiliation, religion, and class, there is considerable similarity in the values American students in my classes express in this exercise. For example, three American values are particularly prominent. Consider the following responses:

"One of the worst things would be going through a bad marriage and a bad divorce – that's why I really want to make sure I am in love enough to last a lifetime."

"I have trouble supporting my family on the poor wage they're giving me at the fast-food joint."

"I will drive a black Saab turbo 900, and our beautiful house will be 5,000 to 6,000 square feet."

"I couldn't just be a mother, nor could I only work."

As these responses suggest, the individual in America is virtually forced to negotiate some kind of relationship with the society's dominant cultural values, such as occupational achievement and success, materialistic affluence, and the romantic love/marriage/family syndrome. The ways they do so vary considerably but involve some ambivalence. Even acceptance of dominant values is often tinged with the concern that all is not well here. This ambivalence is itself part of the contemporary mainstream culture; each value is debated and problematized in the public discourse, and this is reflected in individual conceptualizations. Drawing on her own experience and statistics about the prevalence of divorce, Gina often expresses humorous cynicism about love, marriage, and male-female relationships, joking that she should tell the couples she counsels, "It won't work, stop dreaming, bail out now!" But in fact she rarely says anything like this. Despite her own marital difficulties, she still hopes to find a "good relationship" herself and expresses hope that her children will make "good marriages." Even respondents who want to avoid involvement with one or another of the dominant values are likely to mention them in doing the future autobiography. As one woman noted, "I don't know if I'll get married, but it's something that's done in America. If you don't, people think there's something wrong with you." As such statements suggest, Americans know that others *expect* them to accept these values and will require an explanation for noncompliance.

Exercise 14: Negotiating Cultural Values
How do you and your research participant position yourself in relation to dominant American values like occupational achievement and success, materialism, and the ro-

mantic love and nuclear family syndrome? How does each of you define the value and your relationship to it? What does each of you want here? If either of you resists a value, how do you seek to evade the expectation?

Americans do not just negotiate a relationship with the dominant culture's values; they must also negotiate a relationship with the values of each of the half dozen or more additional cultural traditions they work with. All cultural traditions, whether those of work, religion, politics, ethnicity, or therapy, contain explicit and implicit conceptions of the desirable and the undesirable. One of the complexities of life for all of us in this society is the problem of working out a relationship with the competing values of our various cultural traditions.

The presence of competing values is likely to show up in Exercises 13 and 14. Look at how you and your participant imagine handling value conflicts in the future. Younger middle-class students in my classes, for example, often imagine balancing career, love, marriage, family, children, pets, civic responsibility, leisure interests, and particular religious and ethnic values much more successfully than is typically the case in real-life America. Once you have a general picture, ask questions that directly probe the values of the particular traditions you and the other person operate with.

Exercise 15: Values in Multiple Cultural Traditions

List the major values (ideas about what is good or bad) in several of the cultural traditions that you and your research participant are working with. What are the attributes of a successful person in terms of a given tradition? What gratifications and rewards do successful people generally get out of their engagement with this tradition? Is the way you or your participant handles the value different from how you think the average person deals with it? Now consider how this tradition relates to the other cultural traditions each of you uses. For example, how do the attributes of a good or successful person in one tradition fit or clash with those of other traditions? Explore how the rewards and meanings you have sought to get from different traditions have changed over time and how they fit together now.

Claire's experiences illustrate how all this can work. Claire originally hoped to make a career in music. As a musically talented young adult, she trained extensively to be an opera singer: "I identified my self-worth with my ability and wanted to be a singer." As she sees it, the general values of this career, which come to those with a high level of talent, ability to perform under pressure, extreme dedication, good luck, and astute political maneuvering, include the winning of competitive musical scholarships and awards, training at the most prestigious schools of music, selection for high-level companies, and eventually the aesthetic satisfaction, acclaim, and financial rewards of performing at a high level and being recognized as among the "best" in this profession. Claire had the talent and competitive drive necessary to make success a real possibility, but for a variety of reasons, including ambivalence about performing in public, she eventually gave up on this career. Years later, after becoming a psychotherapist, she returned to her music and began taking voice lessons again, but not with the idea of making a career or publicly performing as a singer. I wondered why.

At first, I thought this activity might be simply a minor hobby, but it turned out that her return to music was more important than this and quite revealing of the values she holds. First, there was an important aesthetic dimension. Speaking of one of Schubert's pieces, she says, "It was a tragic song. . . . The melody was sublime, I *loved* the song, I *adored* the song and I wanted to do it justice." But there was much more as well, for her return to singing involved a hard, sustained effort at self-mastery.

> It was like conquering something – um, for a lot years when I wanted to be a singer I struggled a lot with really going against my nature because I am not an extravert and I am not a performer – and I would be just terrorized at the performance and in part because of that I had other difficulties with my singing. And when I started studying [again], I had to undo a lot of bad habits and there was a period of time when I really couldn't sing at all. It was like taking something apart and putting it back together . . . [eventually I was] able to return and to say I want to work on this because this is a challenge and I want satisfaction from this and I want the pleasure of knowing that I can take a piece of music and express myself, you know, in a beautiful way. And so the lessons from then on when I was out of the running were really to conquer my own mountains. And there were things that I began to be able to sing that I never could sing previously . . . and I got a great deal of gratification, a sense of self-mastery, because it was not only a technical challenge but it was a mind challenge, you know, those balances between being not too self-conscious but being self-conscious enough to keep on top of things.

Claire's new relation to opera was meaningful aesthetically and also expressed and blended values from other traditions that are important to her, including dimensions of her Buddhist psychology such as "letting go," "going to your own truth," and "staying focused inside." Even more closely involved are the values from her psychotherapeutic tradition, as in overcoming and mastering a psychological challenge. Clearly, Claire's attitude toward singing parallels her psychotherapeutic practice. Interestingly, she also equates the difficulties and satisfaction she gets from doing therapy well with the satisfaction she gets from music.

> Psychotherapy requires stepping out of my own ego and then letting it be – whatever it's going to be – letting it unfold without trying to maneuver it from an intellectual level, and in that way it's very similar [to music] . . . and I can get into the same dances around it and getting perfectionistic sometimes and giving myself a hard time and *hating* it like I would hate music sometimes – and yet when it goes well – when I am in there when somebody leaves [a good therapy session] – I say, "Boy I'm glad I do this."

Here we see how Claire balances, blends, and integrates the values of an aesthetic tradition with two of her other major meaning systems.

Balancing more diverse systems is sometimes very difficult. For example, the national cultural systems of Pakistan and mainstream America that Salma switches between offer fundamental value contradictions around the goal of marriage and family. Should one strike out in the singles world and look for a spouse through dating rituals and marry "for love," or should one defer to the wisdom of one's family elders and submit to an arranged marriage? Similarly, Gina believes in both Italian American working-class mainstream culture and upper-middle-class cultural systems, but one says that women should be stay-at-home mothers who endure unsatisfactory marriage to serve men, while the other says that women should fulfill themselves through careers and that if a marriage is "not working," divorce is an appropriate solution. If people have a sympathetic feeling for two or more strongly contradictory cultures, how do they handle the contradictions? The following strategy of questioning can be useful.

Exercise 16: Managing Contradictory Values
Review the list of cultural traditions you and your research participant work with. Where are the strongest contrasts among the cultures you work with and among those that your research participant operates with? What exactly are the major contradictions? What does each of you think about how other people you know manage these

conflicts? What strategies do you yourself use? What strategies does your participant use? What questions could you ask to learn more about this?

Cultural conflict can be disorienting and emotionally painful, as evidenced by the difficulties adults usually have in trying to adapt to an unfamiliar society. Studies of culture shock indicate that after an initial "honeymoon stage" in which the migrant to a new society feels exhilarated by cultural differences, a period of "disintegration" typically follows. Here the person trying to manage two contradictory cultural systems is *expected* to undergo confusion, disorientation, loss, apathy, isolation, loneliness, inadequacy, anger, rage, nervousness, anxiety, and frustration.[1] So how do people manage?

In an essay on "Conflict and Accommodation of Mainstream and Minority Values," George and Louise Spindler analyze the patterned strategies that individuals often seem to use. Their discussion is based on ethnography with Menominee Native Americans who are exposed to both traditional Native American culture and mainstream American culture. The problem is that these systems involve "irreconcilable differences."[2]

Both groups value something we might call "power." Mainstream Americans define power through control over others in hierarchical structures or aggressive, competitive manipulation of social situations and the accumulation of money. Such behavior is so negative in the traditional Menominee view that individuals who act this way are subject to negative sanctions such as gossip and witchcraft. Traditional Menominees value a noncompetitive, self-effacing style of behavior; for them, "power" refers to spiritual power obtained through the vision quest and other relations with supernatural allies. Similarly, mainstream Americans value exploitative use of nature, while the Menominees seek harmony with nature. While some of the Spindlers' examples are simplified, they correctly identify many drastic contradictions between the two cultures. What does a person who is heavily enculturated in both systems do?

The Spindlers report several standard resolutions. One involves giving primary allegiance to one system. Hence some Menominees reaffirm the traditional Native American culture and denigrate the American mainstream, while others reject the traditional Native American culture, conceptualize it as "primitive," and pledge their allegiance to the "modern" American mainstream. Others try to simultaneously hold both systems by separating them and by code switching – for example, by being Menominee at home and mainstream American at work. Still others deliberately seek to synthesize or blend elements of both cultures, as by using home decorations that are both Indian and American. The idea of "hyphenated Americans" (for example, Italian-Americans or Chinese-Americans) sometimes implies this kind of mixing and blending. In yet another patterned solution, "constructive marginality," individuals try to avoid identifying with either culture. Using detachment and cynicism, they place themselves at a distance from both systems and identify with a marginal or outsider position. Finally, the Spindlers discuss "personal withdrawal," where the individual who is "torn by conflict" withdraws or escapes through alcohol, drugs, fantasy, or the hallucinations and delusions of mental illness.

The Spindlers' analysis suggests that knowing or having more than one cultural tradition is a terrible burden that can lead directly to suffering, alcoholism, and mental illness. However, it is clear that most individuals not only manage multiculturalism but often handle it well and even thrive on it. How can this be? What is the good side of having multiple cultures? Actually, many of the adaptations the Spindlers mention can be positive. Multiple frames of reference offer many advantages as well as problems. Knowing more than one tradition loosens the stranglehold that a single culture may place on our understanding. Multiple cultures offer multiple possibilities, and by offering choices, individual agency is supported. The multicultural situation can make for a more varied, autonomous, and interesting life.

Lila Shah, like Salma an immigrant from South Asia, describes this positive outcome in the first reading in Part Two of this book. At first she experienced the differences between American culture and Indian culture as hard to handle, but later she found them advantageous: "Instead of regretting the fact that I was a part of two cultures, I began to enjoy it. I was a much richer and more balanced person because I knew of two different cultures. I had the advantage of picking and choosing aspects of both cultures that I wanted to retain or discard."[3] Other solutions can be at least somewhat adaptive, as when the individual successfully plays at a noncommitted but creative level with a set of traditions to which he or she grants no full personal allegiance. Even personal withdrawal, which the Spindlers portray as a pathological defense mechanism, can be creative and effective. Temporary escape can be useful if it is not too damaging, and all individuals who experience cultural contradictions probably make some use of withdrawal and fantasy.

Fantasy resolves cultural contradictions that are difficult to manage. This vicarious experience is pleasurable, and out of it one may find real solutions. For example, Gina sometimes resolves several of the contradictions of her actual social situation through fantasy identification with a fictional movie figure that magically resolves some of her cultural conflicts. This identification provides temporary escape and has also helped her develop functional solutions.[4]

Imagination is much more than mere escape. It is often the place where creative synthesis or aesthetic balance can be achieved, where one can mix, blend, and balance different cultural traditions. Indian psychiatrist Sudhir Kakkar, who moves back and forth easily between Indian and Western traditions, describes one form of this solution:

> A degree of alienation from one's culture, a deep exposure to other world views . . . may indeed be necessary for heightening one's perception about the culture and society one is born into. . . . "Marginality," "alienation," "ambivalence," "boundary," are perhaps not the right words to describe what I mean here, since they connote a subjective experience of pain and exclusion without indicating the presence of a corresponding heightening of the self . . . and the curious comfort that comes after the first unease has been accommodated.[5]

Exercise 17: Benefits of Multiple Cultures

How and to what extent is having the resources of multiple cultural traditions positive for you? Do you think your multiple traditions may have helped free you from being dominated by one particular system of values? How would you explain this? Have you discovered ways of balancing and blending different systems that is more positive for you than what you might have experienced with fewer cultural resources? Give an example. Do you use some version of any of the solutions, such as code switching or fantasy, identified by the Spindlers? Are there other methods you employ? Describe how one of these works. Now consider these questions for your research partner.

Use of a Meaningful Tradition

One common method for dealing with the conflicts among one's multiple cultures is to devote primary allegiance to a religious, spiritual, philosophical, or political tradition. Here the person deliberately makes such a tradition paramount and mentally and emotionally uses it as the key to balancing contradictory values. Such a system can serve as a moral guide for decisions, a basis for social criticism, a reference point in confusion, and a consolation for problems and difficulties.

Gina, for example, ultimately grounds the meaning of her life in liberal Catholicism. She uses this as an overarching explanation for her life and views issues in her other worlds through the lens of this system. Thus, she sees the arrival of particular clients as a manifestation of God's will and views her work helping them as a form of religious service.

Exercise 18: Use of a Primary Value System

Do you ground you life in a religious, spiritual, philosophical, or political meaning system or a combination of several such systems? If you do, what is your relationship to the tradition, and how do you use it in dealing with decisions and value conflicts? Does this tradition serve as a basis for social criticism? What social problems or evils does it highlight, and what social action does it support? How does this orientation fit with your other cultural traditions? If you do not have such a key tradition, where do your most important values come from, and how do these relate to your various cultural traditions? Now consider how all this works for your research partner. Given what you know so far, what questions can you ask to probe this area further? Finally, consider how these meaningful traditions may be affecting your life history project.

If either of the participants in life history is strongly committed to a particular religious or political frame of reference, this may pose certain complexities for the project. For example, a committed research partner may seek to persuade you of the validity of his or her religious or political beliefs – or even try to convert you. Usually it is possible to sidestep this problem through emphasizing your interest in *understanding* what the person believes. Conversely, if you feel strongly about a particular political orientation – a social justice issue, perhaps – you may find, to your discomfort, that your research partner has very different beliefs, perhaps even beliefs of which you disapprove. In such a case it is usually best to reaffirm that the goal of life history research is to *understand* your research partner's points of view, not to judge, confront, or change them. The understanding we gain may then be useful in other kinds of projects where social change is the goal.

Media Systems and Multiple Cultures

Contemporary Americans not only pass through many different social worlds that involve actual face-to-face interaction; we also vicariously participate in many different media worlds. After beginning the day with a newspaper, we may subsequently tune in to radio, television, film, books, magazines, chat rooms, and websites. As we engage with any particular media form, we slip mentally and emotionally out of the "real" world and enter mediated cultural worlds. Usually our use of media has something to do with our actual social and cultural worlds. Sometimes a person's use of media is mainly "escape," a mental vacation from the stress and strain of ordinary life, including the clash of cultural traditions. In other cases the use of media functions as a vicarious return to a currently missing social world – as when South Asian immigrants to the United States seek out films, novels, cable television programs, and newspapers from India. In other instances people supplement their actual relationships to particular cultural traditions through media, as when Claire reads Tibetan Buddhist texts or Gina listens to a Christian radio program. Sometimes such media even address the problem of conflicting values, as when Gina's radio program discusses living a Christian life in the midst of a secular culture or when Claire's book discusses applying Buddhism to issues in everyday American life.

Exercise 19: Media Worlds
List the media worlds you typically enter in the course of a given day or week. Which of these worlds are most important to you? Do you have a favorite book genre, TV program, or magazine? How do these media experiences connect, directly and indirectly, to your actual social worlds and multiple cultural traditions? Now consider these questions for your research participant.

Our use of media often has complex connections to our actual social and cultural worlds. One way of exploring this is to consider the relationships we develop with particular figures from our media worlds, such as politicians, musicians, sports figures, authors, talk-show hosts, and fictional characters. Sometimes, as with Gina, understanding a person's use of a particular media figure is important to understanding how the person negotiates multiple cultures.

Gina surprised me when she told me that one of her heroes was Ste-

ven Seagal, an actor who has starred in a series of violent martial arts action films: "He's great! He doesn't say much – but he's smooth. He's my
ideal. He walks through a crowd – and without even hardly breathing – he's
breaking bones. . . . I'll be watching videos and my kids are calling about
dinner and I'll say, 'Get your own dinner, I'm watching Hard to Kill.'" Why,
I wondered, would a social worker who deals regularly with the victims of
all-too-real violence be attracted to films like Hard to Kill and Out for Justice,
where the character portrayed by Steven Seagal is vividly shown beating,
maiming, and killing dozens of villains?

In exploring a person's connection with a favorite media figure it is useful to consider how the person relates to the figure. Often there are several
dimensions. Gina considers Seagal attractive, so in that sense he is a kind
of romantic figure. At other times she conceptualizes him as a kind of
brother, a male ally-protector. But mainly Gina conceives of Seagal as an
idealized self, someone she imagines she would like to be like. Thus she
identifies with Seagal in his films and imagines being someone like him
in some of her daydreams. But why? It turns out that there is a variety of
important cultural connections.

In puzzling over her attraction, Gina is sure, first, that Seagal's appeal
"has something to do with the fact that he is Italian." She enjoys the fan-
tasized representation of Italian American culture (however stereotypical)
in the films and is amused by Seagal's Italian flourishes, such as his adept
use of respect etiquette in dealing with a Mafia don in Out for Justice. But
she is equally impressed by his willingness to go against the Mafia don
and the judgments of Italian American culture. Thus Seagal represents
to her someone who is loyal to and fluent in the culture but independent
of its judgments and social pressures, pressures she feels all too strongly
in her own life. In addition, Seagal – a black belt in aikido – serves as an
ideal in her martial arts practice, and her teacher even works this connection into his instructions. Finally, Gina imaginatively equates the people
who have abused her own female clients, usually men, with the villains of
Seagal's films. In watching the films, Gina can thus imaginatively meld
her own work in supporting her clients, whom she treats as family, with
Seagal's out-for-justice actions.

In some of Gina's daydreams, these connections to her cultural traditions are seen to be at play:

Well, [in my fantasy] I'm downtown, in a city, I guess, it's DC, with my sisters and some friends, and they don't know that part of me. There is an old lady being bothered by a gang of four or five bullies, they are older teenagers, maybe eighteen or twenty years old. I tell them to stop but they discount me. They think I'm just this little woman, they don't stop. So I pull a Steven Seagal . . . a chop, a block . . . and they all go running off. The people with me are so surprised that it was me. Meanwhile I was perfectly cool, I kind of kept on walking. I didn't even break a sweat.[6]

Exercise 20: Media Figures and Cultural Traditions
Make a list of figures from your media worlds – political figures, authors, musicians, sports figures, fictional characters, and so forth. Take one of the figures you like and consider how you relate to the person. Does this figure represent some kind of ideal for you or some kind of idealized other to whom you would like to relate? What kinds of connections can you find between your relationship with this figure and the social situations and cultural conflicts of your actual social worlds? Now consider if your research partner has unmet media figures – political figures, authors, actors, musicians, fictional characters – that he or she admires. How might this admiration relate to his or her negotiation of multiple cultural traditions? What kinds of questions might you ask to explore this further?

Multiple Cultures in Dreams

Most of us keep our different worlds somewhat separate. We use one cultural tradition in church, another at work, and a third at home. However, all our traditions are "housed" together in our heads. Here our religious, work, and family traditions and concerns are all simultaneously present, jostling together in our minds. When we are asleep and dreaming they may come into direct relationship with each other. Traditionally, life history researchers tried to use dreams to analyze the psychological patterns of their informants, but dreams can also be valuable for cultural explorations.

Exercise 21: Dreams and Multiple Cultures
For the next five days keep a pencil and paper by your bedside and try to record a dream or two immediately upon waking. Describe the narrative or story of the dream from the inside as precisely as possible. What was the dream like as an alternative world? What were the characteristics of the dream self, dream settings, other dream

figures, and dream action? How is the dream world similar to and different from your cultural experience in your waking social worlds? Does the dream reflect your particular mix of cultural traditions and roles? Can the dream be read as a commentary on the stresses and strains of your waking social worlds? What meaning do you see in the dream? In the dominant American culture, dreams are often dismissed as meaningless, yet there is a lurking suspicion that they may be psychologically revealing or premonitions of the future. Given these prevailing notions, how do you read your dreams? How are dreams interpreted in the religious, ethnic, and psychological traditions you know? To what extent do you use such traditions in thinking about your own dreams? Now consider asking your research participant about dreams and, if the person is interested in them, try exploring this area along the lines suggested above.

Multiple Cultures in Internal Dialogues

Strange and interesting as they are, dreams remain murky and problematic. What people make of them is clearer and more revealing than what they "really" mean. Certain waking states offer more promise for cultural investigation.

Just as the language, concepts, symbols, and ways of thinking from different cultural traditions appear together in dreams, so also do they come into relationship during waking states, particularly in the mental wandering sometimes referred to as "stream of consciousness," "daydreams," or "internal dialogues." When a person is not engaged in rational, focused thought or in some compelling activity, his or her consciousness tends to wander "away" into a flow of inner imagery, feelings, and internal conversation. Here we find a spontaneous, semi-conscious flow of alternating memories, fantasies, anticipations of the future, idle musings, and forms of internal talk. While the dominant American culture teaches us either to ignore this pervasive dimension of experience or to conceptualize it as a mildly negative "psychological process," the stream of consciousness is frequently a functional and always a highly cultural phenomenon. Since the individual conducts memories, fantasies, and internal conversations in terms of the language-concept systems of the cultural traditions he or she thinks with, the stream of consciousness is revealing of the individual's personal version of these subjective cultures and of his or her methods of negotiating among them.

After I asked Gina to keep track of her internal dialogues, she reported several examples, including the following one that occurred while she was driving to Washington DC:

> First I experienced detailed memories – again and again – of the phone call I received [that morning] from the high school counselor who said A. [her son] was in trouble again: "He's in danger of suspension . . ." I felt tension, concern, and anger [toward her son], "I'll kill him." I also felt guilt [about "failing" as a mother], "What's wrong with me?" The traffic was running smoothly so I decided to pray, to try and calm down; "Hail Mary full of grace the Lord . . ." At this point a blue car suddenly cut in on me and I had to brake, "Blessed art thou among women . . ." "You son of a bitch!" . . . "And blessed is the fruit of thy womb . . ."

This brief segment provides an amusing illustration of how we mentally jump back and forth from one cultural meaning system, one role, and one mode of discourse to another. Here Gina shifts from the language of her family tradition to her psychological tradition, to her religious tradition, to her feisty Italian American competitive tradition, and back to her religious tradition all within a few minutes in the same situation.

Research suggests that internal dialogues typically reflect an individual's current concerns, so they can be very useful in identifying values and value conflicts. However, not everyone is open to talking about this dimension of experience, and it is best explored with a participant with whom you have worked for some time and where good rapport exists. If you are working with such a person, it is well worth trying to explore internal dialogues. As with dreams, we can ask ourselves and our participants to monitor this activity and to write down records of what can be remembered. As always, try this exercise on yourself first.

Exercise 22: Internal Dialogues and Multiple Cultures

During routine moments of the day, such as driving to work, taking a walk, washing the dishes, or waiting for a friend, ask yourself the question, "What have I just been thinking about?" Write down as complete a record as possible of the words and images that you can remember experiencing in your mind. Try this at least five or six times over the course of several days. After you have collected several records, ask yourself what areas of current concern are revealed and how these are related to your cultural traditions. Consider the particular cultural traditions, languages, and values that show up in a given segment and how you switch from one to another. Does the segment express conflict among different systems? Is there any sense of resolution? Now consider asking your participant the same kinds of questions.

Internal dialogues are typically *about* dramas in the person's social worlds and are always conducted *with* the cultural meaning systems the person has at his or her disposal. Often you will find that internal dialogues are about alternative ways of coping with problems and that they help us to deal with or repair identity damage and to balance and synthesize the very different ways we think and feel about our social worlds, other people, and our identities and values.[7]

CHAPTER FIVE

Writing Multiple Cultures in Life History

Every human life is mysterious and complicated. But having spent the time we have with our research partner, we have learned something about the cultural dimensions of this life and our own. We know our understanding is incomplete, but it's time to finish. As a cultural portrait of an individual, a life history can include photographs or drawings, but mainly it will be a representation in language, words on paper, a text. So how are you going to "write it up"?

The problem is that there are so many possibilities. The ways individuals think and act with multiple cultural traditions plays out here in several ways. First, we want to portray how our subjects negotiate their various cultural traditions and how these impinge on the theme we are investigating. But the act of writing is itself a culturally constituted practice that is enabled and constrained by multiple cultural traditions. How you negotiate the relationships among the cultural points of view of your subject, yourself, and your audience within the life history tradition will shape the text of your portrait.

Setting out to write within or along the margins of the life history genre leaves a lot to be decided. We know we are not writing a short story or a poem, but we may well want to borrow from these and other genres. Unlike some forms of academic discourse, ethnography in general and life history in particular are relatively open genres. Some earlier, scientifically oriented life history work was rigid in its form, chronological, analytic, and often boring. But even in the earlier phases there were interesting alternatives and experiments. Since Vincent Crapanzano's 1980 classic *Tuhami*, an experimental portrait of a Moroccan tile maker, things have opened up a great deal.[1] There is no narrow, constrained formula for presenting cultural portraits of individual lives. We have the opportunity to be creative in how and what we write. However, as I see it, the life history genre includes several basic expectations, and part of your work will be deciding how to deal with each of them.

Exercise 23: Questions for Writing Life History

Consider how you will answer the following questions in your life history:

1. Why is this life, or this aspect of it, worth telling? What intellectual theme will you emphasize, and what is the relationship between your subject's life and this theme? How can you best portray what is interesting and important here?

2. How will you use the phases of your participant's life or his or her current social worlds to convey the cultural influences he or she negotiates?

3. How does this person see the world, and how does he or she express these views in language? How can you show how the person uses cultural traditions to construct a sense of self and to understand the external world?

4. How does the person cope with his or her social roles and social worlds? How and how successfully does the person negotiate the various traditions of these worlds?

5. Who are you who tells us this? What kind of relationship did you develop with your participant, and how did your cultures affect that relationship? What perspectives of your own are involved in your story of you and this other person?

One way of thinking about how to put all this together is to examine the kinds of material you have at your disposal and to consider how they might be appropriately mixed or blended to accomplish the purposes you have in mind. Very roughly, three kinds of materials are used in writing a life history:

1. Your interpretive, analytic, reflective, or descriptive voice. In summarizing the person's life, in presenting a scholarly theme, in describing and interpreting cultural traditions, and in telling us how this person manages them, you will be composing in your own reflective cultural-analytic voice as influenced by the various traditions you think with.

2. Your participant speaking with his or her cultural traditions. This material includes verbatim records of the person's spoken words, including the stories told, especially as these are embodied in transcripts of tapes of your interviews, and possibly other kinds of materials such as letters, diary entries, or e-mails your subject has written and shared with you.

3. Depictions of scenes of your person in action. This material includes observational records of scenes you witnessed and descriptions of scenes offered by your subject or someone else.

A few life histories rely almost exclusively on one of these devices. Some life history in professional journals is mainly the scholar's generalizing and interpretive voice with little use of informant quotes or depictions of scenes. By contrast, other writers offer edited transcripts of the research participant's statements with little author comment. Here all the reader has is the individual's voice. Still other life histories unfold as stories involving scenes and dialogue with little or no additional comment. Any of these forms can work, but it is usually best to mix all three.

Audience and Writing Life History

In thinking about the essay you will compose, it is useful to consider to whom you are addressing this life history. While you are trying to say something *about* your research participant, you will be trying to say this *to* someone else. Selecting the audience helps us to choose and establish our voice and to determine what we do and do not want to say in the life history.

Exercise 24: Audience and Writing Life History
Pick someone to whom you might write your account, perhaps an old friend, your aunt, or a writer you admire. How does this choice affect what you would say and how you would say it? What cultural traditions influence the relationship between you, the author, and this audience? What do you want to tell your audience in what form and to what end? Draft a one-paragraph introduction and consider the style that emerges. Think also about occasions when you have already told something about the life you are investigating to classmates, friends, or family. How did you do this, and how did these people react? Does this help you plan your written composition?

Another basic question concerning audience involves selecting the major intellectual frame of reference you will use to address your audience. If you are writing for an academic class, your primary audience may be your instructor and your classmates within the context of the cultural traditions of that course, including whatever guidelines you have been given. Writing life history for a class in Ethnography, American Studies, Anthropology, Women's Studies, English, Journalism, Deaf Studies, Queer Studies, African American Studies, Psychology, or Education will significantly affect the way you write – including the particular theme or issue you will choose to focus on, whether this be immigration, disability, race, gender, sexuality, religion, reading practices, media consumption, or political orientations.

But how can we say something about large social issues with a sample of one, a single person – or two if we count ourselves as one of the subjects? In the first place, a case study of how a particular cultural issue works in something of its true complexity, at the level of individual experience for one or two individuals, is often an important and valuable contribution. Second, such studies not only help us see how things work for this person but automatically raise useful questions about the extent to which this person's experience is similar to or different from the experiences of other people in similar social locations and beyond. Obviously, we shouldn't generalize one person's experience to a large set of persons of which this individual is but one member, but any one member is one instance – a kind of baseline – from which we can legitimately begin to think about how this life compares to the lives of others. One approach we can take here is to ask our research participant about this: "To what extent do you think your way of handling this issue is similar to or different from how other people you know who are in this role are handling it?" We may also think, for example, "Hmm, Gina talks to herself in a variety of dialogues. Do I do this? Oh, yes, I do, when I'm driving I do talk to myself, and yes, I do use several distinct languages." Or, "Hmm, Claire thinks of her work partly in terms of opera. How interesting. But is this unique to her? No, that defense attorney I worked with was also a huge opera fan, and that may well affect, probably does affect, his 'theatrical mode' in court." And do I and others I know use particular traditions we are familiar with as a metaphor for thinking about our work?

Findings in life history case studies, like those in ethnographic studies of particular communities, automatically raise questions about issues that are broader and wider than the case itself. We have to be careful about what we say about this, but raising questions about possible wider implications is an important and legitimate aspect of life history. We need to remember, too, that generalizing forms of research have their own problems. Survey research by its very nature suppresses, obscures, and distorts individual variation. By doing a case study of one person, we are adding to the understanding of the complexity of lived individual experience. For example, by looking at the way in which one social worker, Gina, understands her work, I obtained a detailed portrait of one person within the large sample of American social workers. Such a portrait helps reveal the complexity of a given case, showing, for example, how her ethnic, media, and religious traditions affect her orientation to her work. This case then raises larger questions of how other social workers orient to their work and suggests that understanding these orientations may well require attending to how seemingly unrelated aspects of life may affect their practice. Such issues may then be factored into larger-scale ethnographic or survey research in the future.

Exercise 25: Scholarly Issues in Writing Life History

What have you learned about your research participant's life that contributes to the ongoing conversation about pertinent issues in the scholarly discipline or intellectual field in which you are working? Does this person's life connect to a scholarly issue or theme you have dealt with in your class? Does it show something significant about how the issue works at the level of individual experience? How can you write about this person's life and cultures in a way that speaks to a larger theme? Can you raise a question or puzzle about your subject's life and then explore it throughout the course of your narrative? Outline one possible way of doing this. Does your study raise questions that might be important to consider in future studies? Can your research subject be asked questions that might help suggest wider implications? For example, "I'm interested in how your religious background influences your orientation to social work. Do you know other social workers who are also influenced in this way?"

As you develop your intellectual theme you will use your own analytic voice, but your life history will be more effective and interesting if it includes specific case material – that is, if it "shows" as well as "tells." An important part of life history is giving the reader a vivid sense of your subject's feelings and thoughts. The most effective device for doing this is providing paragraph-length indented quotes of your participant speaking. As your argument unfolds it is good to quote sentences and phrases in the body of your text, but longer quotes are even more powerful. In describing how your research participant balances two cultural traditions, you might quote her speaking from within each system and then quote her on how she balances the two. For example, Claire told me about a session at her Jungian dream interpretation group where she experienced a conflict between her Buddhist and Jungian traditions. In writing her life history, I could present her words on this clash of interpretations.

> I had a dream actually about the [Buddhist] temple, which I brought in [for analysis in the Jungian group]. And I did not like that experience. The dream was about being at the temple, there was going to be a parade. . . . I went to

put my gift on the table and it started to collapse. . . . J [the guru] was sitting on her throne and everybody was in white and . . . I talked with her and, you know, it was difficult to know whether she was a God or woman. . . . And the group interpretation like sort of ignored the cultural issues. I mean my feeling afterwards was they didn't hear me in Tibetan Buddhist terms, they heard me in Germanic [Jungian] terms . . . it felt so off the wall. And then they kept saying that "the reason it's so off the wall is that its sooo unconscious in you that you don't recognize that it has to do with your giving up your power as a woman." Ah, and I was trying to say, "Look, in this context what devotion is about is recognizing your own divinity and using the guru as a symbol of the Buddha nature in all of us, and it's not about, 'She's going to know all the answers and take care of me.'" Ah, and I mean they didn't *get* it!

By conveying the person's voice, so that we directly hear her sense of her experience in her own words, quotes help bring the person to life for the reader. Quotes illustrate points you are making, and provide useful and convincing evidence that the person does indeed think in the ways you suggest.

Similarly, at times you will need to generalize about patterns and events in your subject's life, but it is important and effective to also provide descriptions of illustrative scenes. In Reading 4 in Part Two of this book, Douglas Harper might have chosen to describe his meeting with his hobo-informant, Carl, in a summarizing voice, but the vivid scene he presents us with is much more effective. As discussed above, you can draw on scenes you participated in, observed, or were told about by your research participant.

An important aspect of many scenes has to do with what the person was thinking and feeling in the midst of the scene. A useful technique is to interview our subjects about their thoughts and feelings during the event and then to write their answers into our presentation of the scene. I had been working with Gina about the influence of the Catholic tradition on her thinking, so when she described scenes I was able to get her to discuss what she was feeling, thinking, and saying to herself as the scene unfolded and to write this back into her description of what happened. In the following example, Gina was getting ready for work in the morning, her partner asked where his beeper was, and she said she didn't know. Rewriting this interaction with attention to her thoughts and feelings makes this simple scene illustrative of the interior battles of her meaning systems.

"Where's my beeper?" her partner asked.

Gina recalled where it sat on the bedroom table, but, still feeling annoyed with him, she thought, "Find your own damn beeper." Out loud she said, "I don't know." A few minutes later, feeling guilty, she silently criticized herself, saying, "That was so selfish!"

Scenes, like quotes, engage the reader in a way that a generalizing voice alone can never do, and they help us feel the person's presence as an individual. As forms of evidence for the points you are trying to make, scenes also invite the reader to join you in trying to make cultural sense of the biographical material.

In planning your life history, think about how to present your material in innovative, engaging, and convincing ways. Study the life histories in Part Two of this book to see how you might adapt their methods of presentation to your own project. You may also want to consult the Suggestions for Further Reading and to consider examples from literary journalism and fiction. How do novelists whose work you like use dialogue, scenes, and narrative to construct their portrayals of fictional lives? In your notes and memory are real examples of the same kinds of raw material, actual scenes, descriptions of places, conversations, and records of internal dialogues. Look to novelistic strategies for inspiration about how to put your material together effectively.

The possibility of using novelistic techniques raises another issue central to life history. Some scholars not only advocate the use of literary techniques but also characterize life history writing as "fictive." By this they usually mean that an account of a life is an interpretation from a particular point of view, a selective and selected account by a particular person particularly situated in relationship to the subject, very much a construction, composed, and rhetorical. While all this is accurate, life history should obviously not be fictional in the sense of dreamed up, imagined, or fabricated. It would be a violation of academic integrity to invent a person and present the fictional account as a real-life history. Similarly, in describing a real subject it would be unethical to make up dialogue and scenes that did not occur.

An interesting marginal case here is the so-called ethnographic novel. Just as a historical novel is fiction set in a historical period that the author knows well, an ethnographic novel involves a made-up story of made-up characters in the context of an accurate portrayal of a cultural world. But why make the story up? Good fieldwork yields all the materials that fiction invents. Why make up a character when our participants are such interesting characters? Why make up thoughts and feelings when we can interview our research participants about these aspects of life and work their real answers into scenes and stories?

Much of the power and value of life history for the audience comes from knowing that the account is a real portrait of a real person. Yet we also know that our life histories are selective, constructed accounts filtered through our particular relationships with the individuals we are writing about.

Writing about Your Relationship with Your Research Participant

Without information about the author's relationship with his or her subject, it is difficult for the reader to understand and evaluate a life history. In outlining a way to describe your encounters with your research participant, consider the following questions.

Exercise 26: Writing about Your Relationship with Your Subject
How did you approach your research participant, and what role(s) did you play in relationship with each other? What did your participant seem to want or expect from the relationship? When, where, how often, and under what circumstances did you interview the person? How did you get along with each other? To what extent was the person wary and evasive or open and cooperative? How did your cultural traditions mesh or clash with his or her traditions? What breakdowns and rich points occurred? How did each of you come to define the relationship? Did you become friends? If not, why not? What explicit or tacit agreements were made about withholding and suppressing information? Outline your answers and consider where in your life history you can best tell your readers what they need to know about your relationship with your research participant.

Also consider carefully your obligations, as author, to your research participant. The ethical rules we discussed in Chapter 2, such as those formulated by professional associations and human subject review committees, provide important guidelines for writing. Because your participant helped you by voluntarily opening up his or her life, you have a significant obligation to protect this person in what you write. Borrowing a perspective from medical and legal traditions, consider whether some of what the person told you should be treated as a kind of "privileged communication." If, as is typical, you learned about sensitive areas of the person's life, you need to be very careful in writing about those areas. On the other hand, you both entered into this relationship with the understanding that your purpose was to learn and write about the person's life. The issue here involves what not to tell and how to tell what you do tell.

Decisions about what to include depend partly on the kind of life history you are writing. Is this a seminar paper that will be seen by no one but your teacher, or is this a thesis or scholarly journal publication that will becomes publicly accessible and potentially – if picked up by the mass media – very public indeed? Unless the person explicitly wants you to do so and gives you written permission, you should not use the person's real name. You also need to carefully consider whether you are providing information that might allow readers to figure out who the person is. Ethical guidelines mandate that if you are using names or other revealing identifiers, you should not disclose information that might put the person at risk of liability or that is generally defined as "sensitive." On the one hand, this includes material the person is concerned about revealing; on the other hand, it includes information about sexual conduct, drug use, or illegal conduct, all of which is widely defined as sensitive in the dominant culture. How you write about such issues is also important. It is one thing to write that "During this period, as Joe says, he sowed some wild oats and nearly got in trouble with the law"; it is quite another to write that "Joe stole a red BMW on Georgia Avenue on August 3, 2004." Consider carefully what your participant told you about what he or she is willing to have you reveal. But even if you are following standard guidelines about sensitive material, and even if the person is generous about giving you permission ("Go ahead and use anything I said," Gina once told me), you will want to keep thinking about protecting your participant. Check back with your subject as you write, and use your own best judgment in considering whether or not something you learned should be included in your life history. If you're still not sure, consult with someone familiar with ethical problems in fieldwork such as the teacher of your class or the chair of your Human Subjects Review Committee.

A fundamental way to safeguard the rights and sensitivities of research participants is to show a draft of your life history to your participant. The agreement to do this should usually be part of the initial discussion of the project. The participant's suggestions about the draft will be helpful to the interpretive success of the project, but having the person read your draft also provides an opportunity for him or her to check on what you have written. Although this usually works well, there is sometimes a conflict between the point of view of the author and that of the subject.[2]

First, people are usually sensitive to characterizations that seem to carry explicit or implicit evaluations. Since most cultural traditions are laced with value judgments, even an account that is intended to be a neutral description of what someone did with his or her life may be interpreted by readers, including your subject, as evaluative. Second, the ethnographer's analytic, interpretive frame of reference may be partly or completely outside the set of traditions with which the subject customarily thinks. If the subject is not familiar with the language and jargon of esoteric, scholarly frames of reference such as cultural studies, feminist theory, or postcolonial theory, the very medium in which the portrait is painted may seem alien and inappropriate. So in writing keep in mind that as authors we want to try and construct a portrait that fits the purposes and goals of our project but also one that is considerate, respectful, and sympathetic to how the subject sees things, including him- or herself. Knowing that you will show your account to your participant helps keep judgmental aspects and esoteric jargon out of your account.

In most cases, your relationship with your participant, and hence what you write about that relationship, will involve a mutual sense of trust. Your research partner will trust you to be respectful in what you write, and you will trust that your participant is telling you the truth as he or she understands it. Occasionally, however, an interviewer may become concerned that what the participant is saying is deliberately distorted. This might happen if the person tells the same story in very different ways or in ways that suggest exaggeration or duplicity, or when you learn information from other sources that seems to contradict what the research participant has told you.[3]

If this occurs, it will be difficult to deal with. Much will depend on the purposes of your project. A few ethnographers, such as those in investigative sociology, are committed to the assumption that people routinely put up false fronts and that the ethnographer's job is to penetrate deceptions to get at the "real truth" behind the facade. Like most ethnographers, I view this formulation as an inappropriate and distorted way to think about our relationship with our research partners. On the other hand, it would be naive to take a credulous stance toward material that seems patently false. Sometimes, of course, this might involve issues of belief. If the participant believes in a religious tradition and you do not, his or her point of view should be honored in what you write. In the unlikely event that you become concerned about deception in relation to factual information, remember that our primary obligation is to our participants and give him or her the benefit of the doubt. You might want to ask tactfully about a seeming contradiction, but it may not be worth pursuing. Since we are primarily after point of view, it may not really matter whether everything the person says is literally true. What matters more is what a statement reveals about the person's values, schemes of interpretation, and narrative strategies. Remember, too, that this is an unusual situation. If your relationship with your participant is good, you will usually get a pretty accurate account. But occasionally, depending on your purposes, the person's responses, and the kinds of question you are trying to explore, you may need to think about this carefully.

In handling these and other writing issues, remember what you are trying to do. Your goals will partly depend on the nature of the project and your analytic perspective, but they will always include the investigation of cultural point of view. What points of view does this person hold, how does he or she manage them, and how can this understanding be conveyed in your life history? Going back to this purpose will help you sort out issues of concern.

Even though we are interested in point of view and are seeking to avoid value judgments, life history, like other forms of cultural biography, inevitably raises questions about whether or not the life in question is a good, successful, or meaningful one, both in general terms and in relation to the theme of your essay. For example, given an interest in multiple cultures, we may want to consider how "successfully" the person manages his or her multiple cultures. It is important to remember how profoundly such questions are related to point of view. "Good," "successful," or "meaningful" from whose point of view, by whose definition? The definitions most clearly involved will be those of your audience, yourself, and your subject. In life history you may want to respectfully offer your own assessment, and you will want to consider audience expectations, but your participant's points of view should be primary in questions like this. Focus on how the person sizes up his or her own life and success in negotiating multiple cultures.

Writing Yourself into Your Life History

Since we owe our readers a description of our relationship with our subject and an account of the cultural traditions we brought to the project, we will necessarily be writing about ourselves as well as the research participant in the life history. Thus, self-ethnography is a *methodological* and genre requirement. Throughout these chapters I have suggested that something more is also worth pursuing. The process of doing life history with someone whose cultural background differs from our own can shed important light on the cultural dimensions of our own experience. This can be useful to your writing in at least two ways. First, your analysis of your own cultural traditions and how these have affected your experience of a theme you are focusing on can serve as an effective contrast to your subject. Second, your experience in the life history project can also provide a narrative device. Your life history could be written as the record of a journey in culturally understanding both the other person and yourself. What happened to you, including what you learned along the way, can be a useful plot line in developing your life history. Perhaps you can write about how you learned to see some aspect of your own social location more clearly or learned something important about how to deal with multiple cultures. Done well, such narrative devices will also lead the reader to reflect on the cultural dimensions of his or her life.

Despite such advantages, writing yourself into the life history is a tricky process. Critics of postmodern ethnography often complain about the self-indulgence and narcissism that characterize some personal narratives. I think self-ethnography is a legitimate and useful practice, but in your essay you need to be careful not to dwell too much on your own feelings and experiences. Since you are likely to have large amounts of material about your own experience with this project, far more than you can or should include, you will need to use it selectively.[4]

Exercise 27: Writing Yourself into the Life History
Of all that happened to you in this project, what might you write into the life history,

and for what purpose? Ask yourself the following questions: Does the personal material about me reveal aspects of my relationship with my research participant? Does it illuminate how my cultural traditions impinged on my interviews, observations, and interpretations? Does it offer contrasts with my subject that illuminate both lives? Does it contribute to understanding issues that are directly pertinent to the theme of my paper? Does it provide a really good "story" that might hook the reader into the account? Unless it does something like this, you should probably leave it out.

Casting yourself as a figure in the life history parallels the issues involved in characterizing the person you interviewed. Like your cultural assessment of your participant, this will be a partial portrait, a take, one interpretation among many by a peculiarly located person working a particular theme while mired in an unruly set of complex cultural traditions. Melissa Landsman uses a common strategy in Reading 2. She presents herself as the initially naive investigator who moves past early misunderstandings, confusion, and ethnocentric stereotypes to gain some new understandings and to win a degree of sympathetic acceptance from her subject. Since this is usually the reality of a reasonably successful life history project, it is a good narrative device. You might also consider casting yourself in the third person. You might write in first person when writing as the ethnographer and analyst, but refer to yourself in the third person when treating yourself as a subject. This device can help you maintain some critical edge over your own self-presentation.

Writing Strategies in Life History

The act of writing life history, the cultural practice by which our "thoughts" appear as words on the piece of paper or computer screen before us, is a curiously mysterious process. Manuals on writing life history, ethnography, and memoir are worth consulting, and you will want to consider other life history models such as those in Part Two of this book. But you have to discover your own method – and hope that the muse is beneficent when you try to compose. The following suggestions may be useful.

1. Review your file of outlines, key interviews and observations, and the exercise you have done, and develop a final, one-page outline. Review your summaries of field notes and consider where to place the materials you want to use. How can you arrange your quotes, stories, and scenes

effectively in a narrative sequence that speaks to the issues you wish to address in the lives you are telling from the points of view you are developing? Now consider a different arrangement. A chronological account of the life might work. A sequence that follows the chronology of your research and gradual understanding might work. But what if you shook it all up and organized it completely differently? Would a key scene in the person's life or a key moment in your dialogue with the person make for a dramatic introduction? If you started there, how could you make your essay unfold?

2. Write a rough draft of the different sections of your paper. Writing a rough draft in life history often seems easier than in other kinds of composition because you have good material you have obtained yourself and to which you have a personal, experiential connection. On the other hand, the rough draft is challenging because you are making the initial excursion into unknown territory. There is no previous trail of words to follow, modify, or react against. Also, by definition, a first draft will seem unsatisfactory to you. But once you have it you're more than halfway done.

Give yourself a block of time and tell yourself that you must do a draft of this section in the allotted time, as you might do in taking an essay exam. Using your outline, write the basics of the story. What can you say about the basic points and examples that go in this section? Be open to discovering something new as you write. Trying to articulate what we have to say often leads us to grasp connections and understandings we hadn't quite noticed or realized. In order to accomplish a rough draft you'll have to work past your own dissatisfaction with what you first write. If you get caught up in premature editorial tinkering you won't get the section done. But dissatisfaction is useful because it impels us to improve the draft. If you can quickly figure out what feels wrong, make brief side notes such as "seems to lack clarity," "need a better example here," "could be saved for later," or "too much about me." Ordinarily you will want to finish the section before going back and tinkering too much.

3. Reread critically from different points of view. As the author, are you satisfied with how this is coming out? Consult your side notes. Articulating what bothers or pleases you will help you shape the manuscript into something better. Now switch and read the draft from the intended audience's point of view. Is this going to engage them, or do you need to explain more? Will they get this point better with an illustration? Would

this paragraph work better later? And then switch again and think about your draft from your subject's point of view. Is this portrayal accurate, or do you need to check? Are you doing him or her justice here? What might the person feel if you write this way?

4. Reread your field notes with your narrative and argument in mind. Check back over your notes for the way your material speaks to the argument of the draft you have constructed. Does the argument hold up against your rereading? Can you account for counterexamples, or do you need to modify your argument? Most patterns in individual lives have lots of exceptions, so the inclusion of exceptions makes an account more convincing and shows the reader that you have taken all the material into account. As you read, look back over your notes for additional quotes or scenes that speak to your theme. Use them to test your argument again, but also look for how you might work more quotes and scenes into your account. The more of these you can include, the more convincing and engaging your life history will be.

5. Show your draft to your research partner, and work his or her reaction back into your life history. It is always useful to have someone else read your life history for clarity and editorial suggestions, but the most important reader will be your research participant. As suggested earlier, he or she can check for accuracy and help you remove factual errors or off-the-record material. It is also important to see how your participant reacts to what you have written. If he or she thinks your portrait is a good one, that will be useful and affirming of what you have accomplished. After reading, your participant may also offer additional reflections or examples that may be helpful. Finally, if your participant disagrees with what you have written, you can discuss this together and write an account of the disagreement into the final draft.

6. Reflect again on the wider meanings of this life history project.

Through increasing our understanding of how a particular theme or issue works at the level of individual experience, life history can help us understand the cultural dimensions of the topic we are concerned with – whether this involves media use, identity issues, or social justice concerns such as forms of oppression. A few writers have argued that life history may deflect attention from cultural understanding and criticism, but it seems to me that cultural change and social justice work require attention to how social problems are experienced at the individual level.[5] Have you learned something about this that you might work into your paper?

Doing life history has a value and power in opening up our thinking, not only about the method itself and the specific issues we have focused on, but also about the cultural dimensions of the problems of life that we all struggle with. A good life history project partially frees us from the cage of our customary, culturally constituted ways of thinking. By increasing our awareness of the ways culture works on us, by acquainting us with alternative meanings, and by shedding new light on our customary ways of thinking, life history helps us obtain more freedom, agency, and choice in negotiating our cultural traditions. Did some of this clearing and deepening of perspectives occur during your project? How might you express some of this in what you are writing?

PART TWO

Readings in Life History

Introduction

Each of the nine life histories in this section of the book illustrates how particular Americans negotiate their cultural situations. In the first reading, Lila Shah, an immigrant from South Asia, describes how she balances her Indian and American cultures. In Reading 2, Melissa Landsman, an American college student and waitress, discusses her friendship with Paolo, a dishwasher and immigrant from El Salvador, and compares his understandings to hers. In Reading 3, anthropologist Barbara Myerhoff portrays her relationship with Shmuel, an elderly Jewish tailor, and explores his sense of his past and his philosophy of life. In Reading 4, Douglas Harper reports his first meeting with a hobo named Carl, who became his mentor on the ways of American railroad tramps. Jenny Thompson, in Reading 5, describes her experience of participant observation with World War II reenactors and the meanings this hobby has in the lives of several of her subjects. In Reading 6, Joshua Woodfork investigates the complex multiculturalism of a biracial college professor. Elizabeth Clark-Lewis, in Reading 7, reflects on her life history work with African American servants and the challenges their lives presented to her. In Reading 8, anthropologist Ruth Behar describes her friendship with a Mexican American woman. Finally, in Reading 9, Sandra Patton-Imani explores with her research partner, Lynn, how the experience of being adopted complicates their cultural identities.

Even listing these accounts suggests the complexity that emerges when we shift our perspective from group-oriented ethnography to person-centered life history. All of the individuals involved here – the interviewers as well as the interviewees – are entangled in multiple and complex systems of meaning that require them to negotiate their way through diverse beliefs and values. As these accounts demonstrate, an adequate account of individual experience in the United States requires attention to multiple cultural traditions.

As you plan and conduct your own life history research, these accounts will be useful in several ways. First, each one may help you assess the cultural situation of your research participant. If your participant is adopted, a reenactor, and/or an immigrant from South Asia, some of these accounts will be directly pertinent. But even where they do not describe a cultural situation similar to your participant's, each of these accounts can help you gain a feeling, by contrast and similarity, for the situation of the person you are interviewing. If your participant is not a reenactor, perhaps he or she has a strong interest in some other hobby that is personally meaningful, or perhaps his or her imaginal experience takes a parallel direction. Even if your participant is not adopted, Patton-Imani's account may help you think about other ways in which social institutions structure your subject's experience and sense of self. While it is unlikely that your subject will have the same set of traditions as Professor Stewart, Woodfork's portrayal of the chameleon-like manner in which he negotiates his traditions may be helpful in exploring how your research participant manages his or her various traditions. So read these accounts for what they may suggest, directly or indirectly, about the cultural situation of the person you are interviewing.

These accounts should also be helpful as descriptions of the life history research process. Each can be read for suggestions about how to go about conducting interviews and participant observation. They offer models for issues to think about and ways to explore them. They suggest strategies for asking questions, for uncovering different cultural values, and for handling the life history research relationship. These life histories also offer models for self-ethnography, for how to think about and explore your own cultural situation. What does each account suggest about your cultural traditions and your relationship with these traditions? What does the account suggest about how to use contrasts between your own traditions and those of your subject as leverage to understand both lives better?

Finally, these accounts should be useful to you as examples of how to write life history. Notice carefully how the author organizes the material and how he or she makes the story unfold. How does the writer use dialogue, scenes, and interpretive writing? How does the author portray the participant's different cultural traditions and his or her relationship to them? How does the writer describe his or her relationship with the participant, and how does he or she provide us with a sense of his or her social and cultural location? To what extent do you find a particular mode of portrayal effective? How might you incorporate such forms of writing in your life history?

Being Indian in America
My Ethnic Roots and Me

Lila Shah

Like Salma, with whom we began this book, Lila Shah is an immigrant from South Asia who explicitly defines herself as bicultural. She is conversant with the very different mainstream cultures of both India and the United States. Here she speaks to us about the problems and benefits of this situation. This selection provides a good introduction to our readings. The author is not a scholar theorizing biculturalism; she is a young woman, a college student who has personally lived this radically bicultural experience, speaking directly to us in her own words as she reflects on her attempts to cope with what she sees as good and bad about her situation. Listen to this text as you would a research participant's voice. Pay careful attention to her words and try to read them as a key to her changing point of view. For example, what does she see as positive or negative about her experience? Note how her biculturalism involves a critical relation with what she constructs as American culture. How does she assess its benefits and problems? Also, as practice in self-ethnography, pay attention to your own reactions to her story. Try this as you read each of the readings here in Part Two. In this case, what "rich points" arise in the encounter between her points of view and yours? For example, how do you feel about what she says about her parents' "disagreement" with American practices such as drinking, dating, and divorce? Can you identify the cultural roots of your reaction?

"Being Indian in America: My Ethnic Roots and Me" was originally published in Becoming American, Becoming Ethnic, *ed. Thomas Dublin (Philadelphia: Temple University Press, 1996), 206–12. It is reprinted here by permission of the author.*

My heritage and ethnic roots are the foundation of my self. I am fortunate enough to know my roots and appreciate them. My life changed dramatically thirteen years ago when my family and I emigrated from India. The immigration experience transformed my life and me, personally. I have had the advantage of enjoying both cultures and understanding how they have shaped my life.

My family was part of the Indian middle class. Unlike America, middle class in India meant a life of daily struggle and marginal economic mobility. Typically, the rich got richer and the poor got poorer, and the middle class got nowhere. This situation and pollution problems, which aggravated my father's health, compelled us to leave India. My aunt (father's sister) sponsored us in 1976, and my parents decided that my father would precede us to America where he would look for job opportunities and a place to live. While my father was gone, my mother would begin to pack up our apartment.

On a rainy evening when the smell of rain hung so heavy in the air that I still remember it today, my parents told us of their plans. My father stressed the lack of opportunities for my sister and me in India and the wealth of opportunity in America. Naturally, my sister and I were completely against the move and we were very vocal. My sister was ten and I was six, and India was all we had ever known. Opportunities, education, and careers were remote ideas.

My father left, and for the next year, I prayed that he would not find a job or housing. I had no desire to move to a country ten thousand miles away for concepts I could barely understand. However, my father did find a job and a nice apartment in Syracuse, New York. So in 1977, I left with my mother and sister. At the airport, all our relatives and friends came to say good-bye. The departure was one of the most traumatic experiences of my life. I felt I was leaving behind everything I knew and venturing into an unknown chapter of my life. The resentment I felt against my parents that night was almost tangible.

Upon arriving in America, we were reunited with my father, and he attempted to explain all the good he had discovered in this country. Our apartment was the first thing I marveled at. In Bombay there had been an acute water shortage for as long as I could remember. This resulted in twenty minutes of water a day for all those living in Bombay. Even now, this seems tremendously difficult for me to comprehend. In our new apartment I quickly discovered that running water was available twenty-four hours a day. Many times I awoke in the middle of the night and watched the water run out of the faucet.

Besides these small amenities, it took time to adjust to life in America. School was a new experience as I quickly realized that I was the only Indian in the second grade and in my whole school. Luckily my school in India was conducted in English, so I was completely fluent. Aside from speaking English with a British accent, I was very much like other second graders.

My elementary school is the institution I credit with my assimilation. It was there that I learned about relationships and American customs. For example, a foreigner in my school in India would have been respected, and everyone in the class would have tried to become friends with that person. In the United States, instead, I was looked on as something of an oddity due to my darker skin color and different name. Although people were not outwardly cruel to me, they were not friendly either. I was treated with polite indifference. Relationships between boys and girls were also much more forward than in India. The way school was conducted in America was also different. In India, I had to stand up to answer questions, and there was always the chance of being hit by the teacher at any time. After coming to America, I really believed that students did not respect their teachers since they did not stand to answer questions. At school, I began to learn American customs and jargon as quickly as I could. The different qualities I possessed were not appreciated in a country where uniformity was stressed.

Uniformity manifested itself in many ways in American life. Reciting the pledge required everyone to stand in a similar fashion and place their right hands over their hearts. My fellow students dressed basically the same, and there was always a rush to buy whatever everyone else was buying. Those who looked or acted different, like me, were regarded with scorn. As soon as I realized this, I attempted to change all the things about me that made me different. For a period of five to six years, I completely denied my cultural and ethnic roots. At home, I was an Indian girl who spoke an Indian language and ate Indian food. When my parents socialized with their friends (all of whom were Indian), I was Indian. But at school, the shopping mall, in restaurants, I was as American as I could be. I dressed in American clothes and would flatly refuse if my mother or father asked me to go somewhere dressed in my Indian clothes. I spoke slang and tried very hard to be viewed as an American. I would speak only English when I was out of my home and insisted my parents do the same. Suddenly, I was fourteen years old and I felt like two different people.

The following year was very difficult for me as I tried to be one person or the other depending on the situation. I spent months thinking and finally came to the conclusion that I had to resolve this duality. I was no longer capable of being two people; somewhere inside of me was the real me. I spent the better part of that year rediscovering my ethnic roots. I realized that I was Indian and the blood of a ten-thousand-year-old culture ran deep in my veins. I began to participate frequently in Indian activities. I participated in the Festival of Nations, a Syracuse program that allowed different countries to set up booths for a weekend selling their native food and clothing. At the end of each evening, each country would perform an ethnic dance before an audience of hundreds of people. I was filled with pride that by participating in the dance, I was enabling others to enjoy my culture. I came to the startling conclusion that instead of hiding my Indian roots, I could share them with others. I was surprised at the number of people who were interested in my culture and wanted to know more about it. Rather than hiding my differences, I could reveal them. It was nice to be a little different from other people.

In spite of finding my Indian roots, I also realized that the impact of America on me could not be denied. It would have been completely incorrect of me to believe that I had not taken anything from this culture. America had also contributed to my development. Some of my values I realized were American, and I had adopted some aspects of popular culture. My taste in music, clothes, and television was quite American. On the other hand, my religion, food, and most of my morals remained Indian. Instead of regretting the fact that I was part of two cultures, I began to enjoy it. I was a much richer and more balanced person because I knew of two different cultures. I had the advantage of picking and choosing aspects of both cultures that I wanted to retain or discard. Many people would never have the opportunity to make such choices. I realized I was a more interesting and well-traveled person because I had experienced things many of my peers never would.

My parents' situation is a bit different. My parents are staunchly Indian in their beliefs and in the way they lead their lives. My family is decidedly patriarchal, and though my father is not domineering, he does have the power in the family. We eat only Indian food in the house and speak, largely, in our native tongue. All my parents' friends are Indian, and neither of my parents feels deprived because of this. They find the morals of this country generally lacking and believe that American popular culture is the only culture of this nation. Perhaps this may sound as if my parents do not like Americans, but this is not true. They like my friends and my father's co-workers. They simply do not agree with some of the aspects of American culture, like drinking, dating, divorce, and the style of American individualism that stresses the "me" over anyone else – including parents.

My father has a deep, abiding respect for America, resulting from the fact that he came to this country with only thirteen dollars and has since achieved success on a large scale (monetarily, socially, etc.). Of course now my father believes that anyone, no matter what their circumstances, can achieve the American dream. My mother also believes these things and the idea that women are equal to men.

In the past, friction has occurred between me and my parents as I attempted to assert my American characteristics that were directly opposed to their Indian beliefs. On the whole, however, my parents have assimilated very well to this country and culture. Rather than being too liberal or too conservative, they have handled each situation individually with a mixture of Indian and American tools. I consider myself very fortunate when I see some of my other Indian friends who have very strict and conservative parents who do not realize that this country is not India.

Today, I am part Indian and part American and not sorry about it at all. I enjoy all the opportunities and avenues of mobility provided by this nation. I am an aspiring lawyer and frequently compare who I am here to who I could have been had I remained in India. I have realized that I could never live in India again, but this fact does not upset me. I feel as if I belong, and I believe I have carved out a niche for myself in this country. I feel tremendous gratitude toward my parents when I think about all the upheaval they went through for their children. My ethnic roots are something I want to give to my children so they too can see how their heritage can weave itself into the fabric of their lives and enrich it.

Conversations with Paolo

Melissa Landsman

Written when she was a junior in college, Melissa Landsman's life history recounts her interviews with Paolo, an El Salvadoran immigrant to the United States. Melissa's account shows how an undergraduate life history project can effectively open up the author's and the reader's understandings of individuals whose lives our own cultural perspectives and routines may lead many of us to overlook — even when they are present to us on a regular basis. Melissa effectively shows how the life of this initially "invisible" person was a complete mystery to her, and then she proceeds to unravel something of the mystery.

Read this essay for what it tells you about the cultural complexity of individual experience in American society, but read it also as a model for your own work. What, in your reading, does Melissa do well? How might you adapt techniques she uses to your project, including the way you write up your account? To me, for example, Melissa is effective in using her own emotional surprise to show how ideas about punishing children can vary so drastically, such that what seems like appropriate discipline in one cultural context can appear abusive in another. I also like the way she uses her investigation of Paolo's images and dreams of the United States before his arrival. Conversely, look also at what the writer does not include or does not develop that you would like to see in such an essay. Consider how you might bring these aspects of life history into your account. I would like, for example, to have heard more detail about Melissa's own cultural perspectives.

Originally written as a paper for an undergraduate class in life history at the University of Maryland, this essay is published here by permission of the author.

"I haven't had a table in two hours!" I said as I walked into the restaurant's kitchen. I approached Ted and Samuel, both of whom are cooks at this establishment where I've been employed as a waitress for eight months. As I continued through the kitchen, I passed the dishwashing station, where I was suddenly overwhelmed by a deep, passionate voice accompanying the sounds of Latino music. I looked to find a young man no more than seventeen years old with thick dark hair and bright black eyes, singing in Spanish with the music. His eyes were closed, and he appeared to be completely immersed in the essence of this music.

As I continued to watch him, I found that his intense involvement in the music allured me. Never have I seen an American so deeply moved by music. I then walked over to this young man and introduced myself. It occurred to me that I'd been working with him for the past eight months but had never greeted him or told him my name. "Excuse me," I said. It was obvious he didn't hear me, because there was no response. I excused myself again, and this time he looked in my direction and gave me a puzzled look. After I had his attention, I introduced myself.

"Hello, Melissa. I am Paolo. It is very nice to meet you." As we started to talk I couldn't help noticing the large gold cross on a chain that embraced his neck. That made me aware of the fact that he was a religious young man.

"Where are you from?" I asked.

"El Salvador," he replied.

"Oh, that's very interesting." Then, just as I was about to strike up a conversation with him, I heard the voice of my manager in the background, signaling to me that I had a table and must get back to work. I excused myself and told Paolo that it was a pleasure to finally meet him and that I looked forward to seeing him again soon.

During the next few weeks at work I began to develop a friendship with Paolo. I started to realize that I was one of the only employees at the restaurant who engaged in conversation with him. I began to wonder if anyone at the restaurant even appreciated all the hard work he did for us for just a meager sum of money.

Our conversations were always about work. We exchanged our "secret" looks when a manager would complain about our performance on the job. One issue began to disturb me. I was eager to ask Paolo about his culture, yet every time our conversation headed in that direction we were interrupted. Then I would reconsider asking him about his past for fear of violating his privacy. At this point, all I knew about him was that he was seventeen years old, had lived in El Salvador for fourteen years, has been working at the restaurant for two years, and cannot stand one of our managers.

Two months later, I was assigned a research project that involved selecting an individual from another cultural background and conducting a series of interviews in which we investigate another culture. Paolo came to mind. However, I feared that asking him about his personal life would jeopardize our friendship.

I considered asking other acquaintances of mine who were from other parts of the world. However, Paolo's intense personality and sense of humor interested me so much that I decided that there was no one else I was more interested in interviewing than Paolo.

I was nervous because I knew the next day I would see Paolo. I wasn't sure how he would react when I asked him if I could question him about his culture. I was afraid he would feel like the subject of an experiment, being probed at and questioned for hours. Most of all I feared that he would think the only reason I took the time to talk to him earlier was because I wanted to "use" him for a project and that then I would continue to ignore him like so many other employees did.

When I saw Paolo, I pulled him aside and told him about the research project. I explained to him that I was taking a class that studies culture. I told him that I was curious about his culture and that I hadn't met anyone else who interested me as much as him. I reassured him that the interviews would be completely anonymous and that if I asked a question that made him uncomfortable, he wouldn't have to answer it. "Sure, Melissa, I'd love to," he said. I was relieved. Not only was my search for an informant over, but now I could begin to unravel the mystery of Paolo.

Our interviews began on a Saturday afternoon. We arranged to meet at the restaurant, since that was the most convenient place for both of us. I didn't prepare a set of questions, because I wanted the interview to run as though it were a casual conversation, knowing that it would make it more comfortable for Paolo. I did know what I wanted to discuss, though. I wanted to ask him questions about his homeland and family as well as his reactions to the American culture and American people.

Paolo was born and raised in El Salvador and has lived in the United States for approximately four years. He lives in an apartment in Prince Georges County with his mother and a cousin. The neighborhood where he lives is predominantly Latino, but most of the Latinos in his neighborhood are of Mexican descent. When I asked him what that was like, he explained that it was challenging.

There is a young woman he has really taken a liking to, he told me, but her parents do not accept him. He said there is a lot of discrimination by Mexicans toward El Salvadorans, even though they speak the same language. Apparently, this young girl's older sister had previously dated a young man from El Salvador. He got her pregnant and then left the community, never to be heard from again. This only enhanced the hostility toward El Salvadorans by the Mexican community. I found this particularly interesting because I was under the impression that all Latinos regarded themselves as one community and did not discriminate against one another. This was only the first of many instances when Paolo made me aware of my ethnocentric beliefs.

I couldn't help but notice the enthusiasm Paolo demonstrated when talking about his girlfriend, so I asked him to tell me more about her. He reached into his back pocket for his wallet and revealed a picture of an attractive, robust young Latino girl. He told me how much he misses her and how much he looks forward to seeing her soon. I assumed that by "soon" he meant later that day or perhaps tomorrow. He told me that he would probably see her in two weeks. "Two weeks. Why so long?" I asked. He told me that she wouldn't be able to sneak out of her house without her parents' being aware for another two weeks, when they'll both be away at the same time. He could see I looked puzzled, so he began to explain the institution of courtship.

The Mexican and El Salvadoran cultures are very similar with regard to courtship. In order for a young man to take a young woman out on a date, both must be eighteen years old, and the young man must be responsible and have a good job. The most challenging aspect of courtship is that the young man must have the permission of the young woman's parents. If the parents accept the young man, then they are free to engage in a "typical" date, which consists of dinner and possibly a movie or a dance. They may do this under one condition: they must abide by the designated curfew, because if they do not, the young man has proven himself to be irresponsible, therefore not worthy enough for the daughter.

As I mentioned, before the date can take place the young man must get permission from the girl's parents. If her parents fail to consent, the answer is a definite no. Paolo told me that because his girlfriend's sister had the problem with the young man from El Salvador, her parents have decided that El Salvadorans are just not suited for their daughters. The young girl fought for months with her parents to accept Paolo and told them repeatedly that he is an honest, hard worker and that he treats her with nothing but respect. Still, they will not budge on that issue. For months she wouldn't date Paolo against her parent's wishes, but then something happened. She became the first person in her family to graduate from high school. Her graduation from high school increased her sense of independence; however, she still didn't have the will to leave her parents. She began to sneak visits with him whenever she could break free from her family. "It's hard to only see her once every couple of weeks, and for awhile I wanted to stop seeing her altogether because we were breaking her family's wishes," Paolo said.

"What do you mean?" I asked.

"In the Latino culture, the family always comes first," he said. "Your parents are very important in decision making. If you don't do what they tell you, they'll punish you. It should be like that in this country."

"Haven't you ever heard of free will?" I asked him.

"There is no such thing in El Salvador. If you don't obey your parents, they'll get the belt out. I can remember my mom would say, 'Take off all your clothes and then get down on your knees!' then before you know it WHAM!"

I asked, "Didn't that hurt! Didn't you scream or cry?"

"Are you silly? Of course not. If you cry they will hit you more. All I ever did was just keep quiet and take it. It usually didn't last long, one or two hard hits was all. But, boy did it hurt. I'll tell you one thing. Parents should do that in this country."

I was amazed. I couldn't believe what I was hearing. In my terms, Paolo was rationalizing the brutality of corporal punishment and then telling me that parents in the United States should beat their kids too. "What does stripping a child down to nothing and then whipping him accomplish?" I asked.

"Well," he said, "whatever the kid did, he will never – and I mean never – do it again!" I then turned off the tape recorder while he told me a story about his childhood. We decided to keep a part of the interview "off the record" while he sat back and told me all about his family and how much he misses them, as well as El Salvador.

"Do you ever miss El Salvador so much that you want to move back there permanently?" I asked.

"Of course I miss it there," he said. "I miss seeing my family. The family in El Salvador is very important. It is very large. My father, I do not know. He left my momma long ago. I have nine cousins, four aunts, and five uncles that I miss very much. I used to see them on weekends when we would all go to church."

"Did you go to church much in El Salvador?"

"Oh yes," he said, "every week. Not a lot of people did, though. My family was very religious. Some families never went to church. Just about everyone is Catholic in El Salvador."

"Would you consider yourself a religious person?" I asked.

"Well, I believe in heaven and hell. If a person doesn't live his life properly, he could go to hell."

If there's one subject I love to discuss, it's definitely religion. I wouldn't consider myself an expert, yet I've always been intrigued with the subject and the different belief systems of various religions. I've also been fascinated by the different belief systems within a particular religion.

"Since I've been in America, I've been going to church much more," he said.

"Why is that?" I asked.

"Everywhere I look I see temptation. If one gives in to temptation he will go to hell. It is easier to go to hell."

"How, why?" I asked. "What can make somebody go to hell?"

"Well, using drugs, using alcohol, what the Americans call partying. I want to go to heaven, but that is much harder."

"Why?" I asked.

"In order to go to heaven one must read the Bible. It even says that we were created in the image of God. I think that people in America forgot what the Bible is. All people talk about is drinking and marijuana and having sex."

"Yes, but don't forget we work in a bar in a college town. Most of these young people maybe do not understand all of this yet. There are many parts of the country where there are religious people."

Paolo looked at me and asked if he could ask me a question. Naturally, I agreed. After he'd answered all my questions, it would only be fair for me to answer his. "Are you superstitious?" he asked.

"Well, yes, a little bit I guess. Why, are you?"

"Yes, I believe that there are people out there who have ESP and can see the future. I also think that dreams can be revealing." I was amazed at how bright this young man was. He never finished high school and has only lived here four years and is extremely intelligent, as well as articulate.

Paolo proceeded to tell me about the many dreams he'd had about America while he was still living in El Salvador. The images he had of this country were filled with both promise and fear. When his mother told him that they were moving to America, he had some very disturbing dreams. One that stands out most clearly is what he calls his "murder" dream. As he described it, "I had this reoccurring nightmare that I was standing in the middle of a city street, with a pistol in my hand and a dead body lying on the ground in front of me. An even worse nightmare that I had was that I was the dead body lying in the street." His response disturbed me very much. Where was he receiving this message about America? What disturbed me even more was that I knew the answer to that question. It must be from the media.

In El Salvador, the public is at a great advantage because they have not only their own media programming but also programming from the United States. Some of their most popular television shows are American talk shows, sitcoms, and soap operas that are translated into Spanish. Most of the movies that are popular in El Salvador are American-made movies like The Terminator and Lethal Weapon. Unfortunately, American society is represented through depictions of violence in motion pictures, which sends the message to other cultures that America is a militant society that thrives off murder and revenge.

Paolo explained to me that although he had always been aware of the drug problem in the United States, he never knew how severe it really was until he moved here. "It seems that the American people are obsessed with drugs, murder, and violence," he explained. "What upsets me the most is how the media portrays blacks and Latinos as big dopeheads. We are always portrayed as victims and the ones getting involved in illegal dealings. I think that's what reinforced my fears. While I was still living in El Salvador I was twelve, maybe thirteen years old. I knew I was going to be living in America soon, and the movies were telling me that I was going to be a 'gang banger,' blowing people's heads off and being in and out of prison throughout my life." He explained how the media had affected his belief system so traumatically. He made an effort to become more religious while still in El Salvador in order to secure his belief in God and "to protect his soul" from giving in to temptation.

Paolo had other dreams with a more positive outlook. His favorite dream about America was about snow. "I would dream that I was standing somewhere out in the countryside of America," he said, "and all of a sudden it would begin to snow. White flakes would fall all around me and I would look up at the sky, hold out my hands, and feel the cold snowflakes on my fingers." I asked him what his fascination with snow was about, and he explained that in El Salvador it never snows. The summers are very hot, and the temperature often reaches above one hundred degrees. The climate there is similar to how it is in the desert, except that during the winter months it rains practically the whole time. He explained that sometimes it rains for a week or two at a time.

Paolo described snow as representing something peaceful. "The beauty of the white flakes is proof that there must be a God," he said. "They represent everything pure and delicate, just as God wants things to be." He said that although he has seen representations of how America can be evil, the snow was symbolic of the beauty of the freedoms and opportunities that are offered to every individual who lives on American soil.

"If you were still living in El Salvador now, what kind of occupation do you think you would have?" I asked.

"I'd probably be working in construction or welding. If I wasn't doing that for a living, I'd probably be a farmer. The more popular occupations in El Salvador are working in a factory or an auto shop. Some men are painters, but most men seem to work in construction." I noticed that during our conversation about El Salvador, Paolo would refer to men and never women.

"Paolo, I noticed that you did not mention much about women's occupations there. Would you say that comparatively speaking, women are given the same opportunities as men?"

"The most common jobs in El Salvador consist of manual labor," he said. "Most women do not engage in that unless they work on a farm with their husband or in a factory. There are many women teachers and some women doctors; however, most women in El Salvador attend to the needs of their family."

I was curious about how he feels about a woman's place in the job market. Did he believe that a woman is as capable of performing successfully in a job as a man is? His response was refreshing.

"Why do you think my mother wanted to leave home and come to America?" he said. "She is a very intelligent lady and knew that she would have the opportunities here that she did not have in El Salvador. In America, she could receive a better education and choose her own destiny and not have it chosen for her. If there is one thing you should know about my mother is it this. She is a lady who never forgot where she came from. My family in El Salvador was poor. We would spend many months at a time struggling. My mother's decision to move to America has not only given us more opportunities, but it has also given us a little more money in our pockets. Each month my mother sends my relatives back home some extra money and gifts. We have some money for ourselves and some money for all my relatives. My mother is a wonderful lady. She is the closest thing to a true Catholic that I have ever seen.

"Melissa, I don't know about you, but I'm starving. Do you want to order some food?"

"Sounds great," I answered. As we waited for our food to come up, I asked him how he liked the Tex-Mex food at the restaurant compared to the food from his homeland.

"Some of the food is familiar, while some of the food is very different. We eat a lot of beans and rice. Our main food is called pupusas, which is a combination of tortilla, cheese, and chicken or beef. Even though a lot of the foods sound the same, it is prepared differently. In El Salvador, people do not watch what they eat as closely. We just eat! Some girls watch more than others, but generally, if it tastes good, we just eat it."

As we were talking, Fernando walked by. Fernando was born in Venezuela, but he's been living in the United States since he was three years old. He was what Paolo considered "almost too Americanized for his own good." Fernando has been a waiter at the restaurant for two years. He's a member of a college fraternity and affiliates only with American youths. Fernando is fluent in Spanish, since that's the only language his parents speak in their home, but when he's not at home he never speaks the language, not even when he's addressing other Latinos.

Paolo is very disturbed by Fernando. "He never speaks our language to me. Every time he addresses me, he only speaks to me in English. Is he not aware that we are brothers? The other day he asked me why I never responded to him when he was talking to me. I told him in Spanish that we are both Latino, he should know better. Now every time he needs to talk to me, he will only speak Spanish. He owes me that much respect."

Our dinner was ready, and we both tore through our dishes like a couple of savages. We had been so immersed in the conversation that we didn't realize how hungry we were until our meals were placed before us. "Thank you for all of the time you've given me," I said. "You have no idea how much this means to me. I am happy to say that the interview is now officially over."

He then startled me with his response: "That is what you think. Now it's my turn to ask you some questions."

Paolo asked me basic questions about the size of my family, what I was studying in school, and what I aspired to be. Then he began to ask me more complex questions. He was curious if I viewed El Salvador as a "battle zone" because of how badly is it misrepresented by the media. He was also curious about whether or not I stereotyped him before I met him and assumed that he was a "sex-crazed, dope-dealing immigrant," similar to the way many movies depict Latinos living in the United States.

When he first asked me these questions, I had no response. Paolo is very intuitive, and he is aware of the stereotypes about him because he has to deal with them every day. Although America has provided him with the opportunity of advancement, he must first face many years of being stereotyped, which is a result of the media. The media is very insidious in that respect. Its messages become engraved in an individual's mind, and even though one might not believe its messages, the messages have already been presented. Once these stereotypes exist, it's very difficult to escape them.

Paolo helped me recognize just how ethnocentric I am. I've formed all these opinions about other societies – and even my own – simply because of what others have told me. As a result I haven't been aware of all of the stereotypes and judgments I've made. We are all subjected to this pressure to conform that molds our minds and affects our ideas, yet many of us accept such stereotypes as being true.

Learning about another culture directly has enabled me to become more aware of my own. I'm beginning to recognize what some of our culture's assumptions are and how realistic they actually are. Perhaps this is more of a political criticism, but it seems that "culture" in an American perspective consists of structured and defined ideas, whereas in other parts of the world the term "culture" does not even exist. Their way of life is all they know and all they need to know. Perhaps the recognition of other cultures makes our own culture more valuable, yet it also enables us to be more critical of other cultures and of our own culture.

My friendship with Paolo has been a tremendous learning experience for me. Each day we see one another, we know that we share something special. He and I have learned a great deal from one another. Not only have we learned about one another, but we have learned about ourselves as well. We've broken down the ethnocentric barriers that keep us from seeing one another for what we really are: human beings.

Needle and Thread
The Life and Death of a Tailor
Barbara Myerhoff

First published in 1978, Myerhoff's life history of Shmuel remains one of the classics of the genre. It gives us a sense of the potential power of life history. As beautiful and moving as good short-story fiction, the essay gains even more power because we know it is not fiction but a real account of a real life. Myerhoff takes us subtly and yet very deeply into Shmuel's and her own concerns with life's meaning. Showing us how successful life history can be, her account throws light back on our lives and memories of childhood and makes us ponder, question, and reflect.

Read this account once for its beauty and value. And then read it again to see how she composes it. Notice how Myerhoff shows rather than tells, how she mixes quotes, dialogue, scenes, observations, and reflections to create the effects she wants. Note how she paints herself as a character and uses her own thoughts, feelings, and reactions to such telling effect. How could you adapt some of these techniques to the life history you will be writing?

Abe pointed out Shmuel Goldman as one of the most educated and interesting people in the community. I was looking for someone to study Yiddish with and Shmuel seemed ideal, if he would agree. We attempted a few Yiddish lessons together, but he was too impatient with my ignorance for us to continue. Still, we both enjoyed our time together. Shmuel loved recalling his childhood and eventually I decided I would like to record his life history at length. He was doubtful at first, but finally agreed and for the next two months we met at least once a week for formal, prearranged recording sessions, nearly all of which were taped. These were long and often taxing for both of us. In between, we met casually in and around the Center and Shmuel provided a running commentary on the people and events there. Abe was right. Shmuel was a philosopher, and an outsider, though he had lived in the neighborhood for thirty-two years. His psychology and principles made him intolerant of formal organizations, and ideologically he was at odds with nearly everyone in the Center. But he was too sensible, too learned, and too deeply rooted in their common traditions to be ignored by them. He and the Center people could not leave each other alone, but neither could they find peace together.

My friendship with Shmuel troubled many of the Center people. They were fearful lest I adopt his often judgmental, stern attitude toward them. Paradoxically, I usually ended up defending them and Center life to him. I, the newcomer, was more participant and enthusiast, and he the critic and observer. He was my foil and teacher, goading and challenging my interpretations at every point. In time, our differences became sharper and clearer and more often than not a source of mutual amusement. We knew each other for eighteen months. At the end of this time I could see things from both our perspectives at once. I have often wondered if this was his chief purpose in agreeing to work with me. Certainly it was one of his most valuable lessons.

What follows are extracts from our recordings and conversations. I have preserved the chronology and whenever possible, Shmuel's exact words. Those conversations that were not taped, I reconstructed from the notes I made either during or immediately after they took place. This constitutes what I regard as Shmuel's intentional lessons.

I have a friend. A woman I know already many years. One day she is mad at me. From nowhere it comes. I have insulted her, she tells me. How? I don't know. Why don't I know? Because I don't *know* her. She surprised me. That's good. That is how it should be. You cannot tell someone, "I know you." People jump around. They are like a ball. Rubbery, they bounce. A ball cannot be long in one place. Rubbery, it must jump.

So what do you do to keep a person from jumping? The same as with a ball. You take a pin and stick it in, make a little hole. It goes flat. When you tell someone, "I know you," you put a little pin in.

So what should you do? Leave them be. Don't try to make them stand still for your convenience. You don't ever know them. Let people surprise you. This likewise you could do concerning yourself. All this, I didn't read in any book. It is my own invention.

Invented, I was afraid, specifically to warn me. Shmuel delivered this speech as we trotted down the boardwalk on the way to his house, our arms linked tightly, less for closeness than to regulate our gait. He set a fierce pace. He didn't believe in strolling. I didn't mind. It gave me courage to walk with him in this way, regardless of his reasons.

Shmuel had agreed to let me record his life history. But clearly he was full of doubts about revealing himself to me and about my ability to understand him. I shared his fears but was prepared to put doubts aside and try. The differences between us seemed less formidable as I contemplated our long shadows running before us in the clear afternoon light. Many people believe taking their picture captures their soul, and taking a life story is even more threatening. Inevitably, in trying to know him, I would be putting pins in him. Our shadows were exactly the same size – small, compact heads enlarged by wiry curls. Despite the forty years that set us apart, despite our differences in sex, history, knowledge, belief, and experience, we resembled each other. Same big nose, dark eyes, sharp vaulted cheekbones. It could be seen that we were of the same racial stock. Shmuel had a way of reckoning all differences between us in his favor, mocking but without cruelty, yet in a way that always made me feel somewhat apologetic. I was grateful for all our similarities and read them as signs of hope in the validity of my attempt to comprehend him. It didn't help that I was a professor with a PhD, for both of us were aware that his self-directed education was much broader than mine, not to mention his greater experience.

I had explained to him what anthropology was, how it was a way of attempting to penetrate someone else's world from within, to enter another person's culture imaginatively and experience it as he did. I talked to him about the methods of participant-observation, where by sharing a segment of his life – and Center life – I would try to know it firsthand to some degree while at the same time preserving my separateness and a measure of objectivity. I explained what a "key informant" was and said that I had selected him to be a teacher about his culture, if he would agree.

"So you want me to be your 'native.' No, that's flattering but not good," he said. "I'm not typical. Get some of the others at the Center. I'm not like them. I don't join clubs. I'm not a Zionist. I don't believe in God. Find someone else."

Eventually I convinced him that I was drawn to him for his learning and philosophical approach, not for his typicality. He had thought more about his experiences than most, had struggled to make sense of them. He yielded to this argument. I added that this work had personal meaning for me as well. I had not had the opportunity to learn about the world of my grandparents directly. I wanted to hear a firsthand account of Yiddishkeit and the shtetl. My grandparents had not taught me this, and now they were dead.

"Your grandparents did not speak Jewish to you, or to their children?"[1]

"It was the usual story, Shmuel. They talked Yiddish to their children and the children answered in English. What there was to learn they ran away from as fast as they could, to become American."

"So now that you are big enough to choose for yourself, go talk to them."

"Too late, Shmuel. They're all dead. I can only get it in this roundabout fashion. When I hear Yiddish and Hebrew, often I don't know what the words mean, but I know that they are part of me all the same."

"What you ask, we will try. But it needs patience and time. How much I have of that, I don't know. Now I begin by telling you to see something you would not notice without me at your side." He pulled me closer and I stuck my ear close to his mouth to catch his quiet words.

"Look at those women sitting there on the benches. Sturdy little grandmothers." I had noticed them. As usual on a sunny day, each bench held a brace of old women. Motionless, they emitted great resolution. Their mere existence, then as now, was a political social attitude. Their continuing survival mocked their historical enemies, and time itself.

"Look if you will at something important about these women," Shmuel whispered. "Each one is wearing a coat. What's so special about a coat? you could ask. These are poor women here. But still everyone has a coat. A coat is not an ordinary garment. It was our people who brought coats to the world. Before the little Jewish tailors came to America, what poor person could have a coat?"

I never knew if Shmuel's attitude toward his work came from his Socialist beliefs, from some Judaic elements, or were entirely of his own making. Creativity and seriousness belonged to work. It was both religion and play. When he worked, his imagination was freed.

"The mind must be alive when you sew, if you are in a good shop or a bad. I have been in both, and all those in between. The outside conditions do not apply. You must bring it up from the inside, looking always for a way to express yourself.

"Do you know what this means for me? When I am in a shop, I am told to make a whole coat for a dollar. It must be done. You can't tell the boss he is crazy. You can't quit. In my shop, the other men would say, 'Nu,[2] I can do it.' They put down the little screw on the machine to make bigger stitches. But such a coat doesn't last the winter. This coat goes to a poor woman, her only garment for warmth. You wouldn't know this but it gives out in the Bible that a pawnbroker cannot keep a poor man's caftan or cloak for deposit or for pawn overnight, because a Jew can't profit from someone else's need. 'You shall not sleep in his pledge. When the sun goes down you restore to him his pledge, that he may sleep in his own cloak.' This comes from Deuteronomy, which no doubt you have not read. No, it is not the way of a Jew to make his work like there was no human being to suffer when it's done badly. A coat is not a piece of cloth only. The tailor is connected to the one who wears it and he should not forget it."

Shmuel's garments had lasted. He had always made clothes for his friends and his wife, Rebekah, saving shop remnants of his finest material for her. Rebekah still wore the long velvet skirts and frilly blouses he had made. Years after his death, she cut a fine figure in his garments.

We arrived at Shmuel's house, a single-story duplex a few doors from the boardwalk. "Do you want some tea? You are tired?" He knew I was and it pleased him that he was not. "Well, come in then, Rebekah will be glad to see you. By now she will be home from all her meetings."

We went into the large, rather bare living room, furnished with the landlord's castoffs. Two golden Naugahyde couches were pushed against the wall, and in between them stood a brave little table bearing heaps of magazines and papers – *Jewish Currents, Yiddishe Kultur Verband, Morgan Freiheit, The Nation, The People's World*. In one corner was a kitchen chair and a child's school desk, the drawers crammed with scraps of paper – Shmuel's poetry and essays in Yiddish, Hebrew, Polish, Russian, French, and English. Rickety bookcases held dictionaries, novels in all those languages, plus used college textbooks on political science, history, art, psychology, sociology, economics, and philosophy. In the center of the room, a huge bare-breasted ceramic woman in yellow harem pants held aloft a tiny fluted lampshade.

I fiddled with electric sockets and my tape recorder while Rebekah put up water for tea. Shmuel waited quietly, wearing his quizzical monkey look. He didn't look eighty. Time had sharpened his facial planes, paring off all nonessential flesh. The lips were a thin neutral line, the eyes deep and close together, unclouded by cataracts or glaucoma. His smile was restrained and rare. Only his hair and ears and cheekbones were exuberant. His teeth were jagged and stained, but they were his own. I liked them and realized how depressing I found the false white sameness of others' dentures. The cables of his neck wired his great, gaunt head onto a springy, tidy frame.

Rebekah came to the couch and sat down next to Shmuel. She too had her own teeth, and like him lacked the equipment that makes so many among the elderly look alike at first glance – the heavy glasses, hearing aids, dentures. Rebekah was also small, energetic, and erect. Even their hands were the same size, the backs blotched with brown spots but the fingers uncrimped by arthritis. Rebekah was seventy-four.

Both were healthy, apart from Shmuel's heart condition for which he frequently took nitroglycerin pills. "My doctor tells me not to have emotions," he said. "I should damp down everything. Is this philosophy? To live longer by not being so much alive? Now, in honor of your tape machine, I take one of his pills.

"So you are here in our modest home. You see we are not poor. We do not have too much money, not too little either. When this is so, you pay attention. Spend carefully, eat carefully, you think about what you wear, what you eat, chew slowly with pleasure. So you end up paying attention to being alive. This is not such a bad thing. I don't envy the rich. When we were young, in my little town – that was poor. That was hunger. But because we didn't know anything else we didn't think of ourselves as poor. Everyone lived the same in the town. One was hungry, all were hungry. Not so hard as here where you see there are very rich and very poor."

"Shmuel, can you tell me more specifically how much you spend for your life now, and where the money comes from?" I asked.

"For this house, we pay one hundred dollars a month with utilities. From the Social Security we get two hundred seventy-six dollars and from the union pension seventy-five dollars. For food we spend thirty-five dollars a week and our medical bills come under insurance, costing us maybe two hundred dollars a year. Clothing, still I make mostly. I have my sewing machine. What else is there? Entertainment – I have books and papers.

Sometimes we go to a concert, we have a radio. This house is the best we ever lived in. Our son does not give us money. We send money to him for the grandchildren's presents. This is how it should be. In Jewish we have a saying, 'When the father gives to the son, both are happy. When the son gives to the father, both weep.'"

"Shmuel, do you think being a Jew makes the life of a retired person different from others – easier or harder in any way?" I asked. My questions came haltingly. Shmuel was wary, waiting for me to prick him. He was polite, seeming always to defer but guarded. How much of his life must he have lived this way, I wondered. I had seen this stance before, in Indians who hold off the intrusions of powerful outsiders with dignity and persistence, not allowing entry where it would deeply touch them. Would I ever be more than an outsider to Shmuel – presumably one of my own people?

But my question had interested him. When he could draw out a moral he was at ease.

"You can see this is not an observant home," he answered. "So, you would ask, what kind of a Jew is it that lives here? My son is a better Jew than me. But I am not a Jew like my father. He believed blindly. For me, acts more than beliefs make a Jew. Judaism means you know yourself, your traditions, your history, you live them. To be a good human being, in the Jewish way, to believe in life, to believe in humanity, to follow the Ten Commandments, that is enough to be a good Jew.

"Now you will ask me, does this approach make life in retirement easier? How can I answer? It is how I have always lived. I'm doing what I have always done. My thinking hasn't changed, so my attitude hasn't changed. You could say I'm still working. Am I retired now because nobody pays me for this? The only thing that happened was when I was sixty-five I took off my watch.

"Now if you ask me the right questions I could tell you the man who doesn't like his work is a slave, a slave to boredom. Maybe for him retirement is a different kind of life. But in my life I have never been bored. If you cannot tell a story to yourself when you are sewing, you are lost anyway. The work has no beginning and no end, but the story is told, it goes on in the head. A needle goes in and out. You hold a thread in your fingers. It goes to the garment, to the fingers, to the one who wears the garment, all connected. This is what matters, not whether you are paid for what you do."

Rebekah interrupted us. "Shmuel, you are telling her the questions. You should stick to the answers. How can she do her job this way? Come now into the kitchen for tea." The kitchen was messy, fragrant, no signs of the landlord here. The tea was poured into jelly glasses. Shmuel drank his with the spoon in it, sipping it though a sugar cube he held in his teeth. Rebekah put out a plate of almonds, sunflower seeds, and raisins. Here it was easier to ask different kinds of questions.

"Rebekah," I asked, "how did you and Shmuel meet?"

She answered, "You see we had the same background. Shmuel was in the Bund with my brother. One night we were at the same meeting and that same night we walked out hand in hand. That's how we walked."

Shmuel nodded. "Since then, that was fifty-four years ago, we've been holding hands together. That's why I could never make a lot of money. I wanted to hold her hand always."

"Do you have any family members nearby?" I asked them.

"There isn't anybody left of our family except my sister," Rebekah answered. "She lives downtown and sometimes comes to visit us when she can get a ride."

"Do you see your son often?"

"He lives in Philadelphia," she said. "Like you he is a PhD, with a degree in sociology. He loves his work, has four fine boys. During the war he was a pacifist, a radical. He used to scold us for not teaching him Yiddish and Hebrew, so he studied these himself when he went to college. Now he keeps a kosher house and all the boys made Bar Mitzvah. When the children were younger they came here a lot. Now we go there, maybe once a year. We have a good life here. Thirty-two years ago we moved to the beach. Shmuel worked on costumes for the movie people and got a good pension when he retired. For thirty years I have been active in the Emma Lazarus Club, this was one of the first progressive political organizations for women. We belonged to the Freiheit Chorus and all kinds of reading and discussion groups. A few years ago we stopped many of these things because the clubs meet downtown and it's too hard to take buses after dark. Our friends are getting on and don't drive so much to the beach. Still, I wouldn't complain about our life, if only I didn't miss those grandchildren so much. It's like the heart is cut out of me."

"Why don't you live back there with them?" I asked.

"This is not so easy. There, we can't go out in winter. No exercise, no work to do. Here is our life, our friends, our home, and the ocean. Except for those little boys, this would be all I want."

"No, Rebekah," interrupted Shmuel. "It's not worth talking about. He is our son and we are proud of him, but that's his own life, and this is ours. It is a fact of life to be hurt by your children. It doesn't matter how good they are. That must be accepted, so if you have only your children in life, you will have only pain. And after the children – it's still no-man's-land on the other side. I know that. But still I sing every morning in the shower."

"It's true, he does," Rebekah agreed. "For all our life together, every morning I wake up to the sound of Shmuel singing. He's still a *chazzen*[3] and this house is our own *shul*.[4] Look at our home. It is nothing fancy but filled with books, filled with ideas and love."

"It's not a disgrace to have a life like this," added Shmuel. "My son a PhD, from me, a tailor, son of a tinsmith. It could be worse. All this we have arranged and none of us have ever crossed a picket line."

The following week I passed the Center on the way to Shmuel's house for our appointment, and Hannah walked along with me for a while. "I saw you talking with that linkie, Shmuel," she said. "He's no good. He's a Jew-hater, you shouldn't hang around with him. I know, I know he's a very smart man. A filosofe. He knows a lot of things, but what does it do for him if he hates himself?" She gave me a warning poke as we parted, and beneath her question was the veiled threat of exclusion from her and her friends' confidence if I persisted in my friendship with Shmuel. It made me very angry that I couldn't afford to take the threat lightly.

Shmuel opened the door for me with exaggerated courtesy. "Oy vay, the lady professor is here for more questions. Rebekah, warm the tea, she looks cold and she's covered all over with machines." I bumped past him feeling ridiculous, encumbered with camera, notebook, tape recorder, purse, and a box of cookies. Rebekah was about to leave for her Spanish class. She studied Spanish, she explained, because of her work with Mexican migrant laborers. After the class she would be passing out petitions supporting their strike.

"Do you enjoy that work?" I asked as I was setting up my equipment.

"Who could enjoy standing in a parking lot on a cold day, arguing with ignorant strangers? You don't do these things to enjoy. It has to be done, that's all." It never occurred to her, evidently, that her age might excuse her from political responsibility.

"Shmuel, a disturbing thing happened on the way over here," I began. I told him what Hannah had said.

"Yes, I warned you what they think of me. I am persona non grata over there. I will tell you what happened. I have always had mixed feelings about Israel. I told you I'm not a Zionist.

"Here is what I believe. Only life itself is sacred, not a nation. A nation is no different from any other – not America, not Israel, not Russia. 'Behold, the nations are like a drop from a bucket. All are counted as the dust on the scales.' This comes to us from Isaiah. If those ignoramuses would know the Bible, they would understand things better. They think I should fall on the ground of America, of Israel. I kiss no country's ground. According to them, this makes me an anti-Semite.

"Those people at the Center forget their own past. Most of them were at one time Bundists, internationalists, at least Marxists. We all got along all right with our differences until the Six Day War in Israel. Then they went crazy with Zionism. There was one of them, Weidman, a real peasant he is. He shows me a picture from a newspaper. There I see an Arab soldier. Dead. An Israeli solider, smiling with his foot on the Arab's chest. By me, this is an ugly sight. This Weidman says, 'You see, how we have crushed the enemy!' 'Shame on you,' I tell him. 'Are you proud of that? Do you think that's not a man lying there? Are we less brutes than them? In the Talmud it warns us not to treat even our enemies this way.' To him I quoted this: '. . . You have turned justice into poison, the fruit of righteousness into wormwood.' From Jeremiah, the prophet."

"I suppose they didn't thank you for your opinion," I remarked.

"How could they understand? They haven't got the view, so uneducated. The weight of Jewish history, Jewish thought, is too heavy for those people. They are too small to bear the Covenant." Shmuel sighed heavily and reached into his pocket, where he kept the nitroglycerin pills.

Rebekah added, "What do you think they said to him about this? They spat at him. They throw curses at him. This he wouldn't tell you. He protects them. Disgusting are those people, am ha-aretz[5] all. Shmuel, I don't know why you go in there."

"What could I expect them to say? Should they thank me? My presence pierces them like a polished arrow. This happened also to our prophets, especially to Jeremiah. With him I felt a great kinship always. 'They hate him who reproves at the gate. They abhor him who speaks the truth.' At least, I have the satisfaction of knowing I am in good company."

"I can't stand around here talking about such people when there's serious work to do." Rebekah left.

"Shmuel, I wonder too. Why do you go back when they treat you that way?"

"That's not so easy to explain. You see in the old days, this neighborhood had plenty of room for everybody's opinions. We had our discussion circles, poetry circles, Yiddish organizations, union groups, all those things. Now the urban renewal pushed most of them away. Our neighbors die or go to Homes.[6] Every day, our world shrivels. It frightens people. And now those that are left are all thrown together at the Center. Many of them have nothing in common, but they have to stay together. They remind each other of what they are reduced to. There is no place for them to go except to the parks and social clubs for old people where they don't hear Jewish words or see a Jewish face. So why do I go there? I too need to hear Jewish sometimes. And, maybe, it's because they need me. You know, I am like the fly that pricks a sleeping mule. Now we work."

Shmuel held up a batch of papers covered with Yiddish. He had prepared for today's session by writing out some of his recollections from childhood. He put on his reading glasses and signaled that he was ready to begin.

"Oh, how often in our dreams, like a bird, we fly back to the place of our birth, to that little Polish town on the Vistula, which would be to you a small speck on the map, maybe even too insignificant for a map. A few thousand people huddled together, hidden in the hills, but with a view in sight of the beautiful river. In this place, the population was nearly equal Poles and Jews. All were poor. There were the poor and the poorer still.

"If you walked through the Jewish quarter, you would see small houses, higgledy-piggledy, leaning all over each other. Some had straw roofs, if shingles, some broken. No cobbles on the streets, and you might not even want to call them streets, so narrow and deep rutted from wagons. Everywhere, children, cats, geese, chickens, sometimes a goat, altogether making very strong smells and noises. Always, the children were dirty and barefoot, always the dogs were skinny and mean, not Jewish dogs. They came over from Gentile quarters looking for garbage and cats. You would go along this way until you crossed the wooden bridge into the main platz. Here were the women on market day, sitting in the open, or in little wooden stalls if they were well-off. Around the platz, a few Jewish stores, a stable, the pump with a roof and bench.

"Most important, you would see here two buildings, facing each other on opposite sides of the platz, without smiling. There was on one side the Catholic church, enormous, two big towers of bells, and across from it, the synagogue, small but dignified, topped by pagoda-like roofs covered with sheet metal. The church was built with splendor inside and under the sun it was shining like silver, like a sparkle in God's eye. Otherwise it was all wood. The church stands there sternly, the synagogue's historical enemy – those two looked at each other all the day. The church was built with splendor inside and out. Its glittering beauty displayed itself when the great portals opened. The Jewish children were afraid even to look inside."

Shmuel warmed to his subject and broke off reading. "You see, that church was the biggest thing we ever saw. From everywhere in the town you could see the towers. You could never forget about it. It was such a beautiful building, but when the great bells tolled it meant trouble for us Jews. When we heard that, we children would run home as fast as we could, back into the Jewish streets. On Sundays and Easter, those were the worst times. The processions came out from the church. The peasants were drinking all the day and night, staggering down the road behind those pictures of the saints they carry. Then if they came across a Jewish child or woman, it could be murder. The hatred would pour out.

"You see, matters were never simple there. The pogroms were all around us. Then the soldiers on horseback would tear through the town and leave dead Jews behind. One time, we heard the big bell ring out and there was no reason for it. We were so scared we hid in the synagogue. That was probably the worst place to go, but we were small boys. All night we stayed huddling together there and heard terrible noises outside – horses, screams, shouts. We were afraid to light the lamps or stove. In the morning some men came to get us. Someone, it must have been a Pole, had warned the Jews with the bells that the soldiers were coming through. Everyone got away very quickly, hiding in the forest and in neighbors' homes. Who knows what would have happened without the warning? As it is, the soldiers tore up the Jewish streets, broke windows, threw the furniture out. We came out into the sparkling sunshine and the streets were white like in winter. Everywhere were feathers from where those Cossacks cut up our featherbeds. Dead animals also on our streets. From all this you can imagine our emotions when we walked past the great doors of the church. We would hardly throw a glance inside, even though the beauty would draw us like moths.

"Now, by comparison the synagogue you might not think was a beautiful place. It would be misleading to say it had any architecture. But do you think I noticed that? This synagogue was my first introduction to Judaism. The first time I went there I was with my beloved father, who up to the present moment I feel is with me, so that when I think of the synagogue, I can still feel his hand in mine as he introduced me to the world it held.

"I will tell you a littler bit what it looks like. You walked up ten broad steps to the door. Why ten? I don't know, but probably it had some meaning. Then to enter, you walked down again, ten steps more. Why? The reason I think is symbolical. Because from the depths of your heart, you seek God, and you should feel that brings you up. But right away, you realize you are in the presence of God. Your body vibrates with how high He is, and how you are very small. Of this you are reminded by the steps down. That is how I thought of it.

"But like most things symbolical, there is also a practical side. You see, the Poles had a law that the church must be the highest building in the town. So the Jews, to make their buildings high, built it up from the inside, very quietly. You could not see from the outside what was happening. This was typical of the way the Jews lived with the Poles at that time. Everything done inside so as not to attract notice. Oppression made us very cunning. In this here case, the floor of the synagogue was lowered. They dug down into the ground, so from the inside only it was a very tall building.

"Inside the synagogue, no saints, no gold. There is no big beauty. It is an empty room. Benches, a bima,[7] the ark, not very bright. Now here is another thing. In the top by the ceiling, there were murals. Animals, Hebrew characters, flowers, birds of all kinds, and signs of the zodiac. There was also an elephant. Who had ever seen an elephant in Poland? Actually, he looked more like a deer with tusks. I raised my small head and looked up at that elephant until I thought my neck would crack. Some painter, some obscure fellow who never saw an elephant, he was the one who brought me all of a sudden to a thing I had never known before, You see, it was not a Jewish custom to decorate our homes. No pictures in our books. No carvings on the furniture. You know Jews forbid making religious pictures, and everything in those days was for religion. Why the synagogue was decorated at all, this I cannot answer. But in our little town, the only beauty which we could look at was the murals in the synagogue and the ones in the church, which you were too frightened to have a good look at.

"Now, if you have enough tape, I will give you the best part. I will describe my favorite picture in that mural. OK. This one was covered with musicians and angels playing horns and flutes. In the middle was a picture of Abraham in his devotion to God. He took his only son and got ready to sacrifice him for the sake of God, until the Angel took ahold of his knife and saved Isaac. It seems strange, but there have always been people who are ready to make sacrifices on an altar without reservation. So the Bible in this story is showing us that people have always been ready to sacrifice the younger generation. We still send the innocent out to be slaughtered.

"Now you see, these pictures formed me. I never forgot that. There is no such thing as a small place. Some people would call that little town a small shtetl, or say it was a small synagogue. But people are formed by their passions, in the same ways, no matter how small or big is the place they live. They become who they are, with all the troubles, all the passions, with all the things which are bound to come up and face them, from these childhood pictures. That picture of Abraham is such for me. So that to this day, when I see children being sent out for slaughter, with those bugles playing and drums beating, while the angels are flapping their wings so you shouldn't hear the cries of the children being killed and shouldn't smell the blood, it stinks in my nostrils. But that is mankind. You cannot cut it out."

"Tell me, Shmuel," I asked, "didn't it confuse you, to love Judaism as you did, but see it condoning the sacrifice of an innocent victim for God's wishes?"

"Do you think that Judaism saves us from being men? Even as a boy, I saw Abraham's fault and knew it was his responsibility, not God's, to decide what was right.

"Like I said, sometimes things happen that make you realize how helpless you are. Not only were we children. We were Jews and the outside would come up against us. This was like being a child twice over, you felt very small, very weak. To give you an example, sometimes the Polish nation would step into our hidden little world in the synagogue. This was when the governor, appointed by the czar, would visit our little town once a year on the czar's birthday. When we knew he was coming, we cleaned everything, the best way we could. The women would come in and scrape all the candle wax and ashes off the benches and floors, oil the wood, make the books line up on the shelves. All the children would wear their best clothes, borrow shoes if they had to.

"The leadership of the synagogue was so afraid, they wanted not to displease the governor. Everything was done to impress him. A rug was put down, from somewhere we got it. And a big chair put in the middle where the bima should be sitting. We, the boys, the cantor, the rabbi, would stand up there, straight and stiff, full of palpitations to receive him, as he entered the door, dressed in a beautiful jacket, gray, with red lapels and gold trim, with a huge cross hanging from his neck.

"As he entered we turned and faced him. He never smiled. We never smiled. He had little glasses that glittered. Very straight and big. He was much bigger than any of us, maybe six feet tall.

"The rabbi would make him a receptional speech. This rabbi was very short and bent over, a frail old man, nearsighted and scared to death. He held that paper right up to his nose, trembling all over from the ordeal. He delivered it in Russian, careful with all the words, to make it to the satisfaction of the government. It filled my heart with pity to see that kind old man so frightened, like a small, unloved boy.

"After the speech, we children began to sing the Russian hymn, a hymn on the dull side. But we sang with gusto. This hymn was also a delicate business, because it was introduced after Poland was partitioned by Russia. And we were Jews – not accustomed to placing any man superior to any other, except God Himself. But this was the way we were required to pay homage. I will never forget this hymn. All mixed up with it was the fear if we make a mistake, something terrible will happen. I can hear still our beautiful clear voices, and see that tall man's fine uniform, with the synagogue so sparkling clean, and always I come back to the old rabbi's terror. I get it all back together with the hymn."

Shmuel abruptly pushed back from the table. He tore his glasses off his nose and pulled himself up to his full five feet two inches. Voice trembling, but sweet and grand, he gave forth the Russian hymn. I applauded when he finished and shouted bravo. For a few moments his tears and laughter spilled out freely. I had never seen him so unguarded. Neither of us heard Rebekah come in. Shmuel quickly reached for another pill.

"What am I hearing? Is it possible? Why do you sing that terrible song, Shmuel?" Rebekah asked sharply. "Those things only meant unhappiness for us. You shouldn't let him talk about those times," she reprimanded me. "It makes me shudder."

"Rebekah, Rebekah, it was there," Shmuel protested. "You won't make it any different if you say it wasn't there. The hymn, the czar, the fear, the beauty, it was all there. It must be kept all together. To take out one part and lose the rest, to try to keep the good parts is to make every day the Sabbath. So far, the Messiah has not come. When every day is beautiful, we will be in Paradise."

"Shmuel has no understanding in some things." Rebekah turned to me. "He thinks because he has these ideas about things the world is changed. He will try to tell you living with the Poles was not so bad. He maybe hasn't told you what happened to him? Did he show you his scar? He met a boy, a *shaygets*,[8] and it was wintertime, after Christmas. Shmuel wore a heavy sweater and scarf. This boy took out a knife and stabbed him in the neck."

"No, he hasn't told me. What happened, Shmuel?"

"I must have been about eleven years old. I was coming home from another village. I didn't see anyone. It was just growing dark and I was hurrying and took a shortcut through the woods. All of a sudden, something was on me with a knife, from the back. I felt a terrible pain in my neck and fell to the ground. He left me for dead. But it's not so easy to kill me. You know, they say that Jews are a stiff-necked people. He picked the wrong place to stab me. You could say my scarf saved me, or you could say maybe it was the characteristic of our people." Shmuel made his mischievous monkey face, eyes wide and round, eyebrows jumping up, mouth pulling down, nostrils flying open.

"Well, this happened. It is true. I carry the scar to remind me till now. I never saw this fellow's face, but I knew who it was from the voice, one of our neighbors. Not a bad boy, but an ignorant peasant. But this is not characteristic. I cannot depict this here like it was a regular part of life in our little town."

"Did you see him again?"

"Of course, every day."

"Did you talk about it ever? Why do you think he did it?"

"No, we never spoke about it. After that, he was a little afraid of me. I think he thought I was some kind of a ghost. For why he did it, I can't say. He was a bully and a small Jewish boy was like a fly to him. But it must be remembered that there were Jewish bullies also. Who knows what they would do if they wouldn't be caught and punished? Without the law to govern them, do they find it in their hearts always to behave? Because they were the Chosen People? Not even the Messiah would expect that. Without consequences, do you think men ever find it in their hearts to do what is right? If that was so, why would we need the Torah?"

"Why are you undoing your tape machine? Are you getting ready to go? I just got back." Rebekah was very disappointed. She had wanted to make a tape recording of a poem she had translated. I was already late for dinner, but I knew if I left now, Rebekah would be annoyed with me for weeks.

Shmuel sensed my conflict and intervened. "Leave her alone, Rebekah," he said. "She'll come another day. She's a busy lady and I'm a hungry man. Come, I'll walk you to your car. This is a dangerous neighborhood and my neck is stiffer than yours." He winked, gathered up my packages, and held open the door.

Lessons on the Road
The Life of a Hobo
Douglas Harper

Since the Civil War, hobos or tramps have been a continuing feature of American life. More than in the world of the urban homeless, some of the individuals in hobo culture seem to be there by choice. The culture of tramps has been of considerable interest to sociologists because it is a rejection of mainstream values such as materialism, career achievement, marriage, and family and yet simultaneously an extreme embodiment of other American values such as freedom, individualism, and self-reliance. Focused on the general culture of hobos, few of these studies convey much a sense of what it is like for an individual to actually live this way of life.

Harper's study is unique in the amount of time he spent traveling with tramps on freight trains and living with them in their "jungles," or encampments, and in his focus on a year in the life of one individual. In order to understand the subjective experience of this complex world, Harper established a very close bond with the tramp who became his mentor and friend.

In this chapter, Harper takes us along during his first meeting with Carl, the tramp who became his teacher in the ways of tramp life. Notice how he represents this encounter through vivid scenes of action and dialogue.

This reading is chapter 5 in Douglas Harper's *Good Company* (Chicago: University of Chicago Press, 1982), 28–35. It is reprinted here by permission of the author.

The afternoon's travel was broken by a two-hour wait on a siding only an hour north of Missoula. Finally an Amtrak passenger train sped past and we reclaimed our tracks to begin another ascent of the Rockies. The late afternoon sun kept slipping behind the mountains, then reappearing as we climbed higher and higher. The train worked hard and the ride was slow. Hours were spent without conversation, and in the privacy of our trip I felt a deep loneliness. As we passed one of the few towns on the route – Thompson Falls, Montana – the train veered close to the houses and I watched people through their windows, sitting down to supper. The tramp crouched in his corner, by now just a dark shadow. I felt lost in the din of the train and the approaching darkness.

It was completely dark by the time we reached the top. The extra engines were left on a siding and then we careened down the other side of the mountain. The freight moved faster than any I have ridden and our boxcar threw us around like the wood chips that covered the floor. For hours we sped directly northwest; then the train turned west and the ride became tamer as we crossed the flatlands of Idaho. City lights appeared in the distance, and we entered Spokane. I felt done in by the ride and the long day but the tramp seemed newly energized. We jumped the train as it idled into the yards and hiked to a huge bridge where there was freight in the making. I guessed that it was after midnight.

The tramp wandered off, again leaving me with all our gear, to determine the destination of the train. I felt immobilized and vulnerable. I tried to shrink into the shadows, but passing figures, if they noticed me at all, paid me no heed. A yard engine idled by, illuminating me in its glare and startling me with its bell. Boxcars loomed as black shapes as they creaked through the yard.

Carl finally returned, satisfied that he'd found the Wenatchee train. I was anxious to find a place to ride but we were out of water and Carl wouldn't think of traveling dry. He again disappeared into the darkness to return a few minutes later with two gallon bottles full to the brim with ice water.

"Where in the hell did you get those?" I asked.

"Shhh," he whispered, "not so loud." He started pouring the water into our canteen and hilex bottle. "See that tail end dragging the crummy around the yard? I knew nobody would be riding that crummy while they was pushing it through the yard so I jumped in and borrowed this here water. I knew it would be in the refrigerator. Always is."

"You mean you went right into a caboose to get this water? Isn't the door locked?"

"Naw, the door's never locked."

"But the light's on inside of those things. It's like daylight!"

"You can do a lot of things in the light of day," he answered, "providing you move real quick! Now hold steady so I can pour!"

We left the bottles in full view ("We don't need the bottles – just the water," the tramp said) and began walking down the train, each to a side. We learned quickly to adjust our pace so we would meet at each coupling. We found an empty boxcar near the end of the train and boarded.

Carl spoke in whispers: "I been through this yard for years but I know the other yard, the old Great Northern, better. Back where they used to run the high line. That's the old N.P. It's only lately – since they merged – that the Big G comes through here. . . . That's a good yard over there. Store nearby. Water easy to get. Then there's the "Yardley Tavern" a half block down the street. An old woman run it."

"I guess these yards aren't so complicated," I said, "but sometimes I walk into one of them and I don't know where in the hell to start. I waste time, and I miss trains that way . . ."

"But you don't even know what to watch for!" the tramp interrupted. "Half the time you don't even know where the mainlines are! You got to learn while you're hanging around! For instance, in this yard they make up all the trains right here. The rest of the yard don't mean a thing to you. The hotshot stays on the main line. They just check him on the main line – maybe reshuffle his cars over the hump – and send him right back out."

"But even the hotshots bust up here, don't they?"

"Not here! They go right on through. They're made up way east – Minneapolis, Chicago. That Seattle train's made up right in St. Paul. It doesn't bust up in Minot – they just shuffle the train over the hump and the same cars go out again. It's ninety-seven and one-ninety-seven – that's their numbers. Odd numbers going west; even going back east."

"Do those numbers mean the train leaves the same time, travels the same route? Or is it something else?"

"It's the same train. It's the 'time freight.' That's another name for it. We were on a drag – that's the local we've been stuck on for the last couple of days."

"Last year they told me I was riding a hotshot and it busted up all over the place," I said.

"Well, they said it was the hotshot. The only real hotshots are ninety-seven and one-ninety-seven. The *through* freight; the *time* freight. They got to keep time. The others, they just fuck around, go onto 'hold' and let the hot ones go through . . .

"There's a lot of tricks to it. It's always better not to have to ask anybody nuthin'. After you done it a few times you can recognize the engines and tell where the train is going. Look at that engine over there – that's a 'square nose.' Out of Laurel they go to Salt Lake. If it's a 'round nose,' they'll go up the high line. It's what we had on tonight. The round nose'll have a headlight right out in front. A single light. The new Burlington Northerns – they're sort of pointed but we call them square nosed because the angles are sharp in front of those engines . . .

"Now usually the S.P. & S. comes up here. They'll put the S.P. & S. and the Great Northerns together. But when they go down to Salt Lake they put a Western Pacific on it. So there you are – the next time you ought to be able to get out of Laurel!"

"Well, what about Salt Lake City – that a hot yard?"

"No, no that's a good yard. A lot of guys go there. You'll find a lot headed for Ogden – that's outside Salt Lake – because they get a hundred and fifty-some dollars a month welfare. And out of Salt Lake you can go anywhere you want to. Denver, you catch the Burlington. Or, if you want to get to Denver you can go down through Billings. You got to know your connections. You can go through Wyoming from Laurel, or you can go through Nebraska. Or you can go north to Great Falls – all that from Laurel, right where we were."

"I liked that land between here and Laurel," I said, "I really liked it this time. I wanted to see it that way – to go through the mountains during the day – and I'm glad I did."

Carl surprised me by replying: "That north route's better; I like that ride through Glacier Park. You can see the whole canyon. You can see all the way up to the top, and then when you go down the other side, through west Glacier, you get another view of that whole goddamn valley. But then once you get past Cutbank you don't see much scenery any more, just wheatland all the way past Havre, Shelby, all the way to Minot. All of a sudden, bang! Corn country. Corn and those goddamn sunflowers."

"That eastern Montana on the high line is a barren damned area . . . Glasco, Wolf Point . . . doesn't seem to be much there."

"Had good crops there last couple of years. But before that, too much rain, not enough rain – nuthin' would grow up there!"

I broke the lull: "That ride last night – I'm sore! Boy . . ."

"Tonight was worse!" Carl said. "That dirty cocksucker, rocking all the way. Why, my insides were goin' back and forth, bouncin' like that and then that damn slamming back and forth!" He looked at our bags along the walls in the front of the car and said: "It's dangerous layin' the way we are now. If we stop real quick, our heads are goin' right up through the wall. If he stops quick and you're layin' sideways, you roll – hell, I already lived through one wreck! That was in California. Feather River. He throwed about a dozen cars off and I didn't even wake up! Shit, I woke up in a siding the next day and we stayed there for three days – in a snowbank. It was just gettin' spring. Lucky I had a whole sack of french bread and rolls, some lunch meat, and even some old coffee. No tobacco though. Spring nearby so I could get water easy. But dammit, it was cold! Couldn't do much except sit!"

"I always stayed out of California when I've been on the freights. I sort of assumed that those yards would be hot."

"They're all right – again, that's if you know them. What I do sometimes is, if I'm in Oakland, which is hot, is to hitchhike, or if I got the money, take the bus up to Stockton, or even Oroville. The yard's smaller and it ain't hot. You can pick up a hotshot out of there that goes two ways. One goes to Salt Lake City and the other comes up here.

"You can get down there, all right. Catch out of Portland, which can be tricky, or better to go through Wishram. Pasco to Wishram and then the S.P. & S., or the Western Pacific to California. Wishram is the next division goin' down the river out of Pasco. Breaks up there in Wishram, puts it back together and away he goes! Up the mountain – up the Columbia River canyon – and shit, that's pretty. You follow that Deschutes River all the way to the top. Over a hundred miles. Then you go through Bend, Klamath Falls, Redding, and then down to Oroville. You can ride into Oakland, you just got to be careful. It's going out that's tough."

Our conversation was blotted out by an Amtrak passenger train highballing through the yard. It was a short train, not more than ten cars, with no intention of slowing for the Spokane freight yard. Our train suddenly snapped forward and threw us both off our feet. Carl lost his balance and nearly fell out of the car.

"Don't tell me, I ducked!" he said as the train began idling westward. "I remember the first time that happened. It scared the daylights out of me. About this time of the night and that train let go – I didn't know what was happening! The train snapped and I must have gone three feet into the air . . .

"When you hear something like that you duck. God, I've seen a man get his head cut off! He was stickin' it out and lookin' – door open about this much and it slammed shut – there it goes! That's it! Christ, what a bloody mess! Hands, same thing. I've seen 'em bust off their feet sittin' hanging them out the door and wham! Those switches or those close bridges I showed you. You can't see them coming. *Never* sit with your feet hangin' out the side of the car. *Never!* Even standing here like we are, if that thing jerks – out you go! It don't take much . . ."

We idled near a lighted caboose. "See that crummy over there," said the tramp, "that's where I got the water. Just go over and check if the door's open and if it is, go right in. If they find you rummaging around in there you say, 'Hey, where's this train goin'' while you're making for the door! . . . Naw, there's nothing to worry about. If it's their own crummy, they'll lock it. Some crews ride the same train and keep the same crummy – but they don't do that much any more. Years ago they kept their own caboose a certain way. You didn't mess around with those." The train snapped to a stop. In the distance we heard an amplified voice directing the making of another midnight train. We were still deep in the yards.

The tramp bent over his small bag to roll a cigarette. The couplings creaked and groaned and the train nudged ahead.

"Nowadays everything's mechanized on these jobs so you can't stop and roll a smoke. You gotta buy tailor-mades. Or at least I wouldn't stop working to roll a smoke. I'd think the boss was lookin' at me."

The train picked up speed and the tempo and the intensity of the noise increased. Rock, rattle, bang bang bang. There were dim fires near the edge of the tracks where, Carl said, the Indians and the niggers jungle, and where I'd stay away from if I knew what I was doing.

"See, there's somebody over there!" Carl pointed ahead. The tramp saw us and yelled: "Which way's he goin'?" Carl hesitated before he answered and the tramp was past our car when he yelled: "Seattle."

"I didn't want anybody in this car," he said, "that's why I waited until we went by to answer. He sounded like a drunk Indian anyway."

"I noticed you didn't tell him this was the Wenatchee train, either."

"That tramp won't know if this is the Wenatchee train because it goes both ways to Seattle. I ended up in Pasco that way once. The train was goin' to Seattle but it went the long way around and I missed Wenatchee by a few hundred miles." We passed more jungle fires. "That's where they coop up, under that bridge. You got to stay on the other side of that bridge, away from here. They get their water in those stockyards. That's Armour packing. Then they go up a little ways and get a free meal from St. Vincent de Paul's. They hang around down there, I know. That's why I don't like to bed down comin' out of these yards. Anybody can jump in – and if it's a Negro I won't let him in. Maybe if he's alone I'd let him in. If there's two of them, no way. Either they'd get out, or I would. I'd just tell them there's another car down back. There's more than one empty on a train – they can get their own car! It's bad at night, especially this time of year with all the pickers coming in . . . and if you been drinking, watch out!"

"I don't drink when I'm riding," I said.

"Well, if I do drink I get up the corner of the car. Even when I got a hangover, you won't see me near the door. Fuck no! I stay in the back but I get scared! The speed raises hell with me – I just don't like it anymore."

"I don't drink on the road, and I figure I can handle most that are drunk. Or at least that's what I tell myself. People get crazy when they drink. Sometimes they don't seem rational . . . They just do crazy things . . ."

But Carl answered: "Oh, you can handle a drunk if you know what you are doing. But if you drink yourself – then it's bad. Or if two or three of them that's been drinkin' jump you."

"Yeah, I've been told plenty of times never to let a couple of guys entice me into a car with a bottle . . ."

"No, no, *fuck* no! Don't ever ride with a couple of them. Your best bet is to get with an old-timer, somebody that knows the ropes. Nine times out of ten that old-timer will be carryin' a gun – especially in this country. I used to carry a gun, not no more. Afraid I'd kill somebody. Used to herd sheep in this country – you needed one there. And I carried one for a long time in the army – anyway it's all how you use it. People fuck around with them but I tell you, buddy, if you go pulling a gun you better use it! 'Cause if you don't, you won't be around to tell about it!"

Under another bridge Carl pointed to more jungles. "All along here – you watch during the day. Old fires all over. It's bad here, too, if you come down take the street, or walk along the highway and climb down by that first bridge . . . Yeah, there's a lot of tricks on this road, but only a few important ones. You have to learn to stay away from the rest. Set up camp after dark. I never let anybody know when I'm goin' – I wait until the campfire's out and then I disappear. I don't want nobody to follow me!" Then he looked me straight in the eye. "Some people on this road are helpless. When you start helpin' it's just like having a son – they don't know where it stops! You got to support them – take care of them – you got to provide the hand and I won't do that. If a fella is on this road and he can't learn – then to hell with him!"

"You get tired of me just let me know!"

"I will, but you still don't know what I mean. Don't travel alone if you can help it, but when you get your job, don't depend on nobody else. If you want to leave, then leave! That's it – a lot of these guys say, 'If you quit, let me know and I'll quit with you.' I say bullshit. Before you know it you'll have run out of places to work."

"That why you been leaving all these good jobs you've been telling me about?"

"Usually I get tired of the man. I work hard for a man but after a while he thinks he owns me! He starts puttin' more and more work on me with the same pay. I say to hell with that – that's when I leave. But I don't care how cold and rough it gets, you won't find me on the bum. It might be forty below but I'll find work. Maybe just for my clothes and some warmth, and a little food, but I'll work. And I ain't proud." We passed an intersection in the tracks. "I was right – there goes that Pasco cutoff!" Carl yelled. We crossed a valley on a bridge that seemed to go on forever. Carl said the valley was three hundred feet below but it was all lost in the darkness. The ride was smooth and fast when I bedded down and I was asleep in minutes.

"That Really Happened"
Ethnography and the Hobby of Twentieth-Century War Reenacting

Jenny Thompson

In order to retain social acceptance in their various real worlds, all Americans have to manage their imaginary cultural experience carefully. Here Jenny Thompson investigates the lives of individuals who leave their real-world jobs and families to participate in a make-believe social world based on imaginatively re-creating and reenacting wars of the twentieth century, including both world wars and the Korean and Vietnam wars. An estimated six thousand Americans participate in these reenactments, joining up with their reenacting units across the country to take part in both public and private events. Dressed in period uniforms, they portray Russian privates, Canadian nurses, American GIs, British officers, Vietcong soldiers, and even Nazi SS troops. At air shows and living history encampments they set up displays, perform battles, and try to teach people about the soldiers they represent. Their private reenactments are closed to spectators and take place across the country at camps, military installations, and private sites.

Drawing on her training as an actor and ethnographer, Thompson entered this world via participant observation and took up the roles of a Russian combat soldier, a World War II correspondent and photographer, and a World War I truck driver. She expertly pulls us into the midst of this controversial cultural tradition and then shows us how the individuals who play at what they call "the hobby" make sense of it from their own points of view. Her focus on two individual reenactors, Luke and John, helps us see how participants engage in reenacting in a variety of ways.

Thompson's essay vividly illustrates the power and utility of opening a written life history with a scene. Notice how effectively this scene draws readers into the midst of the reenactors' world and helps us vicariously experience and hence begin to comprehend her subjects' experiences. Her scene also locates her as a researcher in a way that sets up her examination of how her gender and research roles affected her own experience through the course of her study.

Portions of this essay, which was written for this book, appeared in Jenny Thompson's *War Games: Inside the World of Twentieth Century War Reenactors* (Washington DC: Smithsonian Institution Press, 2004). This material is used here by permission of the Smithsonian Institution Press.

Kitted out in my World War II correspondent's uniform and seated uncomfortably in the back of a deuce-and-a-half (a World War II–period truck), I've spent a chilly morning getting to know my reenacting companions at this private World War II reenactment. Dressed as American GIs, they are all wearing olive drab wool trousers, parkas, and helmets and carrying rifles. Tilden Scott, a thirty-something high school history teacher from Virginia; Brian Shore, a mechanic from Pennsylvania; and Sam Adler, a friendly New Yorker in his early forties, have clearly accepted my presence at this World War II reenactment after I was assigned to their vehicle. They have warmly welcomed me, and we've spent the early part of the morning cordially chatting as we move through the site bringing up the end of the long train of period military vehicles on its way to the "battle."

We are in charge of the radios linking together the Allied units. After our group has mastered the code names for each U.S. unit commander linked to the network and schooled ourselves on authentic radio protocol, our conversation turns to contemporary matters.

"So, what field are you in, Jenny?" Tilden asks as the truck bounces over the rough, narrow road.

"American studies," I respond.

They're curious about my project and want to know more. I explain that I'm studying reenacting in order to understand it from a cultural perspective. They nod encouragingly.

"I'll tell you what my wife says about the reenactors' perspective," Sam says, resting his rifle against his knee. "We're fuckin' nuts."

"It is a little strange," I say delicately. "But I think it's pretty interesting."

"My wife's what I call a feminazi," Sam continues. "You know, hates guns, thinks war is bad. She thinks I'm crazy for doing this. She thinks it's sick and testosterone and all that. But look," he says suddenly. "Look at this." He pulls the truck's canvas flap aside to reveal the mass of reenactors streaming across the field. "This is absolutely amazing. You can read, you can watch movies, but try to put yourself in it, you can't. Not unless you reenact."

Several minutes later our truck comes to a lurching halt. We get out and find that all the other vehicles have stopped.

"Waiting around. That's pretty realistic," Brian says.

Up the road, Luke Gardner, our unit commander, is conspiring with his sergeants, pointing in various directions. Several reenactors appear to have been ordered on a reconnaissance patrol, and they move along the road, sliding every few feet on the sheet of ice covering its surface.

"Let's wait in the truck," Sam says. "I don't want to freeze my ass off."

We pile back into the truck and continue talking. A few minutes later we hear a loud churning sound coming down the road. "Jeez, Louise," Sam says, scrambling madly to load a clip in his rifle. "That's them! That's the fucking Germans!" Tilden and Brian unlock their safeties and are on their feet, crouching in the back of the truck. Seconds later, a German truck approaches; two Germans manning a machine gun perched in the truck's bed begin firing at us, shouting wildly as they speed past.

"Shit!" Sam yells as he flings his heavy body up at least half a foot before falling like a mound of dead weight on top of me.

"Awwww!" Sam groans as if really injured. I lie there, listening to his heavy breathing. The only other sound is that of the German truck's churning motor growing fainter as it speeds away. What seems to be an eternity passes before Tilden, Brian, and, thankfully, Sam rouse themselves, all having been killed in what reenactors jokingly refer to as a "drive-by."

"They wiped us out!" Brian exclaims.

"Man!" Tilden says. "That actually scared me. It took me totally by surprise."

"We couldn't do anything," Sam declares in excitement. "We were totally defenseless. The Germans just opened fire," he says, describing what just happened as if he had been the only witness.

I dust off the back of my pants, feeling a little embarrassed. But they're engrossed in recounting the moment. Soon they lapse into a discussion of history.

"That really happened," Sam urges.

"Sure," Tilden responds. "The Germans wiped out GIs sitting in a truck just like this. I can't remember the unit, but another unit came by later and all they found were the bodies."

"Oh yeah, that happened a lot," Sam says, shaking his head. "Guys just parked at the side of the road. The Germans picked them off, didn't matter if they were defenseless, didn't matter if they couldn't fight back. Supply trains, medical trucks, you name it. It was fair game to the Germans."

A pair of eyes peers into the back of the truck. "You guys okay?" asks our driver.

"Yeah, we're okay," Tilden says breathlessly. "We were all killed. Were you?"

"Nabbed me right on the side of the head. I fell right over the gearshift."

"Shit!" Sam says with a level of bitterness appropriate to the real passing of friends. "You know," he repeats to us again, "that really happened." He sits dumbly, his rifle cradled in his thick arms. He is speechless.

Being "killed" as I was that morning was typical of the kind of experiences I had over the seven years I spent conducting fieldwork on a little-known group of Americans: twentieth-century war reenactors. My efforts at participant observation found me within a variety of scenarios that were admittedly odd, confronting a practice that used as its language the trappings of war and violence. It was a territory that was highly guarded, strongly masculine, and, as I would come to believe, largely misunderstood by outsiders.

As an ethnographer, my basic goals seemed deceptively simple: to find out who the reenactors were and why they chose to participate in their hobby. But I soon found that my own expectations as well as the reenactors' initial explanations for the hobby were complicated, and even contradicted, by what I saw actually going on. Not only were the lines blurred between what happened in a reenactment and what happened in the history that reenactors purported to represent, but their very identities seemed to be masked by their elaborate period uniforms and props that range from machine guns to trucks to tanks.

They are, to use one reenactor's phrase, "just people who love history," and they describe their hobby as "fun," "interesting," or "challenging," a chance to experience something different.[1] They say that they want to represent war authentically in order to understand something of the historical war experience for themselves, and often they explain the hobby to outsiders by reciting what I came to call their "public mantra": their intentions are purely educational and commemorative. But as I began to interview reenactors and ask them to define reenacting further, I would most likely hear: It's not golf. It's not acting. It's not paramilitary activity. In fact, descriptions of what reenacting is not rather than what it is seemed to dominate their attempts to define it. "How do I put it?" one reenactor tried to explain. "You can get a lot out of it. You can learn. You can get a lot, and it's really fun. Doing something that you wouldn't think would be possible." Another observed: "It's tough to explain the dynamics of reenacting. There are so many various participants. Honestly, it's often like a historical version of a *Star Trek* convention."

The convention, in their case, is an "event," a private reenactment or public event (such as an air show or parade) that draws reenactors together, bonded by their common interest in war and history. And indeed, nearly three-quarters of reenactors cite history in general or military history in particular as their main interest in reenacting. Yet one has only to peruse *TV Guide* or visit a local bookstore to see that many people have similar interests. So what is it that compels them to take their interests, as one reenactor puts it, "one step further," and actively reenact war?

The uniforms. The guns. The tanks. These are only parts of the hobby's surface – its spectacle, if you will. But underneath the spectacle lies a complex structure. The reasons behind their interests, the meaning of the choices they make in representing war, the rules they attempt to enforce, and their beliefs are not apparent to the casual observer. It was only after I came to know reenactors themselves that I began to see that underlying structure emerge. But it would take a while before I was able to identify the unseen assumptions, the ideas about history and the present, that were at work in the hobby.

It would also take me a while to forge an effective approach to this culture, and even longer to begin to articulate some of the insights that I would later find so obvious. Only upon reflection can I see that as I moved further into the culture, the lines between who I was and my research would also be blurred. I went from "naive outsider," armed with a set of expectations, to an insider, able to read the hobby's symbols, anticipate the reenactors' actions, and discern the hidden connections between reenacting and the larger context of American culture. In the process, I learned as much about what is required of an ethnographer as I did about what reenacting is all about.

As I first assumed my well-defined role as ethnographer, my inclination was to cut to the chase and ask reenactors what I thought to be a fairly basic question: Why do you reenact? The first time I asked this question was during my first World War I reenactment. I stood on a hillside with two reenactors, one of whom was dressed as a Turkish soldier, proudly showing off the details of his rarefied "impression" (the word reenactors use to describe their portrayal of a solider). All seemed in good spirits, so I thought it would be okay to ask him why he reenacts, and I did. He looked me right in the eye, paused, and then responded in what I took to be a Turkish accent: "Zey pay me salary. Plus feed me well. I get uniform and boots for my feet. Very good!" We all laughed, but I was confused. What I thought was a straightforward question was one that many reenactors would refuse to answer in casual conversation. "Aw," one of my informants would say and sigh each time I tried to get him to talk about it, "Reenactors are a bunch of weirdos who never grew up. We like wearing uniforms! It's cool, man!"

In terms of my own meaning systems, I have no doubt that I was drawn to the curiosity of the hobby, unable to walk away from it, and captivated by the task of figuring it out. The excitement, the thrill, pulled me in. My mother would later comment that she thought I was a risk taker. And it was somewhat of a risk to put myself squarely within this hobby. Over the years I would find myself "executed" by several Germans, "hijacked" by a band of reenactors, and asleep on a cot in the woods at night, surrounded by a hundred men in uniforms, carrying guns. I also believe that my earlier experiences as an actor added a dimension to my interest in the hobby. As I played the parts of war correspondent, World War I truck driver, and Russian combat soldier in various events, I relied on my familiarity with the phenomenon of role playing and felt comfortable donning a costume and improvising in a variety of rather dramatic scenes and settings. Still, I suffered a degree of culture shock at first. I would come home from an event feeling that I had visited a strange and foreign land, one difficult to explain. Often, I would have dreams where I found myself at an event surrounded by darkness. I was always trying to find something and always obstructed in my quest.

Perhaps it would have been easy to have remained a true outsider to the hobby, to keep my distance by interviewing reenactors and faithfully writing down what they offered as explanations, and then constructing my own interpretation. But I knew the importance of participating in the hobby myself; I had to experience it fully by putting on a uniform and taking part in all that goes on in events. As I did, I found many contradictions between what reenactors said the hobby was all about and what I saw going on in it: the reenactors' joking, horsing around, and engaging in conversations about contemporary matters despite their claims to be entirely focused on representing war seriously and authentically, and their constant arguing in contrast to their description of the hobby as a place of intense camaraderie, for example. Thus, I came to see that to understand and explain the underlying meanings of their culture required taking an even more open – and vulnerable – stance. So I stepped back to allow the culture to unfold before me, prodding it with questions to be sure, but holding back my expectations. In some ways I see this as relinquishing some of my conceptions of who an ethnographer should be. She is made uncomfortable. She is placed in a foreign realm. She arrives empty-handed, neither burdened by a preordained framework nor bound by expectations. She must relinquish herself.

It was somewhat difficult to withhold judgment in confronting a group that elicits such strong reactions, particularly concerning their portrayal of Nazis, their use of guns, and the whole idea of using war and violence as the basis for a leisure activity. But as a woman raised in a culture that still erects boundaries around her freedom, to be hindered was not altogether unnatural for me. Ignored. Not taken seriously. Treated like a child. From a restaurant job experience when my boss told me that he didn't want a woman running the reservation book because a man commands a better presence, to the time when, after a particularly rousing political discussion at a party, a male acquaintance told me that I was too "emotional" to be taken seriously, I had felt, as have many other women I know, a keen sense of my own powerlessness strictly as a result of my gender. Therefore, it was not an entirely foreign feeling for me to keep my initial reactions and opinions at bay as I worked to uncover the unseen meanings.

As a woman studying a primarily male hobby, I was thus a double foreigner, different not only because I was an outsider but also because I was a woman. While there are women who reenact, there are few, and at some events I attended there were no women present. There was no question that I was encroaching upon a male-dominated territory whose overt and covert opposition to women was often made clear. Most reenactors did not mind my presence; but at times, in certain circles, I felt uncomfortable. In turn, they were sometimes made uncomfortable by my presence.

"I'm sorry" was the embarrassed apology a reenactor would utter after making an overtly sexual remark or telling a particularly dirty joke. After telling reenactors posing for his camera to "Say pussy," and then turning around to find me standing behind him, one reenactor turned bright red. "Oh my God," he said, and launched into a lengthy apology.

Some overcame their opposition only after I had "proven" myself; and others, even though they said they were happy to help me with my research, admitted that they could not understand why any woman would want to place herself in the confines of such a hobby. To be sure, the hobby's martial airs were, in some ways, disconcerting. And no matter how much reenactors accepted me, I never forgot that I was a minority among them. There were times when I felt the gender divide acutely. At one particularly low moment at an event, I watched several reenactors firing their guns madly, circling a vehicle, yelling, falling, laughing. One of them shouted, "Man! I get a hard-on firing this gun!" My notebook bears witness to my attitude, indeed my disgust, at witnessing such a display: "Who cares why they do this!" I wrote with disdain. "They're all just a bunch of warmongers anyway."

I felt embarrassed when I came across those notes years later. Why had I lapsed into the critical outsider's view of them? But I realized that I had reacted out of frustration, not malice. Theirs was a highly masculine world whose every exchange, debate, or interaction seemed to obscure the real meanings beneath them. And I came to the hobby lacking any script to translate two sets of meanings: first, the language of a largely male grouping, and second, the language of reenacting. But there was another script that all of us shared, one written by the larger society, and one that shaped gender roles.

I began to see that, for a number of reasons, being a woman in this largely male world worked to my advantage. First, few in the hobby seemed to recognize the power I might wield as a scholar – at least they seemed fairly unconcerned with any authority I might convey as an ethnographer. Although they would often inquire about my "paper," as some referred to my work, most did not ask much. Even when I would later remind them that I was writing a book about them, they seemed fairly unconcerned with the prospect of my studying them. This allowed me to be entirely upfront about my intentions while observing and participating freely.

Second, because I had my own long-standing interest in war and history, reenactors were often pleasantly surprised and even delighted that I was a woman who was just as interested in "this stuff" as they were. This shared interest thus provided me with a very strong bond with many reenactors. Looking back on these early days of research, I marvel at how warmly so many welcomed me into their midst. Some even confided that they wished their wives or girlfriends would share their interest or at least make an effort to understand it.

Third, I had to work harder and be more precise than a male researcher might have had to in order to understand why things took the shape they did or why reenactors communicated in a given way. I found myself asking an endless stream of questions, taking nothing, even the most seemingly inconsequential exchange that perhaps a male researcher might have overlooked, for granted. I also found that reenactors were forthcoming in explaining things to me – more forthcoming than they might have been with a man. They didn't hesitate to answer questions I hadn't even asked, and most seemed to have no qualms in taking time to respond to even the most basic of my queries. So generous were they in offering their explanations for everything from what happened in a given battle to why so-and-so said what he did that at first I was somewhat offended, feeling that they assumed I knew nothing. But I realized that their willingness to act as teachers and guides was derived from their role of authority granted them by the larger culture. Whatever my personal feelings concerning gender inequality in America, I found a keen sense of pleasure in realizing that, at least in this case, it could work to my advantage.

I also found that the very desire to exercise authority and be seen as an expert was a central meaning system for most reenactors. They wanted to be known and respected, and most happily opened up and shared with me. Storytelling – so central a component of the hobby – is an act related to the construction of identity. As I listened to reenactors endlessly telling their own "war stories" – tales about what had happened in various events – I recognized that they were not intent on "reliving" history per se; rather, they wanted to appropriate history for themselves. One reenactor explained this important factor of the hobby: "No other collection that I can think of – like stamps or coins – you can't just shrink yourself into a stamp and put yourself in the book and go, you know, 'Oh, look! I'm a stamp!' Right? I mean this is something that you can actually collect and actually show off. Be a part of it."

Captivated by the idea of being "stamps" and putting themselves "in the book" of history, reenactors seek to carve out a place for themselves in the long history of war representations and to "feel," as one reenactor put it, "as though you are part of our history of the wars." But, of course, it is not the experiences of actual soldiers that reenactors "own" by reenacting. As one reenactor observed: "There is no way in hell we can ever come close to what they did in World War II – the feelings, the emotion, the hardship. Anyone who thinks that [their experiences in reenactments] are interchangeable with their grandparents at their time is completely misled." Instead of trying to replicate others' war experiences, reenactors are consumed by the process of creating, witnessing, and documenting their own – hence their intensive focus on photographing and filming their impressions and events.

Knowing that reenactors sought to gain a kind of authority over the history of war that they view as their legacy (more than 80 percent of twentieth-century war reenactors have relatives who fought in the wars they reenact), I knew that the benefits they seek in and derive from the hobby must be related to what they refer to as their "real lives." Despite their assertion that the hobby provides them an escape from the real world, I would soon see just how profoundly connected the hobby is to that very world. But in order to understand this connection, I had to get to know my informants as people. Luke Gardner, a graduate student when I first met him, and John Loggia, an administrator in a private high school, were just two reenactors I came to know well over the years. Both were in their late twenties when I met them, and, ironically, both were initially opposed to my participation in reenactments because I am female. And both became my friends. Such a transition would not have been possible had I not come to know them personally; and my uncovering of the meanings of the hobby would not have been possible had I only observed them within the context of the hobby.

Both Luke and John were longtime reenactors, each with his own clearly established reputation within the hobby and the units they led. Like many other reenactors, they attempted to make a distinction between their "real lives" and reenacting. Although they emphasized the scholarly benefits of reenacting, they downplayed their involvement in the hobby to outsiders, somewhat for fear of being labeled "nuts." "All reenacting is politically incorrect," John admitted, while Luke said, "I don't like to let on to people that I am a reenactor for several reasons. One, I don't want them to immediately assume that I'm some kind of nut. Two, I don't want them necessarily to know that I have guns, and thirdly, it's regarded as unprofessional. I think in some circles, like in the historical, traditional academic [circles] it might be regarded as kind of silly."

Indeed, during our initial encounters both John and Luke clung to their "public" explanations for participating in the hobby (it's educational; it's commemorative). And, like many other reenactors, they privately echoed the critical outsider's view of reenacting as "silly" or "unprofessional." "I personally think there is something a little strange, maybe just a little strange with this hobby," as one reenactor admitted to me. "Okay, and maybe it's because I've been brainwashed so much by the media that I'm being forced to think this. But I think it's a little strange that I am into this, and wearing the uniform. Okay? So I don't want people to accept it. The best formula that I've found is apathy. I mean to find someone who could just not care less about it. They know about it but it doesn't bother them."

John and Luke represent so many other reenactors who try to manage moving between the different cultural traditions of the hobby and those of "real life." Another reenactor, Warren Grace, is a very kind man with a wife, two children, and an optometrist practice. He once turned to me during an event and said: "I was just thinking about some of my patients. Very staid, but respectable people. I sometimes sit here at events and think, God! If they could see me now, what would they think?" Ted Morse has a similar feeling as he moves between the hobby and graduate school. "It's kind of like I lead two completely separate lives," he observed.

Leading two separate lives can cause stress for some reenactors. "It's my dirty little secret," Patrick Hart said of his membership in a World War II German unit. He described a terrifying experience he had when he was busy repairing his schemel (German footstool) and an old college friend, who's Jewish, showed up unannounced at his apartment. As the two friends chatted, Patrick sweated, fearing that his friend would pick up the stool and see the swastika painted underneath it.

Aware that people have adverse reactions to the hobby, John tended to downplay the hobby by stressing the fact that it's only a "game." He seemed eager to separate his role as reenactor from his "real" (more serious or legitimate) life, referring to the hobby as "playing" and willingly laughing off the intensity so many reenactors bring to it. On the other hand, although Luke also drew a distinction between his professional life and reenacting, he continuously emphasized the hobby's seriousness. "You really can't get around it. We are pretending to be soldiers," Luke said to me in an interview. "But I think that when you do it a hundred percent and you make sure your uniform is perfect and your knowledge of the period is substantial, that you can do a good first-person impression of the character you're trying to assume, whether it's an American soldier, a German soldier, a Russian soldier, that kind of makes up for it. That dignifies it, moves it to a higher plane. Otherwise it's just a bunch of clowns, running around playing guns."

Both John and Luke were clearly aware of the dismissive attitude that so many outsiders have toward the hobby, and like many other reenactors, they struggled to fit reenacting into their lives, whether by emphasizing its trivial aspect (it's a game) or by dignifying it (it's on a higher plane). And in fact, I found that their use of their public mantra served them well. When pressed to do so, they were able to articulate a set of formulaic goals to reenacting that are not particularly outrageous. The publicly stated goals of education and commemoration are clearly acceptable in terms of mainstream cultural values. But knowing the difficulty they often have in relating their involvement in the hobby to other aspects of their lives, I found that underneath their public explanations, in many ways, they have the greatest difficulty not so much in explaining it to others, but to themselves. "We don't understand," one reenactor admitted; "even we have trouble within ourselves."

But with each conversation I had with them – at events, over the phone – they let their guard down more. I was not serving purely as researcher during those conversations, firing off a line of questions. I let the conversation go where it might, straying away from the hobby and into the terrain of their real lives. This was not an act of treachery on my part; it was an effort to get to know them. They, I believe, were open to me since I had a recognizable agenda (to learn about reenacting). I was neither a confusing nor a threatening character to them. And the more I came to see who they were in other aspects of their lives, the more I became incapable of seeing their lives and the hobby as separate. I listened to them as they spoke of their real-life concerns, even offered advice and encouragement, and they, in turn, learned about my life and who I am beyond the hobby.

And it was out of this foundation of understanding that I felt myself giving up my role as "ethnographer," and they their roles as "reenactors." And we did something that all human beings do when they connect: we became friends.

Those on the outside of this world would sometimes express shock when I revealed the nature of my relationships with my "informants." One of my professors seemed disturbed when I told him that reenactors often called me at home, and a couple of fellow graduate students expressed a kind of dismay that I was "slumming" with these gun nuts. Sometimes I would wonder – am I getting too close? As reenactors began to include me in their lives more and more, confiding in me, inviting me to do things with them, I felt like I wasn't doing research at all. I was living my life. Still taking notes and photographs, asking questions, and writing up various essays, I realized that this was what I had always done, even as a child, when I trailed around with a tape recorder or camera, asking people questions and often being teased – why do you always want to take pictures? A memory of myself as a child in 1972 came to mind when I had asked one of my mother's friends, Who did you vote for, McGovern or Nixon? (I was reprimanded later for asking too personal a question.) And so it was that I realized I had always been something of a natural ethnographer.

It was in this natural role that I learned how my informants' real lives were inextricably linked to the hobby. Each sought a kind of legitimacy through reenacting. John was what he termed an "amateur" historian, who felt inadequate among "real" historians despite his own intensive research on World War I. Although he was clearly embarrassed by the hobby, at the same time, he worked diligently on it, whether studying the complicated maps and battle plans for the Somme or reading histories of British participation in the war. He was, I would learn, devoted to his "men" in the unit he commanded, and he brought to his hobby-related activities a determination and seriousness that belied his efforts to dismiss reenacting as a mere game.

Luke also felt somewhat inadequate as a historian, although he earned a master's degree in history during the time I knew him. Even though he downplayed his role as a reenactor, his efforts to dignify the hobby were intense. He was forever taking up immense volumes of military history to read, visiting the National Archives to conduct research, and planning unit activities. He spent hours on the phone with reenactors, lobbying for a new site, devising a grand plan for a completely authentic event, and cajoling unit members to undertake various projects. At other times he poured over training manuals, made reproduction K-ration boxes, spent hours putting together the unit newsletter, and even carefully sewed himself a pair of overshoes out of an army blanket. He was seemingly driven to the point of obsession, concerned with doing things right and tremendously hard on himself when he thought he hadn't succeeded. In fact, both John and Luke became terribly disappointed when an event did not go well. At first I was surprised at the bitterness they expressed. Through one cold winter I spoke with John on the telephone several times, listening to his complete exasperation with the hobby, the politics and infighting among reenactors, and the low authenticity levels at events. "When I started reenacting, I loved it," he said sadly. "Now it's just hard." And one summer day, Luke showed up at my apartment after an event at Fort Eustis in Virginia, dressed in his GI uniform, filthy, wrinkled, and exhausted. "So much effort for such a disappointing event," he said, pulling off his boots to reveal blistered feet. Perhaps only partially rhetorically, he asked: "Why do I do this?"

Each of them dealt differently with the challenge of making their reenacting experiences successful. For Luke, nothing less than perfection was required, and dignifying the hobby was a burden he imposed upon himself. Rarely was he happy at an event. "He never has any fun," observed one of his unit members. I would come to find out that he was rarely happy with any other aspect of his life. Complaining about graduate school as a "waste of time," his job as a "hell," and his relationships with close relatives as fraught with trouble, he never seemed satisfied. Although he was quick to criticize others, he was hardest of all on himself, citing the fact that he felt like a "failure" who had squandered his life – all by the age of thirty.

Luke's quest to dignify himself took form within the hobby. And while he prided himself on the fact that he didn't care what others thought of him, he was very concerned with his reputation. Most people, however, rarely saw his unrelenting self-criticism. In fact, Luke would often say that the "personal lives of great men are always kept private." Modeling himself upon the "great men" of history and his hero, the American soldier, he clearly attempted to step into the boots of such men through reenacting and to walk proudly around in them for himself. As he did, he showed little of his own sense of failure. Instead, he was quick to criticize others; he never smiled for the cameras always present at events, and he often frowned on his way home.

Luke was unable to see what others – even his closest friends – reminded him: the hobby is supposed to be fun. Yes, they were attempting authenticity – down to the stamps on a mail call letter or the chinstraps of their helmets – but it was a game played by a voluntary membership. The question of authenticity – what is correct, proper, what goes too far, or not far enough – was, to be sure, constantly debated, producing an excessive amount of arguments and animosity among reenactors. But unlike Luke, John maintained a more balanced approach. He imparted this piece of wisdom after his many years of service on the "Western Front": "I learned a long time ago and some people still have to learn this: That people do this for different [reasons] and it's difficult to get the kind of level of cooperation that you want. You can only try and work towards it, always keeping in mind that your perception of the way things should be is not always going to be what everyone else thinks it should be."

The difference between Luke and John was striking. Although they shared a desire to do it right, John possessed a more mature understanding that people did things differently, and he was more willing to assume the role of mediator. Luke, however, would rail against those who didn't do things "his way." John might profess to perfection, but he was far more flexible in his attitude. For instance, when I found out that John had raised his voice in opposition to my joining the unit, I sought to make a connection with him. During an event I called him by name, although we had not been introduced, and asked him to pose for a photograph. He smiled broadly and immediately struck a pose, melting whatever ice had been between us. From that moment on, he was my friend, admitting to his opposition, and then dismissing it by paying me a compliment: "You showed yourself well." He agreed to an interview and shared with me a bit about his life outside the hobby.

He was, he admitted, an Anglophile, who, despite his Italian American background, was obsessed with British participation in World War I. He traveled to the battlefields in Belgium nearly every year and worked at home reading up on the strategies and tactics of the Great War. He had recently suffered through a painful divorce, but his optimism was clear. Rather than wallowing in self-pity, he began efforts to improve himself such as an exercise regimen that slimmed him down and made him feel "good" about himself.

Like Luke, however, John also suffered from a sense of inadequacy. He was less than confident about his abilities as a historian and recounted a conversation with a history professor where he was "nervous" that he would show himself to be ignorant. But rather than taking out his lack of self-confidence on others, John sought to improve himself and work for the group, and in particular for his unit. This I saw firsthand. After accepting me, John proved a generous and loyal friend who was quick to encourage; he was close to his family and seemed to have little criticism for anyone. It may have been an act of flattery that initially forged our friendship, but forever after, John was a faithful friend and a great help to me.

With Luke, however, the more I came to know him, the more distance he seemed to try to establish between us. The pinnacle of this behavior came when he intentionally left me behind at an event. I was furious. To his credit, he apologized profusely, but he admitted that he had done so after being challenged by some other reenactors that his unit was less than authentic for having me around.

But I was not the only one Luke treated so harshly. Another reenactor, for example, found himself ostracized by Luke owing to the fact that he had grown too "fat" to be an authentic member of Luke's unit. For such acts Luke was often soundly (but privately) condemned. Others may have respected him for his dogged pursuit of authenticity, but among some reenactors he earned a reputation as a "ball buster," an "asshole," and, in the language of reenactors, a "Stitch Nazi." Sadly, I realized, having come to know him personally, that the very thing Luke sought – respect – was not forthcoming, since he too often violated the ideals of teamwork and camaraderie so valued among reenactors. On the other hand, John's more evenhanded and even humane approach earned him a sound reputation among other reenactors. He was described variously as a "good man" and an "excellent leader" who was able to mediate, cooperate, and treat others fairly. Modestly, John would only admit that other reenactors "like me as much as they can."

Both John and Luke proved that through reenacting they sought things that were missing in their lives: respect, legitimacy, and authority. And like other reenactors, they used history as a way to shape their own stories, to add a dimension to their "real lives" that had real-world value. Had I accepted their initial explanations for why they do what they do, and had I viewed them strictly as reenactors and myself solely as ethnographer, I never would have seen these connections. Just as I found it necessary to relinquish my role as ethnographer, so too did they relinquish their roles as informants. By getting to know them as people I saw something of their lives outside the hobby and came to see how the two worlds connected and fed upon each other. I also came to realize that there was no such thing as performing a truly distinct role; the many aspects of our various identities and worlds are intimately connected, even if they appear radically different.

Whether conducting ethnography or reenacting, each activity, each role we play, is part of living a larger, total life. The difficulty lies in seeing clearly – and sometimes justifying – the connections among our various and seemingly separate roles and identities. Often that difficulty is related to the larger expectations of a culture that defines roles so distinctly: spouse, friend, employee, woman, man, reenactor. But the relationships among our cultural meaning systems are far more fluid, more complicated, and in many ways, more stressful. Perhaps we want our roles to be clearly defined, our goals easily articulated. But however much we struggle to maintain boundaries around what we do and who we are within each of our supposedly distinct realms, we endlessly violate these boundaries. We are not only ethnographers but also women, graduate students, and friends. We are not only reenactors but also employees, sons, and men. Our dreams, our memories, our goals seem so often (and annoyingly) to drift into other parts of our lives. As much as we try to coax them back into their "proper" places, they seem to have a life of their own, and relentlessly, they seem to blur together.

It is no wonder we need to have stories to tell about ourselves, those with a clear beginning, middle, and end. The reenactors' efforts to "own" history for themselves, I came to believe, are derived from such a need. But the challenge we all face lies in the fact that the stories we tell about ourselves are constantly changed and affected by what happens in our real lives and in our culture as a whole. As the reenactors told their stories and as I told my own, I came to see that just as it is with reenacting, conducting ethnography is in fact living one's life. It just requires being keenly aware of the ways all of us try to give meaning to our lives and understanding the many connections among our many roles. With patience and perception, an ethnographer can uncover latent meanings within a specific cultural tradition, and suddenly particular stories begin to tell another, larger story: one that reveals something about our shared culture. At the end of my journey through the hobby, I would marvel at this process. Ultimately, I would also recognize that however strange or unusual some of my experiences were, they were very real. Sam's words proved to be prophetic: "That really happened."

A Chameleon-Like Approach
Successful Negotiations of Multiple Cultural Traditions
Joshua C. Woodfork

Conflating culture and race, some contemporary studies discuss biracial individuals as if they were bicultural. Here, Joshua C. Woodfork provides a richer, more complex, and more accurate account of how biracial individuals make their way through an array of different cultural worlds. In describing how Professor Robert Stewart moves through family, class, academic, sports, and opera worlds, Woodfork shows his chameleon-like style of negotiation, one that involves changing quite radically to adapt to very different worlds — worlds that vary racially from predominantly white, to racially mixed, to predominantly black settings. Looking at Stewart from his own biracial, multicultural perspective, Woodfork suggests that Stewart's adaptive style proves to be successful but that it also involves some drawbacks and costs.

This essay, originally written for a graduate seminar in life history at the University of Maryland at College Park, is published here by permission of the author.

To assert that one is a "white middle-class woman" or a "black gay man" or a "working-class Latina" within one's study of Shakespeare or Santería is only interesting if one is able to draw deeper connections between one's personal experience and the subject under study. That doesn't require a full-length autobiography, but it does require a keen understanding of what aspects of the self are the most important filters through which one perceives the world, and, more particularly, the topic being studied. — Ruth Behar, The Vulnerable Observer[1]

My foot hit the pedal harder as my cranberry-colored van, affectionately know as "crantastic," raced to make the yellow light. "I'm going to be late," I thought. "Not a good impression for our first interview, and I do want Dr. Stewart to take this seriously." I wanted to accelerate, but another red light stared me in the face. As I waited to see green, I recalled the notes I made the first time I met Dr. Robert Stewart. "Symbolic Logic ended the day. The professor seemed cool and we have no final. After getting the books and syllabus, I'll know if I can handle the material."[2] Those were my recorded journal thoughts regarding the first class meeting on Tuesday, January 16, 1996, when I was an exchange student at a historically black university (HBCU) where Professor Stewart taught my philosophy class. At the time I was mostly worried about finding out whether I could "hack" the class and fulfill my "quantitative reasoning" requirement, an obligation I'd been dodging throughout my college career. But I also remember thinking how Dr. Stewart was the first professor I'd seen with dreadlocks. And I wondered, "Could he – like me – be biracial?"

Dr. Stewart spent the first period going over the format of the class and introducing himself. "I'm not as young as I look" was among his first comments. Perhaps he knew he seemed "cool" and therefore wanted to assure the class that he was qualified to instruct, as he meticulously explained his age and listed his academic credentials. He mentioned that he called students by their last names. Thus, "Woodfork" would become a regular reference for the remainder of my experience, as I struggled to grasp the intricacies of p.q versus p⊃q. Later in the semester, Dr. Stewart shared during office hours that he, too, was biracial. We briefly bonded over the similarity in our racial backgrounds, discussing a book on the mixed-race experience by philosopher Naomi Zack.[3] Then we moved on to a discussion of a radical, lesbian, feminist philosopher who taught at my home school.

Finally, the light turned green and my first life history interview as an ethnographer would soon begin. My choice to interview Dr. Stewart stemmed partly from the fact that I only knew him on the level of professor/student and wondered who he was in a deeper sense. I was intrigued by what it was like to work in a nearly all-black environment of an HBCU. Yet the major impetus behind choosing Dr. Stewart was our shared racial background. I thought that interviewing him would provide me with an opportunity to further my research in American Studies on biracial/multiracial identity, granting me an informant who was a generation older than me. During the 1990s, the "multiracial movement" – the grassroots "group" of activists dedicated to adding "multiracial" as another racial category in places like the Census and school registration forms – brought attention to the growing number of biracial/multiracial people through legislative efforts and support networks. Concurrently, a number of entertainers and sports figures (for example, Tiger Woods, Mariah Carey, and Derek Jeter) have openly claimed their biracial status. Likewise, many books on the multiracial experience appeared at this time, including Zack's *Race and Mixed Race* (1993) and *American Mixed Race* (1995), Lise Funderburg's *Black, White, Other* (1994), and two collections edited by Maria Root, *Racially Mixed in America* (1992) and *The Multiracial Experience* (1996).[4] Thus, biracial/multiracial issues have become a hot topic. Dr. Stewart presented a biracial informant removed from the media spotlight or the multiracial movement. I wanted to explore how he negotiated his racial identity.

"Come in" was the answer after I gingerly knocked on the door. "You want some coffee?" inquired the bespectacled, tall, slender, light-brown-skinned professor.

I had a professor some years ago – a black woman – who said matter-of-factly that to be born black in this country is to be born with a hundred-pound weight on your back. "The question is," she said, "how will you carry it?" To be biracial, it seems to me, is to be born with a weight that is anywhere from fifty to a hundred and fifty pounds. The question remains: How will each person carry it? – Lise Funderburg, *Black, White, Other* [5]

My finger hit the red record button on my tape recorder.I was wondering how long it would be before I would find out how Robert Stewart carried his weight. The first question I asked Dr. Stewart requests that he categorize his life history as though he were writing his autobiography.

— RS: Now this is a – these are the table of contents of my biography/autobiography?

— JW: Autobiography. If you had to write the chapters of your life thus far, what would they be?

— RS: I have um – made a couple notes to myself. This is how I broke it down. '63–'68. Manhattan. Born 1963 and lived there – that stretch. Guess that is the first chapter. Did these kind of literally chronologically. '68–'75. Queens/Nassau. Grew up on the border of that, those two counties. '75–'80 is a – put a note down to myself – cancer and religion. My mother got cancer, which she died from, and that was a time also when I was very religious. Those are very in-depth chapters to me. So high school basically . . .

As I listen to Robert speak about his early years and his mother, I realize that although we share a similar racial heritage, there are other aspects of our lives that we do not share, such as class background. Thus shifting my expectations, I settle down to listen and try to understand his particular journey through his thirty-six years. The loss of his white mother grounds his narrative, but not even five minutes later he shares other losses: the suicide of a college girlfriend and a recent divorce. He explains how these losses have affected him and recalls the thread of depression:

> Depression is wrapped up in a lot of this in a very peculiar way for me. I am not sure how to dissect it all. But Shirley, my first girlfriend, was profoundly depressed, suicidal. She obviously committed suicide ultimately, but she had attempted it before, tried it, so it was already part of her story. And, in hindsight, I think my mother was probably a depressed person. Lot of kids. Very shut down, I am realizing. And probably, almost certainly, when she had cancer became depressed, if not before that. Then Ligia [Robert's former wife] also suffers from depression, you know, I mean like a clinical kind of medication, counseling, in-there depression. Although for the vast majority of our marriage, it was just her struggle with it. She wasn't seeing a therapist. Well, at the beginning for a little bit. So depression has been woven through my story a lot. And I am also for myself starting, thinking of what that means to me and what ways that I am depressed. Pushing that.

Robert's childhood, as one of nine children growing up in a working-class New York neighborhood – the son of a black GI and a German mother – is distant from his current middle-class lifestyle within the academic world. Yet his roots remain close as he shares in the working-class lives of six of his eight siblings who live nearby in New York.

Robert's parents met in Germany just after World War II while his father was stationed abroad during his service in the army. His mother was a white German, while his father was a black American from North Carolina. His parents lived in various German cites for almost a decade, and then toward the end of the 1950s they moved to the United States. They lived on military bases in different U.S. cities, finally landing in Manhattan. Robert's parents both worked. Robert's father was a career military man who advanced to staff sergeant during his twenty-three-year army career. Afterward, Robert's father held other jobs finally settling with the bus company. Before her death when Robert was fourteen, his mother worked at a department store folding clothes and stocking shelves. When asked for a fond memory of his childhood, Robert recalls, "I do remember a fond thing. Every now and then my mother worked at this department store folding clothes until 10 at night or 9:30. There was a McDonald's . . . a few blocks away. Every now and then she would come home with a whole bunch of food that was always – that's a nice memory."

Robert also recollects how, "One Thanksgiving we got food from the Salvation Army, things from charity." There were many mouths to feed and many siblings to compete with in his family. Robert states that he was not particularly close to either of his parents growing up, nor is he close to his father now. He describes his relationship with his seventy-eight-year-old father as "civil and polite." "It's not like we have some sort of argument that keeps coming," he explains. "It's not that kind of thing but it's a – he's a very reserved person. I feel like I don't know him." As for his mother, Robert maintains that although he was young when she died of leukemia, they were not close either. Asked if the fact that there were so many children influenced their relationship, Robert replies, "Partly. Yeah. Like every time I think about her, I think about having conversations with her or somehow being with her, I always have the impression when I remember that there is ten other people in the room, you know what I mean. Yeah, I don't think we were close."

Although the family's size might have detracted from his relationship with his parents, Robert speaks of it fondly: "It was unusual. There was kind of like this special thing about us, there were so many of us." When I asked whether the number of children was a source of strength or a negative thing, Robert replied:

> I don't know. Sometimes my sisters talk about negative issues. When you say negative, the first thing I thought of was what my sisters sometimes say, which is that when they would get to school they would be compared with the sibling just older than them. I didn't quite get that, I think 'cause I was a guy. I have one sister two years older than me, one three or four years older, so I was in school at the same time as a lot of my siblings, but I didn't experience that. I kind of got a kick out of people who knew my older sibling and then knew me. I didn't think of the scarcity of stuff as being connected to so many of us. I think I just sort of thought of that as being the ways things are or something.

Although he enjoyed having people know his siblings and then him, Robert also valued his independence and continues to do so. "My older siblings did do some of that like adopting the little ones," he said, "but I was very independent – I am very independent. I feel like I generally cooked for myself or was one of the people doing the cooking. You know, domestic stuff I feel like I have done my whole life – washing clothes, choosing clothes, making food, things like that."

When asked about his relationship with his siblings while growing up and currently, Robert explains, "I have always been kind of close to the sister just older than me: Shirley, another Shirley. And I am pretty close with the sister just older than her: Julie. Julie is also the other, probably the only other person of all my siblings who is also bookish." As for his only brother, Robert states:

I am not close with my brother. He is six years older than me. This is how I explain it to myself. We were kind of not in school at the same time. You know what I mean, when I was starting seventh grade, he had just graduated; that kind of thing. We never bonded around that, and he is much more of a jock, played football in college. I was more booky, you know. He works with his hands for a living, a plumber, carpenter – well, did construction. So the way that I tell it, I guess on the surface anyways, we never really sort of over-lapped in the things that we did, but I don't know, there is probably some bigger thing, haven't thought about it. But I am pretty close to my sisters. All but one lives close, the other in North Carolina. All live a couple of miles in the Queens/Nassau border where I basically grew up. A little more into Long Island really. Just this past Saturday we all got together. My birthday was in September. One of my sisters has the same birthday but like seventeen years apart. She's fifty-three, my oldest sister.

The two siblings who are separated from the rest geographically – brother Herbert in Florida and sister Alicia in North Carolina – are not as close to the family's nucleus, which has remained in New York near Robert's father. Robert explains his father's role: "He's at all the family stuff. My family has a way of like, I think we enjoy each other's company, and we spend all the holidays together. We create a few holidays like the birthday things and stuff like that. Lots of nieces and nephews, so he's around for his grandkids and that kind of thing."

Robert considers his participation in family events and relationships with his siblings one of his major cultural traditions: "There is family stuff, like my family, all the siblings, nearly all of us still living in the area, which is nearly all of us, husbands, wives, kids, we get together fairly rou-tine, fairly often. Like if two months goes by and we don't all get together on a Saturday at one person's house maybe two months, three months on the outside."

When he speaks of family, Robert is commenting on the family gatherings around holidays and other events, which he regularly attends. These gatherings are multiracial affairs, as Robert's two oldest siblings, Samantha and Sarah, are white, having been born in Germany to a different father. Two of the sisters are married to German men. Moreover, of the married siblings, which is all of them but one, all except one has a white partner. Robert is the only one of his nine siblings with an advanced degree, although others have some level of college. One sister receives public assistance, and the others range in careers from a toy designer to an academic secretary. Thus the family is an interracial, international, multi-class unit.

Robert describes himself and his siblings as "nouveau middle class," a term he thinks encompasses his current middle-class status and his working-class childhood.

> I guess I would say middle class. Actually, I made up a little term for what I think of sort of my generation of my family the nine kids. I think of us as "nouveau middle class." Because like middle class – I am kind of comfortable with that term. There's a regular, ordinary sense at which I am clearly middle class. But I think of myself as being fairly – pretty well connected to being poor, being working class only a generation ago, like my parent's generation and us as kids kind of thing.

When listing his siblings' occupations, Robert notes that some of them continue to lead working-class lives. Thus he manages a shifting class level, which, as he suggests, means more than the amount of money he makes. While explaining his class level, Robert offers an example of his class consciousness:

> So one of the things that I notice in myself or I notice in other people rather that I hang out with sometimes that I don't notice in myself the same way is like romanticizing – this is how I feel and I think of it as a negative thing – romanticizing poverty. You know, like everything poor people do is right. There's something pure about being poor. There's something, you know, to fetishize about that. As opposed to poor – poverty being something most people with choices try to avoid. So yeah, middle class, professional. I think of myself as Bohemian on the inside. I don't know if I mean, the thing is my standard is pretty high 'cause I use to have blue hair [laughs] and no I don't

have blue hair anymore. But I like that I think of myself as playful in certain kind of cultural ways that I like.

Thus, Robert's personal affiliation with the working class and poverty affects his relationships.

Robert considers himself a "progressive" on political issues and calls himself "liberal." He sees his understanding of poverty as deriving from his childhood: "My personal story was very sketchy. I was not a disciplined student. I grew up in my house with no books; there was a lot of people with a lot kids in a very, very small space. We had like a two-three bedroom, a three-bedroom house and the TV on, radio on, no books, no desk, no place where it was nice and quiet and absolutely nobody who was doing anything like academic work." Thus, Robert negotiates his class level, moving from his working-class roots to the elite halls of academia to an art form that he likes to attend: the opera.

As I think about Robert's class levels and other diverse traditions, I am prompted to consider my own. It was always expected that I would attend college. I remember a white student asking me once if I was the first in my family to attend college, as she had heard that this was common for many black students. Her question led me to reflect on the fact that all four of my grandparents and both of my parents have graduate degrees.

Thus, unlike Robert, I was raised in a middle-class household. My parents are both social workers. Accordingly, they didn't make a lot of money, but with three children and sacrificing their own desires for ours, they were able to give us a comfortable suburban upbringing. Like Robert's parents, my father is black and my mother is white. My grandfathers worked together at a veterans hospital in western Massachusetts, with one serving as chief psychologist and the other as chief social worker. One Thanksgiving, my father needed a ride back to Boston after serving in the Peace Corps and my mother was driving there to return to grad school. Thus, my grandparents introduced my parents to each other. My parents were married in 1970, and I was born in 1974.

Is there not something unseemly, in our society, about the spectacle of a white woman mothering a black child? A white woman giving totally to a black child; a black child totally and demandingly dependent for everything, sustenance itself, from a white woman. The image of a white woman suckling a black child; the image of a black child suckling for its life from the bosom of a white woman. The utter interdependence of such an image; the merging it implies; the giving up of boundary; the encompassing of other within self; the unbounded generosity and interconnectedness of such an image. Such a picture says there is no difference; it places the hope of continuous generation, of immortality of the white self, in a little black face. – Patricia J. Williams, The Alchemy of Race and Rights [6]

When I asked Robert about his parent's involvement in an interracial marriage, he wasn't sure what sort of treatment they received:

> I don't know how that played out for them. And I'm not sure if it is because I don't remember much about my mother talking about it, and my father doesn't talk much about it except in very general ways about how things have gotten better racially in this country. He'll say stuff like that, but he's not real specific about actual concerns or how it worked out. Only thing I can think – sort of like filling in blanks – like being in the army. I don't know if that was a better or worse thing because the army – military is an odd thing, integrated much earlier than many institutions, but my gut feeling about a lot of stuff is that people still had their attitudes and they bring them with them. I am not really sure of that whole story, I suspect that.

My father, like Robert's, is also silent when it comes to his experience as part of an interracial couple. Yet, my mother has shared some stories with me. For instance, while my parents were courting they were picnicking in a Boston park when some white teenage boys screamed "nigger-lover" at my mother and scurried away.

Unlike the multiracial working-class neighborhood of Robert's youth, I was raised in a middle-class, nearly all-white suburb north of Boston. My brother and I, with our racially ambiguous, maybe Latino or light-skinned black appearances, were tokenized as merely the "Woodfork boys," good students and athletes, acceptable blacks. My adopted sister, seven years my junior, had a more difficult time, as she was darker-skinned and female. Nonetheless, in third grade I was called "nigger" and had my first and only schoolyard fight. I felt "othered" by race when it came to such issues as dating or people's curiosity about my hair. My parents taught me that I was black, since when I grew up in the late 1970s and early 1980s the notion of a biracial identity was not as common as it has recently become.

Similarly, Robert got into fights as a child. He explains the reasoning behind them: "[It] was usually some sort of slight, sometimes it was racial. There was this one kid, white kid, who was always like, actually he often had derogatory terms like mixed-race derogatory like 'checkerboard,' 'zebra,' words like that." Thus, we share the cultural tradition of resistance. Robert explains for a time he thought of himself as racially mixed and that "I always at some level thought of myself as a black guy who happened to be half white. Which is, I guess, oddly how I still think of myself primarily. I think of myself as a black guy, and one of the ways to be black is to be half white." When I was younger I felt the same way, that my experience of having a white mother was part of the diversity of the black experience in the United States. As I entered college, I explored my identity and became familiar with the concept of being biracial. Today I still identify as black, but sometimes I announce my biracial background. However, I understand that these labels are political and in any particular social context I will consider the appropriate response. On the contrary, my younger brother only identifies as biracial. The popularity of this trend to claim both racial heritages equally may be a sign that people are now allowed more agency in defining themselves racially than when I was raised as a member of an interracial family.

Besides being biracial, Robert also defines himself as bicultural because his mother is German. His pride in his biculturality is seen in a recollection of himself when he was in school:

> I do remember a conversation or class discussion, maybe something in high school or junior high, where I remember making some kind of point – or maybe it was in some kind of writing assignment – maybe in English class, or I don't know what – but some point about how in a census form, anything that asks your race, I remember how puzzling it was to be mixed because there was no box for that. Having to make some comment about it or something. I think there was a sort of kind of pride I had in being mixed. I thought that was kind of interesting, unusual. I do remember discussions, if it would go very far like someone was asking about being black or something, sort of being proud of having a German mother or being half German. I remember that being something really cool.

Although Robert thought of himself as half German in junior high and high school and has German in-laws and sisters, it was unclear how his Germanness currently affects his life. He didn't mention it as an important aspect of his identity or describe any involvement with German traditions or affiliations.

Similarly, the public high school I attended had a large Jewish population, and during the Jewish holidays I remember explaining to my ninth-grade classmates that I was one-quarter Jewish. Indeed, my maternal grandfather, Saul Raphael Rotman, was Jewish, while his wife, Patricia Ann Smith, was an Irish Catholic. Thus, perhaps my boasting about having connections to Jewish holidays and St. Patrick's Day may have been akin to Robert's German pride. Despite my grandparents, my own connections to Jewish holidays and Irish culture are currently nonexistent.

As with Robert and his family, my family plays a central role as a major cultural tradition in my life. We spend holidays together and talk frequently. I, too, have a respectful relationship with my father, and we are becoming closer, yet we don't have a lot to discuss. On the contrary, my mother and I frequently talk on the phone, providing each other advice and support. My brother is replicating the middle-class lifestyle we were raised under, while my sister is taking an unfamiliar route that has caused some familial stress as she struggles to find her way. While growing up we went to church as a family. My father's mother died when he was young, and one of the ways he coped with that loss was through participation in a Protestant church. Thus, religion became a major part of his life and, in turn, our family regularly attended a multiracial, multiclass, urban Episcopal church. I recall driving past the all-white Episcopal church in our own neighborhood each Sunday; it was important to my parents that we drive the extra distance so we could be in a more diverse place.

Robert was also a Christian when he was younger, and he explained what religion meant for him:

> I was a Christian. I guess the time when my mother got sick a lot of the kids, myself included, became – got involved with born-again, fundamentalist Christian beliefs. That involved going to church a lot, reading the Bible. It was very kind of a literal fundamentalist experience – believing in healing, you know. A lot of that kind of texture. My father has always been religious. He was a bit more conventional kind of. He went to church pretty steady like every week since he was a kid, but he wasn't necessarily sort of fundamentalist kind of variety regular Baptist, southern, and he still does that much more of a regular steady mainstay kind of thing.

As for Robert's current religious traditions, he mentions that his father says grace during the holidays. I asked,

— JW: So you don't attend [church]?

— RS: I don't participate in any way.

— JW: No participation in organized religion.

—RS: Yeah, I like that phrase "organized religion," as opposed to the disorganized kind. No, nothing like that.

Thus, through Robert's quip, a sense of his nonparticipation is displayed. Similarly, when my father asked me if I was attending church during my first year away from home, I responded that I was doing "home prayer." I do believe in some type of spirituality, but like Robert, I don't participate in organized religion.

As for other traditions, Robert and I share an academic/schooling tradition. Robert recalls being "booky"; I was also an avid reader, winning the "Battle of the Books" in fourth grade. We've both chosen to make a career in academia. Thus, all of the professional aspects of teaching at the university level play out in both our lives, such as grad school training, membership in organizations, teaching, and journal reading. Robert considers himself a dedicated teacher, almost to the point where all of the preparation and grading requirements inhibit his own research work. I hope to model my own teaching after his student-centered approach.

When asked about other traditions, Robert mentions the New York Mets and cooking. Certain traditions intersect, especially when his family gathers together: "Which I guess as I am talking about it, I am realizing a certain kind of tradition emerges – a lot of cooking around that typically and a lot of baseball fans in the family, so that will often be part of the discussion and we will actually have the game on occasionally or something. That's what I think of, what came to mind when you asked for traditions."

The Mets and the opera provide windows into understanding the meaning of Robert's traditions. Robert's fondness for the baseball team and the opera fall under the rubric of being a fan. As for the Mets, Robert identifies "with some of the ebbs and flows of the season," seeing the team as a metaphor for his own life. Robert is careful to note, "When I go to Shea stadium I am very vocal. I sit in the cheap seats. That kind of thing. I am not sort of sitting there with a jacket and a briefcase in some corporate box. You know"? He immerses himself in the culture of the event or activity he is involved with.

From his meticulous laying out and organizing the ingredients when cooking to "endlessly creat[ing] the outline" of a paper he is writing, Robert likes to have things organized; in his words, "I am really very elaborate with setting things up." His desire to give his all to something moves beyond organizing it to getting fully involved with each step. Thus, he is moving from being a baseball fan to participating in the sport himself. His excitement reveals the way he enjoys involvement: "Like I just found out that there is a softball league forming amongst a bunch of acquaintances next spring in the Lower East Side. I haven't had a glove in years. I can think about it and pop in and out of sporting goods stores for months, just 'cause I want to. Just to marvel at different gloves and stuff." Rather than just being pleased to get on the field and play, Robert is delighted by the entire experience, including purchasing the tools required for participation.

Although opera is usually seen as a white upper-class tradition in the United States, Robert feels comfortable participating in it. He excitedly explains to me the difference between a full-staged opera, an opera concert, and a recital. Although one thinks of the opera as an affair that couples attend, Robert goes by himself. This decision is indicative of a larger tradition of independence in Robert's life that manifests itself in compartmentalization and continued reinvention of himself. Robert describes himself as a loner who chooses to lead a "relationship-proof" life. He explains:

> There's no way I could hook it up with somebody here. It doesn't have to be love interests but friends or whatever. It will never get to, "Oh, why don't you come over tonight, the Mets are on tonight, come over let's watch the game." Like last night, a friend of mine did watch the game. He came over and we watched it at my place and stuff, but there is a huge tract of my life that he doesn't enter, which is my [teaching] life. But nobody in my [teaching] life will ever encounter the huge tract of my life, my New York life. No one who knows me as a professor will ever know about me and my private consulting practice, for instance, and so on. I do go to the opera and I do go to Mets games. There's nobody who sees both those sides of me. And none of my family is part of anything of those things. My family is a big part of me, too, so they don't see those other parts, and no one in these parts sees my family. So it is really partitioned.

Robert relishes the fact that nobody knows his entire life. He prides himself on participating in multiple traditions and on keeping these worlds separate. I wondered, "Why does he like this?"

Robert first understood that he could reinvent himself during his college days. After his mother's death, he was heavily involved with Christianity, and that led to a punk rock, alternative phase that included dyeing his hair blue and hanging out in Greenwich Village with "Jesus people." When asked about who his friends were at this point, Robert reveals:

> I had a variety and I never had – and I still don't have this – I don't have a primary circle of people that I walk through with and I notice that about myself for a while now. Like I am in one group, another group, I am in a few groups and they all sort of – they know one part of me but none of them has the big picture. I always felt like that. It was like even then I may have friends that were into music or sort of the cultural scene but I also have friends who I knew from school who were also studying biology, which I was studying at the time. Then I had philosophy friends and none of those groups sort of impinged on any of the others. I didn't really have a primary – like I don't have friends that I have had since I was like little, you know what I mean?

Since college, Robert has traveled in many circles. He likes the freedom of associating with different people who share similar interests. Therefore, he is able to move from a Mets game to a philosophy colloquia at New York University (NYU) and still feel comfortable.

Switching between the cultural norms of different circles requires knowledge of the etiquette and practices of each group. Through his transformation in college, Robert recognized his ability to change himself. He remembers his thoughts during this time:

> I felt really charged. I learned about myself, I guess, that I can reinvent – I can invent myself as anything. And, you know, walk into those – I can be grand and get noticed and go deep with something. Like if I was into something I could do it 24/7 and I realized that it didn't scare me. I could become that thing and I could do it plausibly and well and all that. I had people come up to me, I would go to punk rock shows or something and people come up to me and say, "Oh man, cool hair, where do you hang out?" That kind of thing, a response which a year earlier – or something I might have said to someone a year or two earlier. I was like, wow, I can do it that way. I am not the guy who is not sure and maybe doesn't have the right look or isn't in the right place. I learned that about myself.

Thus, Robert enjoys his chameleon-like ability to change himself to participate in various traditions. Although he does not suggest that his biracial identity has influenced his pleasure in being able to juggle these worlds, it may be a factor. His pride in his ability to reinvent himself is reminiscent of his claim to be not only black but also half German, suggesting a connection between his biracial identity and his transformations.

For Robert, the key in these changes is keeping his worlds apart. When asked why he wants to keep them separate, he says:

> It really keeps me disconnected. I get to sort of not be tied down or bound up in any particular social group. For some reason it doesn't feel right to me, it doesn't feel good to me to be like a – this is, you know, a pop culture example. The TV show *Friends*, for instance: I couldn't imagine being one of the six or seven or whatever number [of characters] there are, not because their lives seem terrible or anything, but because the idea that anybody could look at me in a group and sort of see a whole lot of me in that group, that never occurs in my life. I feel like I have too many pieces that don't fit, don't flatten out even. If I could be in a group of six or seven people that were totally into each other, but the downside is I don't have any enduring friends or people that have seen me sort of through a long trajectory. I have people I knew like twenty years ago, and I might bump into them, but they haven't known me for the last eighteen, let's say.

Robert openly confides that having many people know his story wouldn't feel right to him. He admits further that this could be because "there is something where like – it is a way for me to feel larger than them or something, something like that." Thus, there is a power element involved in Robert's control over the interpretation of his life.

The power element suggests that Robert finds other positive aspects to sectioning off his life. He believes that this approach enables him to get a lot of work done. Additionally, "The biggest positive is I get to be as intense and self-absorbed as I want to be. I can do projects and same as that reinventing thing. I can pick something up and do it for two or three years or maybe I'll do it for twenty years or maybe I'll only do it for two years." Robert's work is important to him, and being able to launch himself into a project is something he values highly.

Nevertheless, in mentioning the lack of enduring friends, Robert has identified a negative aspect of his compartmentalizing. He elaborates:

> The downside is, it is lonely. I do feel lonely a lot of the time. And there is a certain kind of sourness, like every now then I just sort of, like, just get really pissed off. I don't know what to do with that. That's hard not to do anything

with that. You know that is sort of tailor made for relationship, like to work that through. Or it is nice to work through that with somebody. You could use that energy to do something positive. It is easier to ruminate and brood and get really pissed off by yourself. So that's the downside for me. I am sort of wrestling with that.

Thus, loneliness and the lack of relationships over a long period stand out as weaknesses in his approach to keeping his worlds separate. Robert articulates how he gets "pissed off" and how a relationship might help to alleviate some of this anger. The thread of depression that runs through his story may be seen through his loneliness. Robert briefly mentioned that he has been in therapy to work through some of these issues.

Despite the shortcomings of compartmentalizing, Robert is not trying to merge all of his lives. The sense of power that derives from his sectioning enables him to make up for some of the deficiencies he sees. Accordingly, he interprets the motivation of his reinvention as follows:

I guess some of it is a sense of lack that drives that sort of reinvention thing. I tend generally to think of myself as having less or having like a deficient starting package. I tend to view things that way. I tend to view myself as sort of working uphill against the odds. Having to do some kind of heroic efforts. I mean I think again I am . . . right now. I tend to think of the things I have accomplished in philosophy as things that have happened despite working here because I feel a lot of things here have sort of shortened or diminished my package or, you know, heavy teaching load things like that. I tend to see myself as fighting the odds generally.

In his discussion of his skills growing up and of his current teaching environment, Robert displays his participation in the tradition of the achiever, seeking to overcome obstacles placed in his way.

Each of us is a unique member of the sets of endless groupings that touch us, whether called racial, gender, disability, family, ethnicity, or nationality. Perhaps for strategic purposes we may choose to affiliate along one or a few lines of group membership, but these lines may shift as our strategies and goals change. – Martha Minow, Not Only for Myself[7]

Dr. Stewart thinks that his current work environment has not enabled him to be the philosopher he wants to be.He explains how there are basically two schools of thought in philosophy: those who see it analytically and those who see it historically. Robert falls into the former group. He also uses this analytic tradition to help his clients in his own counseling and therapy practice. Although his specialty is the philosophy of language, Robert has primarily published articles on African American philosophy. He is currently going through his tenure review and believes that, although his publication record is not what he would like it to be, it will probably help him to achieve tenure. Although he may gain tenure at the HBCU where he teaches, Robert has other aspirations.

Robert's ultimate goal is to work at an Ivy League institution such as Princeton, Penn, NYU, or Columbia, but there are specific terms that he wants to be hired under: "I don't want to be hired as the black guy at fill-in-name-of Ivy League school; you know what I mean. I want to be the guy who comes in there who is a philosopher who does philosophy of language, who also has an interest in problems coming up in black philosophy, African American philosophy. I am happy to be that guy. But I don't want to come in as a joint appointment in Black Studies." It is important to him that he is not just an affirmative action hire but that his work is the factor that gets him considered. Robert sees this as paradoxical, since he thinks he cannot do the work he wishes to currently because of his large teaching load and advising responsibilities. Therefore, he can only be considered on the basis of the very work he does not want to be hired for.

When asked why he doesn't want to be that "black guy" hired at the Ivy League post, Robert elaborates candidly:

> I feel like that's – some of it elitist I know. And maybe some sort of tangled-up race thing in there. Like I don't want to be black-identified in my work in the sense that I feel like I am doing a different thing than the mainstream of the profession, but paradoxically I am very interested in putting my work out there as being black-identified. I mean, if I didn't want to be black-identified, I suppose I might not have dreadlocks, let's say, or teach at an HBCU.

Robert mentions the contradiction of both wanting and not wanting to be identified as black in his academic life. As he notes, his degree is in philosophy, not Black Studies. Working at an HBCU and having dreadlocks are both markers of blackness (white people can do both, yet it is not nearly as common). Thus, his desired perception is not a denial of his blackness but rather an imagined ideal for Robert. He admits that some of this may have to do with "some sort of tangled-up race thing," alluding again, it seems, to biracial identity issues. Once again, Robert sees himself as black but not just black. Earlier he spoke of being half white and half German. The tension here appears similar, as Robert wants his scholarship on both race and language to be recognized.

Unlike Robert, I have made peace with my racial identity and my academic pursuits by placing my focus on issues of identity. One of the ways it has played out in my life is through attending a predominantly white undergraduate college but then spending an exchange semester at an HBCU. Thus, I do understand the tensions Robert feels over not wanting to be marked as a "black scholar." Despite my interests pertaining to race and to black people, I've decided to pursue a degree in American Studies rather than in African American Studies, as I think that my marketability as an academic will be better. Nevertheless, at this point I'm comfortable with the stigma that comes with being seen as a product of affirmative action. In fact, while I was getting an MA my funding came through an Affirmative Action Graduate Assistantship. Yet, my pride may derive from the resurgence of African American Studies programs and the recent rise of black public intellectuals.

A theme that begins and ends Robert's story is his divorce and the emotions he still is dealing with over the loss of his wife. Robert is bitter regarding the experience, especially since he did not initiate the divorce. He considers and refers to himself as "divorced" rather than "single," as he thinks that "single" ignores the experience he has been through. He suggests that these emotions provide a fertile area to work through with someone. Yet since his life is "relationship-proof," having such an opportunity seems doubtful. Robert and his wife did not want kids, and he still does not, claiming, "I never had the interest in seeing a little version of me." I am also single, but I have never been married. I think the strain of graduate school makes it difficult to commit to a healthy relationship at this point. Unlike Robert, I might want to have children.

Robert's compartmentalizing influenced our interviewing process to some degree. I was pleased when Dr. Stewart readily agreed to be interviewed. We met four times for an hour to an hour and a half in various locations at his school. He was quite forthcoming in explaining the details of his life. As for our relationship, although Robert told me that I could call him by his first name and contact him at home, I understood that in some sense we were still professor and student, albeit grad student. Since Robert relishes keeping his worlds separate, my knowledge of his pieces might have made him uncomfortable. Thus, I would suggest that we had a good working relationship but that it did not evolve into a friendship.

Nevertheless, Robert and I had a pleasant interview process. Both of us joked frequently. For instance, when Robert told me that he once had blue hair our exchange was a friendly one:

— RS: No, my family is pretty accepting. I have never, ever had the episode where I showed up, I mean I had different color hair and stuff, cut all different ways and had blue hair for awhile. I never had the moment where I came home and like, you know, father says you are disowned.

— JW: Blue hair does –

— RS: [Laughs]

— JW: Are there pictures of this?

— RS: There are, somewhere.

— JW: Someone's blackmailing you somewhere.

— RS: When I run for the Senate.

— JW: In New York, you and Hillary [Clinton]. Okay, interesting. So what about friends then or other relationships?

As I came to understand how much Robert enjoyed his privacy, I was surprised that he had been so forthcoming with me. Perhaps our biracialness made him feel comfortable sharing with me, particularly when it came to discussing race.

In her book *Colonialism/Postcolonialism*, Ania Loomba discusses hybridity. She quotes Robert Young, who informs us that "a hybrid is technically a cross between two different species and that therefore the term 'hybridisation' evokes both the botanical notion of inter-species grafting and the 'vocabulary of the Victorian extreme right' which regarded different races as different species."[8] Although there has been an advancement in thought so that races are not considered different species, the hybrid's racial allegiance is still questioned. The trope of the "tragic mulatto" – the person caught between two worlds because of the mixture of black and white blood – still remains in some sense as well. Both Dr. Stewart and I are technically "hybrids," and therefore the ways in which we identify racially and our racial allegiances are under constant scrutiny for "authenticity" tests of some sort. While looking for the ways in which biraciality affected Robert, I attempted not to reinscribe the same tests.

Instead, I tried to ask the questions that professor John L. Caughey raises regarding negotiating multiple cultures. He suggests that multiple frames of reference offer many advantages as well as problems. Knowing more than one tradition loosens the hold that a single culture may have on a person's being. Multiple cultures offer multiple possibilities and can make for a richer, more varied and interesting life. Dr. Stewart clearly lives in many worlds. From the Mets to the opera to academia to family gatherings, he moves back and forth. Notably, Robert feels that by reinventing himself in each arena he is able to participate fully in these experiences. He wants to keep them separate and is able to achieve this. He definitely feels that he has a "richer, more varied and interesting life" through his management of multiple worlds.[9]

However, although Robert does negotiate multiple traditions skillfully, his way of doing this contains drawbacks, as he himself admits. The manner in which he negotiates his situation leaves him lonely at times and desiring more. It also means his career is not where he would like it to be. Moreover, the loss of his mother, the suicide of a girlfriend, and the end of his marriage have had a profound impact on him. Thus, in assessing whether or not his life is a relatively "successful" or happy one, I would assert that it is. He is realistic about his options and happy with how he is handling them.

Scholar Ruth Behar argues that identity markers in life history are important only when they are placed between the person being studied and one's personal experiences.[10] I learned a good deal about Robert, and in the life history process I learned a lot about myself. Clearly, it is important for Robert to be different from other people and to have space from them. Like Robert, I value my independence, but I also like to blend in. I also have friends for different components of my life (study buddies, movie pals, support networks), but I have had some of these people as friends for many years. Understanding my cultural traditions provided the context Behar suggests is necessary for deeper connections within one's study. Through self-ethnography, I was able to be less judgmental of Dr. Stewart. Seeing another biracial person negotiate his life without exhibiting characteristics of the tragic mulatto – indeed, with a pride in his racial heritage – was uplifting.

As a philosopher, Robert is able to use a highly developed analytical mode to reflect on these issues of identity and life. In mapping out his autobiography, Robert considers his life now and asserts, "So yeah, I don't know what the last chapter so far would look like or what it would be called. I wrote 'professor,' but I don't know what that means actually. I am doing that I guess."

My thumb hits the button again, and the tape recorder stops. I thank Dr. Stewart and think about what he has just said. Yes, he is doing the professor thing, I think, and I hope I can articulate what he has just taught me about his life in multiple worlds. Once again I need to hurry, as I'm out of time on the parking meter. I jump back into my van, this time not worrying about making lights but rather about the hours of transcribing tapes. Constructing our lives awaits.

The Sound of It Stayed in My Ears
Life History with African
American Domestics
Elizabeth Clark-Lewis

In her book Living In, Living Out, *Elizabeth Clark-Lewis recovered an important and neglected dimension of African American history by using life history research to movingly retrace the experiences of African American women who migrated north from the rural South, worked as live-in servants in the homes of wealthy whites in Washington DC, and then managed to move out of that situation into daywork, jobs that helped them achieve their desire for greater autonomy and freedom.*

In this reading, Clark-Lewis discusses how she was both an insider and an outsider to the worlds of these women and how she struggled to reconcile the multiple perspectives involved in her relationships with them. As an African American woman some of whose family had lived this kind of cultural migration, she was an insider to these women, and this clearly helped the research and interviewing. But – as with most life history research projects – the interviews also revealed strong contrasts between some of her own cultural traditions and those of her participants.

This essay was written for the present volume and draws on the research Elizabeth Clark-Lewis conducted for her book Living In, Living Out: African American Domestics in Washington, D.C., 1910–1940 (Washington DC: Smithsonian Institution Press, 1994).

I was forced to travel back to my true foundations – to the very woof of my African American heritage – to complete interviews with ninety-four women who left the rural South "goin' North" during the first four decades of the twentieth century. As the daughter of a woman who spent ten of her forty-five years of employment as a dayworker, the granddaughter of a woman who worked many years a live-in servant, and the great-granddaughter and great-great-granddaughter of slaves, I am mindful of these lines from Mari Evans's poem,

and the old women gathered . . .
and sang . . .
standing
resolutely together . . . .
[Their song] was fierce
and not melodic . . .
although we ran
the sound of it
stayed in our ears . . .[1]

The sound of their voices stays in my ears as I recall my own journey toward and understanding of these women's struggles and successes. I recall clearly the day when I, in the company of my eighty-eight-year-old great-aunt, Mary Sprow, attended a meeting of the Twelfth Street Bible Club in Washington DC. I had eagerly anticipated this event, not only because I was researching household workers, and all the members of this women's group were former domestics, but also because this club has been in operation for over sixty-seven years, and each member has acquired some modicum of social or civil prominence in her own right. Over the years these women saved large sums of money together and assisted each other during hard times. Collectively they have recognized the weddings, birth dates, illnesses, and deaths of fellow members and their families; and, they always attended church programs and community activities honoring their members when the larger culture ignored these events in the lives of people they knew only as "the help."[2]

Mary and I walked slowly toward the house, as each of her steps required a lengthy rest for the legs that had carried her for nearly nine decades. On this sunny autumn she explained why these club meetings were "the center of old women's social world." A slim, demure woman was our hostess, and as she answered the door I could view a beautifully decorated apartment. My great-aunt's eight club members worked hard to help me feel less foreign in this group of elegantly clad ladies, all dressed in expensive, tailored suits and dress ensembles with matching hats and gloves. After a short meeting we moved into the dining room, where a large table laden with exquisite sterling silver, English bone china, and fine crystal awaited us. Trying to appear nonplussed, I scanned the pyramid of seven plates, five forks, four spoons, and three knives set before me. There were at least four different glasses, a cup and saucer, and a bread and salad plate. In addition, there were some odd-shaped, unfamiliar objects on top of the setting, which I didn't know whether to eat, wear, or what.

After the senior member, the vice president, blessed the food, the hostess began serving our meal in courses. I lost count after the sixth. The ladies were adroitly manipulating the pyramid of dishes and processing the proper utensils for each course. But, after about my third faux pas, my poor great-aunt timidly apologized for my obvious lack of manners, noting, "This girl just doesn't know about these things. She didn't ever do service work." They all nodded politely, making it clear that they were fully aware of my embarrassing conduct. It was the first time I felt deprived because I had not been a maid or servant in the home of a wealthy person. With that humble admission, they collectively offered me some pointers on the proprieties of multi-course dining. And, most importantly, they felt free to divulge the migration strategies that families followed, how they learned to work in households – always noting that wealthy persons wrongly assumed that every servant was born knowing how to function at even the most formal occasions. One woman explained in detail why females served certain courses while the male servants were expected to serve others.

They giggled and winked as privileged illusions were drawn off some of Washington's most famous and wealthy families. The women were clever mimics, and it was clear that they knew the mannerisms of these famous people quite intimately. They talked about employers who had tried to "use" them and how they had always managed to use their employers just as much. Each story had an Anansee quality to it; the poor African American girl outwits "Miss Ann" in the end.[3] Like so many of the stories that African Americans tell themselves to establish who they are, each of these posits both who the female household workers were and what they were not.[4]

The women explained how they first felt freedom. One woman said:

When I got to carry clothes I was finally working in what I wanted to. Not in no cast-offs, that's what you'd have to wear down south. Down there [in the rural South] they swore you had some bugs so as soon as they took you to they farms they put some old rags on you. Sometimes badder than your stuff. . . . And not no gray or black uniforms [livery] you worked in up here [in northern urban households]. . . . When I got to work in what I wanted, I knew I wasn't just to serve or belonging to anybody.

> It's a funny thing to tell. . . . I put my stuff in a bag at home. My freedom bag was always from a good store – 'cause that's where it [the clothing] come from. Even if it [the clothing] was secondhand. Who knows? You might have got it there. [laughter] Plus, good places had the strong bags. They wouldn't tear on a street car.
>
> Mostly I guess I wanted to show I didn't wear a uniform. I wasn't a servant.

Another woman added: "I can't tell you how it felt to just walk out of any house and the sun'd still be up. I will remember that feeling as long as I live. To see that sun hitting me as I left." They taught me how small things, such as their desperate desire to attend Bible study class or take in a show at the Howard Theater, prodded their quest for more independence and freedom.

As the meeting progressed, I knew my historical studies of African American women were totally incorrect. I realized you could not fathom the women of this culture by merely studying their degrees of oppression as reflected in the records of employers, government documents, and reformers' studies. I was learning data entirely ignored by major scholars, studies, and research institutions. I was sitting and learning from African American women – the female half of the "peripheral population" – the folks always seen as the objects, not subjects, of events. I learned how, in their personal and employment life, despite constraints of race, sex, class, and very limited education, these women never accepted that they were a corps of powerless, one-dimensional workers who spent their lives as passive reactors instead of active forces in history. At one afternoon "tea party" I finally grasped how restraints they encountered came to serve as impetuses; when courage collided with caution, these women developed the responses that ultimately transformed the patterns of their personal and employment lives.

The older women I interviewed were never what I expected. For example, this was a group of elderly women who had been meeting in a Bible club almost every month for over sixty-seven years. However, they had always enjoyed a cocktail at each meeting and wine at every meal. My great-aunt drolly confided that members of the group had even kept the meetings supplied with dandelion wine and "bathtub gin" during Prohibition. I saw how their lives provided contrast to my mind's portrayals of African American women migrants from the rural South with limited formal educations. They refused to conform to my belief systems or allow me to shape any romantic ideals or images about their role in history. With earnestness and enthusiasm they were able to prod me into accepting that my interpretations and perspectives of the past frequently were not theirs.

As an investigator, I learned from the migrants that nobody drove African Americans from the South or forced these persons to journey northward. I learned how African American migrants were choosers, makers, and doers.[5] With candor and insight, these energetic speakers gave examples of the many ways they had to "throw up a highway through the wilderness" for their children.[6] I heard how these trailblazers "cut roads where there were not even paths" and provided the next generation with life skills and construction information never seen on an engineer's plan. As family, church, and community trailblazers, each stressed the daily victories they created for themselves. With unlimited grace from God and far-reaching assistance from their co-workers, these women built the paths needed to avoid racist employers and oppressive social mores. The roads they constructed took them around oppression individually and also moved an entire race around subjugation. As they unselfishly gave their time, I realized that I filled in the gaps of my own past as they shared their history with me.

I discovered oral testimonies that were dramatic, complex, and culturally stratified. I heard some of the women complain of age-associated ailments; however, I was surprised that their minds were sharp and their conversations crisp. More than I liked to admit, their sharp "mother wit" frequently triumphed over my educated mind as they defied my conventional beliefs about the lives of young women migrants who spent their lives cleaning the homes of others. With ease and accuracy, these women, who generally had less than three years of formal education, discussed local community changes, local politics, and the presidency. Events in their past were discussed thoroughly. They were most focused when they detailed the impact they had on their families, extended kinship, and community networks. With clarity they traced the subtle process of women's rural-to-urban migration and provided me with insights into the impact of these African American migrants on United States history during an era of vast transformation.[7] In each interview it became clear that these women did not see themselves as merely products, but often as major causes of change.[8] Yet each woman stressed, when I initially contacted them about an interview, "Why do you want to talk to me? I didn't do nothing. I was just a mother, wife, and domestic all my life."

My singular challenge therefore was how to write about these women as I saw them, as they saw themselves, *and* as they did not see themselves. I had to develop the ability to respectfully listen and simultaneously decode the threefold meanings informing their statements. After the first few minutes, each interviewee was eager to answer my questions and relate her history to "Miss Mary's niece" or "this friend of a friend who wanted to listen as old folks talked." No book or class could equal the way these interviewees taught me how to build a strong relationship with the people and culture I was studying. Their combination of historical insight, affection, intimacy, and identity made my study possible. Through investigating this cultural group I learned how to fuse the roles of niece, inquirer, and narrator and to "blend the passion of a family member with the skepticism" of a historian.[9]

I was always astonished at the language I had to learn. In the interviews I learned much about the lives of migrants from the things they felt had to be defined to me and explained in pointed detail. My women used a term like "mirate," a word in southern, mainly low-country dialect which describes a situation that is bothersome, petty, and uncomfortable for the person relating the information.[10] Many terms escaped my generation, and after many interviews I could not for the life of me figure out the meaning of many of the terms these old women used in each interview. I developed a pattern of interviewing the women migrants and then calling my culture experts. These adept and skillful specialists included my great-aunt, a second cousin who was in her mid-seventies, and Yvette Aidara, a friend reared by elderly grandparents who knew the language of older African Americans in amazing detail. Not one of these persons studied the theories of language and resistance strategies, bifurcation in analogous phraseologies, or indexical expressions within vernacular idioms, but their ability to decode the diverse social and cultural meanings expressed in each interview was startling. Without expert interpretation, I would never have comprehended the differences in meaning of terms like "pick-up" versus "party work," "aciphidity" versus "freedom bags," and "livery" versus "uniforms." With expert interpretation, the migrants' words were the foundation for a study that allowed African American women to confront the many stereotypes

– written and spoken as fact – that have led to hostile racial attitudes toward African Americans in general.

The myriad ways women devised to show their abhorrence of demeaning stereotypes continually amazed me. Each woman worked tirelessly to never reinforce or internalize an inferior status. Often they placed great emphasis on the use the front doors of homes where they worked and the stores where they made purchases, because this generation believed that there was an intimate connection between the mythology surrounding the use of back doors by America's ancillary class and the unceasing white-supremacist beliefs that serve as the foundation of racism in the United States.

However, they preferred buying food from the back doors of eating establishments where their friends were the cooks. Each woman insisted that "going to the back door means that you get food that is clean, portions which are generous, and better service from a hand you could trust."[11] African Americans who took pride in pushing back the limits others tried to impose on them willingly preferred the safety and assurance of the "Negro doors" of restaurants, insisting that there were special privileges for persons who went to the rear of restaurants. Did choosing the rear of the store affirm or defy the front-door employment equality they fought so hard to create?

The women constantly fought the menacing belief that females had to be weak, embrace societal constraints, and acquiesce to the prevailing conventions related to servants. At every opportunity they stressed the bold new face they assumed after leaving the rural South. Each woman recounted with pride how the move from live-in servant to daily paid household worker translated into more freedom and the opportunity to make the choices that a liberated worker makes. Freedom, advancement, and choice, for every woman I interviewed, came when these workers shed the dreaded uniform. The women indignantly explained how all employers demanded that live-in servants wear uniforms; and some wealthy employers adopted special uniforms to distinguish their "retainers" from those of other employers. And these former live-in servants never concealed the rage they felt knowing that employers wanted to lay claim to the servant as their property when they insisted that servants arrive at and leave their homes in uniforms. Without a place to change clothing, off-duty servants were force to travel on public transportation in uniforms – the outward symbol of every servant's subordinate position.

As the women moved to daily paid work, they simultaneously shed the uniform like an old skin. All the women adamantly refused to wear uniforms when they traveled to and from any job; and, many refused to ever again work in a uniform. The refusal to wear uniforms, those "most visible and valued signs of a white person's social arrival," was of paramount importance to the dayworker.[12] Without question, the sense of power permeated the women's rejection of these vestments of a worker of inferior status. Not wearing a uniform was an important manifestation and consequence of their progress as workers and their determined strength as women.

By contrast, I was never able to understand why at least one-fourth of the women, who all eloquently explained the constricting role of the fiendish uniform, would still perform their tasks as daily paid household workers in uniforms or dresses that were styled exactly like a uniform. Was the uniform permissible as long as other workers never saw them in this garb? Did the fact that dayworkers generally waited until the employers left to put on the uniform disengage the close link between wearing a uniform and losing ground on the path toward improvement? While the women never completely explained how they redefined this garment, clarity came when I remembered what Alyce Gullatee defined as "being in a mind of their own."[13] I know with unequivocal certainty that without these interviews I would have missed the women's ability to reframe the contextual issues of a uniform. Only the women's oral histories conclusively discredit scholars who confidently write that "blacks are more willing to wear uniforms" without ever perceiving the erroneousness of their statements.[14]

Strength, resolve, and a resolute "mind of their own" brought this generation of African American women more than just increased earnings and greater employment autonomy; their fortitude helped them realize their forefathers' promises and dreams. Their strength during the first five decades of the twentieth century would "uplift" the race in the last five decades of the century. They openly revealed a disdain for females who used weakness as an excuse for inaction or debased themselves with "weak-minded" actions to win favors from others. Collectively, they never accepted the double confinements of discrimination and oppression.

So why, before the end of every interview, did every woman proudly share her version of the "act"? I came to know the "act" as a servile, acquiescent, meek pretense that each woman maneuvered with ease; it was the shroud they easily put on to explain how they won a game they found deadly – the game called "fool Miss Ann." I did not understand the "act" or the meanings behind it until I heard each woman, as she was looking back on her life in the rural South, explain how rural southern ex-slave mothers and other female kin *taught* the women how to put on a convincing act for an employer as part of their "hometraining."[15] The support of the family was a primary task for every female by the time she reached seven years of age. The employment of these young women benefited the entire household and occasioned new social experiences. Each woman spoke in detail about being *taught* how to behave when working in the homes of white employers; and, after three to six months of tutelage with their mothers and other adult female family members at their place of employment, the girls by age nine were working with a white family near their homes as live-in servants. With solicitude each described a varied, unpredictable set of servant duties in every household. However, the one universal of every household was the belief that all African American women were always expected to appear subservient, deferential, and humble in manner. Because unemployment threatened to annihilate any hope for the family's economic improvement, the economic survival of the family depended on the young woman servant's ability to convincingly wear the servant mask and emotionally maneuver employers.

It took effort for me to understand this role, which pleased the elderly women I interviewed. A young, educated woman should not have to ever present a "fool Miss Ann" face. It was the face they did not want my generation to see or use. They did all that face work for me, and they hoped the face would remain forever lost to their daughters, their granddaughters, and other young women. But they could always find that face – a reality that was startling for me. It took much reflection for me to empathize with this generation and their uses of a "fool Miss Ann" face. I now know it is their choice to reveal the perfect servant face when they feel it is needed. I just had to accept that for this generation, this face justified their choices, rectified their actions along lines of a larger historical tradition, and fashioned the identity these women felt was appropriate for the workplace.[16]

They perfected an "act," and their respect for workers who could "wear the mask that grins and lies, / hides our cheeks and shades our eyes, – / this debt we pay to human guile; / with torn and bleeding hearts we smile" was genuine.[17] Together, Miss Mathilene Anderson and Miss Pansylee Holmes spoke and really explained "the face."

> You keep moving, dusting, doing . . . but smiling . . . talking and laughing with them all the same. [The servant] was doing nothing, but know how to make it seem so much to whites . . . could get them better with stories!
>
> Now we knew it was nothing and when we were around just us [the staff] we'd laugh. We would get them [make other staff laugh] with stories of how we learned how we'd get them down home. Those . . . from down Virginia? Would get them with better stories. [Virginia people] told how we'd get them . . . good. [Virginians] seems the goodest of good. . . .
>
> The very best? They'd dzern [discern] how . . . to be so busy, so so long, with nothing.
>
> But talking and laughing all the time. . . . And you always smiling. A good live-in servant does nothing more than anybody else. Mostly doing the object things, but they knew how to look busier. It is funny.
>
> But we still know how to get them right back the more-ist part of the time. We'd fool that woman from dawn to dusk.

These women collectively painted a portrait of persons who, with social, economic, and legal practices stacked against them, defiantly believed that you worked "to survive" and that work required the development, maintenance, and promotion of a false face. Their impeccable personal integrity was central to their view of themselves as deeply honest, Christian women. However, the unremitting hard work made employer-directed deception a virtue, and the most respected worker cultivated occupational ingenuity.

But these women never obscured one point: in these interviews, this generation of African American women loathed and viciously assailed workers who allowed the "act" to become a reality. They took issue with the belief that the intersection of race, class, and gender created an environment that made it permissible to in any way genuinely embrace the dictates of employers.[18] I interviewed Eula Montgomery, a household worker who tried to join their club but was viewed as "ment-ly" (mentally unstable, lacking clear purpose). I learned of her obtuseness from other workers who noted she was "happy" to work for abusive employers. They told me about one employer who was so mean that they never let her take any time off and whose demands caused her only boyfriend to leave her. When interviewed, this woman, speaking in a high-pitched voice that has an unnervingly shrill, Butterfly McQueen–type whine, justified how the employer, after thirty-one years of service, simply let her go one day – without notice, severance pay, or pension. Although she is "happy," the telltale wrinkles around her mouth are not from laughter, and the constant twitch in the lower corner of her right eye is suspect. She frequently pauses midsentence to stare vacantly out the window, especially while describing "her people" (the family she served for thirty-one years).

While her family members and senior citizen club members accuse her of letting white folks walk all over her, this worker says she was never disliked or mistreated by an employer. Not even the time when she missed her sister's wedding because "her people" wouldn't give her the day off, even though she had given them four months' notice of her intention to take that day off. But to make up for her having to miss the wedding, didn't they take her on a trip with them (and let her babysit) the very next summer? She never liked how people talked back to white folks. She never spoke up. She never fought back. "Her people" took whatever they wanted from her. She did whatever "her people" wanted, whenever they wanted. The interviewee never confronted the employer's sense of superiority and conveniently overlooked the essential matter of mutual respect between employer and employee.

For me, a more pervasive problem persisted and preceded the respect the workers did not receive from employers. This generation of women spoke with pride about being the "backbone" of the African American community's strongest institutions – the family and the church. I felt it was a term that was telling on many levels. It was apparent to me that the women who proudly used the term were referring to function rather than location. However, I recognized that for most women it was a reference to their location in these institutions, not their function.[19] They proudly insisted that, in their homes and churches, women were always to serve in the background as support workers. Each woman lectured me on the need for women in the home to always be devoted to fathers, obedient to elder brothers, and submissive to husbands. In the church, their responsibilities were in the kitchen, while the pastors and men dictated policy. Women always made up over 70 percent of African American churches' membership, but they were invisible among the church policymaking positions. They were quite comfortable with the fact that men were in charge of the households. Generally women found work as domestics and earned the family's highest income. African American men, as solid documentation affirms, were constantly faced with irregular, unpredictable employment. However, women always insisted that the men were the head of the family and the final authority in a stable home.

In my first five interviews, with relatives and close kin, I posed questions about strong women accepting weak positions. How could these women work in churches that did not give them more power? Does the fact that they are women who are without power make the question of the majority not having equal power make the issue any less of a concern? If, as I tried to contend, having respect was inseparable in workplace and in the church, then a split could not be made between employment racism and religious sexism.

My status as an outsider became more clear as the interviews progressed. Whenever their reflections delineated the importance of accepting sexism, the complexity of these areas of their lives became clear. In every interview with my elderly relatives, and with each woman who addressed my questions and concerns, I was given the final word on my incorrect ideas, wrong opinions, and immoral thoughts. First, the Bible outlines that women are to support the male of the house. Women are to listen and follow the directions of fathers and older brothers when they are young; then, they are guided by the dictates of a husband when they are adults. Second, women knew they were in charge but never felt it was right to move from the background to the forefront in any obvious way in the family or the church. Leadership does not require prominence in public or in the home; conspicuousness causes confusion in both the home and the church. Christian women do not create confusion, because God is not found in confusion. Finally, while underscoring the critical economic and social role played by women, this generation of women accepted the unenviable position of elevating African American men at the expense of African American women. Notwithstanding all the evidence I could present to the contrary, the women refused to recognize and deal with my questions. This generation of women refused to recognize and deal with sexism on my terms.

Every woman with whom I discussed these issues made it clear that I was revealing thinking that was different, very distorted, and wrong. I was showing how my age, educational attainment, occupational opportunities, and status as a person who did not live with segregation warped my capacity to think. And, I was admonished by my great-aunt and other elders – my segue into this community of older persons – to stop causing my family "embarrassment with crazy talk." I continued to ask the questions and learned how to tacitly agree with their answers, because to do otherwise would mean I was pushing aside the directives of elderly relatives I deeply respected. But I could never resolve several questions. Were my ideas a reflection of an outsider's unfair expectations? How does one explain blatant discrimination to people who see your ideas as inauthentic? Does selective equality or silence on specific issues mean conformity?

Months of interviews with migrant women helped this young scholar travel to different places, explore new worlds, and understand life for women reared eighty to one hundred and five years ago. As young women they lived lives filled with family work, community work, church work, work-work, and more work. They migrated northward into cities where they were hedged about by legal and societal prohibitions. When they were able to move from live-in servant to daily paid household worker they were required to perform an ever-tenser balancing act to survive, routinely acquiring part-time "party work" jobs (serving food of cleaning up after a social event) in addition to full-time employment to sustain themselves. However, their oral testimonies explained the rich social fabric and abundant personal joy they found in life. They enriched my understanding of the past and deepened my appreciation of the many ways every African American of my generation owes a debt of gratitude to each of these women. I disagreed with them on a few issues, but in reality, did they need to agree with me? Was my dismay on the "self-limiting" aspects of their lives valid? I knew how hard they worked to move beyond the back doors reserved for servants and the back of every bus this nation reserved for African Americans. I was discouraged because I felt they should have more aggressively moved from other "back" bone positions, should have propelled themselves forward in the directions that were critical to women in the first decades of the new millennium. In balance, was my discouragement tenable?

Their discouragement quickly tempered my thoughts. Women like my great-aunt clearly stressed their disappointment; however, it was a disappointment that was focused on younger women like myself, people who, on a daily basis, never wore hats and gloves. We never had to "show or prove" that we were real women – ladies – and seemed to "have forgotten the art altogether." In a prosperous America where legal segregation has ended, the historical imperatives have changed. We moved from a very limited world to a world of expanded economic possibilities and social opportunity.[20] We benefit from legal protections they never dreamed would become a reality. Yes, there had been many gains "for colored girls," they admitted; but each wondered if there hadn't been some losses too.

For a long time after the end of my first tea party with these women, I sat in my car remembering the lovely ladies with their meticulously attended benevolences and their fashionable hats, gloves, and proper table manners. Staring blankly at my bare, untended hands on the steering wheel, I too wondered about my losses.

My Mexican Friend Marta
Who Lives Across the Border from Me
in Detroit

Ruth Behar

In her essay "The Vulnerable Observer," Ruth Behar argues that there are good reasons for an ethnographer to bring relevant aspects of his or her own life into a portrait of another person. The following reading is an effective example of one of her own efforts at this kind of double portrait.

Behar presents her friendship with her Mexican friend Marta as a story, not an analytic essay. Along the way she explores cultural dislocations and barriers and draws some telling contrasts between her own life, as a Cuban American and a professor, and that of Marta, and between Marta's relationship with her husband, Saúl, and Ruth's relationship with her husband, David. Implicitly, her account also leads us to reflect on the nature of our own relationships, research partnerships, and friendships. Her account is interesting, too, in how she uses her efforts at honest self-observation to craft scenes in which she does not appear as an entirely sympathetic character.

This essay was originally published in *Bridges to Humanity: Narratives on Anthropology and Friendship*, edited by Bruce T. Grindal and Frank A. Salamone (Prospect Heights IL: Waveland Press, 1995). It is reprinted here by permission of the publisher.

Marta and I live a half hour away from each other, but there is a gaping-wide border between the corner house she and her family are borrowing from her brother-in-law in Detroit and my two-story Victorian house in a quiet, tree-lined neighborhood of Ann Arbor. Neither of us ever pretends that this border is inconsequential. Yet the circumstances of our lives have brought us at once so close and so far, and within that space we've managed to build a friendship.

It is June of 1993, and I am preparing for a return visit to Marta's hometown in Mexico, where my husband and I have lived, off and on, for ten years. She herself can't go back, because her husband, Saúl, has just lost his job and their economic situation is shaky. So this year I will be the one to hug her parents and sisters, and to spend afternoons chatting in the patio with her *abuelitos*, her beloved and frail grandparents.

Marta arrives with Saúl to drop off a Sears catalogue for me to take to her family. And she brings their video camera to shoot some footage of my house. For Marta my house is a museum. She goes around talking into the camera as she points out highlights in our living room and dining room. "We come to this house a lot. Our friends like to invite us over," she says, chuckling.

My house is filled with books, embroidered cloths, and antique furniture; and there are clay pots, enameled trays, and bark paintings brought from Mexico. It is a house of many rooms, wood-framed windows, and a garden. I sometimes can't believe it is my house, bought with my own money. As a Cuban immigrant kid, I grew up in a series of cramped apartments in New York, so when Marta tells me she loves to come to my house, that it is her dream house, I understand, but feel odd that the things I have acquired are inspiring wanting and longing in someone else. She takes notice of anything new – a wicker chair, a used piano, a Turkish beaded good luck charm, new tiles in the bathroom with whimsical nopal cactuses, also brought with us from Mexico.

Marta focuses her camera on all of my Mexican wares. "Look at all the beautiful things from Mexico," she says into the camera. She seems to be displaying for her family back in Mexico all the Mexican things the anthropologist has in her house, which the Mexican herself, namely, Marta, doesn't want to have. Marta, for whom Mexico is her grandparents, her seven siblings, and her mother and father, who were always working not to become poor, desires none of these things; she dreams of packages filled with pretty white linens, edged in lace, that you order from catalogues, and she wants elegant, gold-trimmed porcelain dishes, the kind you can sometimes find on sale for fifteen dollars, service for four, at K-Mart.

I am always the one who phones Marta. When Marta decided to marry Saúl and come live with him in the United States, I made a promise to her parents and grandparents in Mexico that I would always look out for her on this side of the border. I haven't been able to explain to her family that another border separates us here.

"Marta, how are you?" I ask in Spanish, addressing her in the informal *tú*. We have spoken our native Spanish to one another since we met ten years ago in Mexico. We may both speak English to our sons, but our friendship is lived in Spanish.

"I'm fine. And you?" Marta always addresses me in the formal you, as *usted*. She won't let me forget that I am ten years her senior; that when we met in Mexico she was a young girl finishing high school, and I was already a married woman embarking on a career as a writer. Even after seven years in the United States, and my continual requests that she address me as *tú*, Marta insists on maintaining certain formalities that acknowledge the age, cultural, educational, and class differences between us.

"And how is Saúl?"

"He's okay. He got that job teaching high school Spanish. Says he's going to earn almost as much as he used to at his old job. Says he's looking forward to the long summer vacations. We're just waiting for them to call about his physical exam."

I have known Saúl for about as many years as I have known Marta. Born in the United States of Mexican parents, Saúl grew up in Michigan, working summers with his four brothers and their parents in the cherry, apple, and cucumber harvests. When I met Saúl, he was searching for his roots in the same Mexican town in which my husband and I were searching for a topic to study. He'd usually visit around Christmas, hosting lively *posadas* at the house of his mother's cousin, where the *tamales* were plentiful and a big *piñata* bulging with sweets was never lacking. On one of his first visits, when I met him, he came with a girlfriend, a *gringa* with long curly blond hair; and years before, he had come with a different girlfriend, also a *gringa*.

But during the Christmas season in 1983, he came alone. Marta, who had won a scholarship to attend a state boarding school, was home on vacation from her job teaching in a rural school. Her hair was permed, she wore a pink knit blouse and fitted pants, and she danced an entire night with Saúl at a fifteenth-birthday party, the *quinceañera*, of a cousin. Soon after, when he returned to the States, they wrote letters to each other every day. Two years later, they decided to get married, against the objections of Marta's father. He described Saúl, thirteen years older than Marta, as a *gallo*, an old rooster, who wanted the hand of a *pollito*, a little chick.

Marta and Saúl were married in a big church wedding in Mexico in December of 1985 and moved to East Lansing, where Saúl worked in the personnel department of Michigan State University. In the university setting, Marta met other women from Latin America and studied English. Saúl, who realized he had taken Marta away from her job, hoped she'd prepare to become a teacher of bilingual education. But Marta soon decided she wanted to have a child and, without letting Saúl know, she let him get her pregnant. What she hadn't expected was that it would happen so quickly.

Their son, Eduardo, was born in 1988, when Marta was twenty-three, and in 1989 they moved to the Detroit area, where Saúl found a better-paying job in a state government office. For the next three years they lived in a garden apartment in Romulus, under the flight paths of the Detroit Metro airport, where few families with children lived. Marta felt unsafe and stayed indoors all the time, shut within the four walls of their apartment, with her baby and the television as her only companions. Marta says she learned English watching soap operas. Later they moved to another apartment in Westland, where there were more families with children, and the stores were within walking distance. It was not yet Marta's dream house, but at least she felt less isolated.

Then Saúl lost his job. To save money he and Marta gave up their garden apartment and moved into his brother's house. It was a difficult moment, especially because they had taken on the added responsibility of caring for Marta's brother and sister, who had come from Mexico with all their papers in order thanks to Saúl's efforts. Polo and Lisandra planned to complete their last year of high school in the United States and then study in a community college. The two of them had learned English quickly and progressed rapidly in their schoolwork. Saúl was proud of them and hoped their presence would cheer up Marta, who had grown depressed and moody in her new surroundings.

"Guess what?" Marta suddenly announces. "I've signed up for a course. Saúl says it would be good for me. It's a course about relationships, about letting go of the anger you've been carrying around since you were a child. Do you know I still have dreams in which I get angry because my mother isn't home to take care of me?"

Women think back through their mothers, and, indeed, Marta wants to become a different kind of mother than her mother. Marta tells me that her adult self comprehends that her mother had to work hard, first as a peddler and then as a schoolteacher, to care for her eight children; but even so, she says with anguish, she can't forget how as a child she felt neglected and wished she could be wrapped inside her mother's arms, those arms which were always busy working. In the United States, Marta imagined she could become the mother she didn't have, the mother who would plan her pregnancy and be exclusively devoted to her child. And so she chose to have one child, Eduardo, for whom she has cared singlehandedly during the early years of his childhood. And she has chosen, too, to make it impossible to ever have another child.

It is October of 1992, five months after Marta's hysterectomy. With some hesitation I have asked Marta if I can write about her operation for a conference on women's health. I fear that treating her as an anthropological subject will hurt our friendship, but Marta immediately agrees to let me write about her. She considers it an honor, she says, that I am interested.

We sit on her bed with the white lace coverlet. A mirror is behind Marta and I try not to look at my own face as I look at her. Little Eddy is in the living room playing with my husband, David, who has accompanied me on this trip because I don't like to drive to Detroit alone. The tape recorder is on the bed and I hold up the microphone toward Marta. We don't know that the tape recorder is not recording anything; only later, when I get home, I will learn that David forgot to put the batteries in the microphone.

On three sheets of lined loose-leaf paper, Marta has begun to write her life story in a few broad strokes. I read her hand-written words and notice how careful she has been to leave out anything painful; but her sense of solitude is profound and it surfaces, unwittingly, several times in her brief text, which ends in mid-sentence, with the words, "I have tried not to be an abnegated wife, but a . . ." She has held within herself all the pain of social and cultural displacement, all the tension of her rite of passage from virgin to wife, and all the anxieties of losing her womb so soon after becoming a mother.

Knowing that she planned to have only one, or maybe two children of her own, Marta tells me she tried to enjoy every moment of her pregnancy. It was a special time that she remembers with joy. But giving birth was a nightmare for her. At the hospital, when she became fully dilated, the doctors told her that the baby's head was too big and that they needed to perform a C-section. They had given her a spinal block for pain relief and later they put her under total anesthesia to perform the C-section. Saúl was not allowed to be present at the birth, and the staff delayed bringing the baby to her. Apparently the anesthesiologist was sloppy, because after giving birth Marta suffered from terrible headaches and body pains for four months. She cries, remembering how she could barely take care of Eddy at first. For Marta, having a C-section, especially one that was botched and alienating, made her feel that her womb wasn't worth much. She told me that the doctor who took out her uterus cut along the dotted line of her C-section scar.

Marta found the doctor who performed her hysterectomy, a board-certified obstetrician, in the phone book. She had already gone to two other doctors, both women, before seeing him. The two previous doctors, she felt, were unscrupulous in their desire for money; after learning what a good health insurance plan she had through her husband's job, they had immediately wanted to perform hysterectomies without even running a single test or analysis. As a rule she prefers women doctors, she says, because she's a Latina and finds it shameful to be examined by a man. But the doctor she found in the phone book impressed her enough that she put her trust in him. He's Cuban, she tells me, which I already know, cringing at the thought that Marta, in a subliminal way, may have put her trust in him because she's learned from me that Cubans are okay. I am holding the microphone that is taping nothing as she tells me that she wanted to have tests done and the Cuban doctor did them. She wanted to be sure she needed this operation and he convinced her she did. Her heavy menstrual bleeding had worried her since she was a young girl, but after giving birth, it had gotten worse. She had to rest during her periods and take iron; during those days, she fell behind on the cooking and cleaning and she didn't like that, because if the house was going to be her only responsibility, she wanted to do it well. The doctor told her if she went on bleeding so heavily, one day she'd have a hemorrhage. He also told her that she had a tumor in her uterus, but after removing the uterus he admitted there was no tumor. He claimed her uterus was abnormally enlarged, that it had not shrunk back to its proper size after pregnancy.

Marta is beginning to question her doctor's advice and motives. She is not so sure anymore that he wasn't out for the money, too. And she recognizes that he's not so honest, perhaps, as she thought at first. When she tells him she's been gaining weight after the operation, he pretends it is her eating habits that are responsible; later she finds out that it's very common for women who lose their uterus to put on weight. But what matters is her health, she says. It's nice not to be worried about her periods anymore or about getting pregnant. She couldn't have gone on taking iron pills forever. And if she is not going to have any more children anyway, then she really doesn't need her uterus. She's lucky, she tells me, that Saúl is educated and accepts her in her new wombless state. In Mexico, she says, there are men who won't have a woman who's had a hysterectomy; they claim those women aren't women anymore.

Marta needs to affirm to herself that her decision was a wise one. She thought about it for a year and she feels she explored her options by getting several medical opinions. She believes her health has improved, that she is really better, much better. But the loss of her uterus has made her aware of all her losses – of everything she has given up, everything she is giving up, to make a new life for herself and her family on this side of the border.

You know, Marta says to me, the last time she was in Mexico she and her mother were joking around and her mother called her a good-for-nothing. Those words – "no sirves para nada" – stung, and the pain was compounded when Saúl recently said the same thing to her, also as a joke. As she recounts this, Marta's eyes fill with tears. Marta was the second daughter; it was her sister, the eldest, who was always the smart one, always the favorite of her father. When she was in Mexico, her father told her how proud he was of her older unmarried sister for having gotten so far in her studies and achieving degrees in two fields. But he didn't say anything to Marta about being proud of her. She longs for greater affirmation from her parents, and yet her deepest wish is to someday bring them both to the United States and provide for them in their old age.

Marta left everything behind to come to the States with Saúl, but she didn't receive a very warm welcome from his family. When her mother-in-law suddenly developed an inexplicable illness, her father-in-law accused Marta of having used witchcraft to cause the illness; later he told Marta that Saúl didn't love her and that she was lucky he had paid any attention to her. One brother-in-law called her an Indian from the rancho because she refused to drink beer; another brother-in-law told her she was "un perro entrenado" (a trained dog), because she was so concerned to keep Saúl happy, having dinner on the table when he returned from work and setting his clothes out for him, neatly ironed, each morning.

She doesn't do those things for Saúl anymore, Marta says, because he never thanked her, never showed any appreciation. If Saúl thought he was bringing back a young and innocent Mexican wife to do all his housework for him, those days are over, she says, wiping her eyes, her face hardening.

As David and I drive back to Ann Arbor, I tell him about how Marta told me she often feels worthless, that her life isn't amounting to anything. Tears come into David's eyes; he says that's how he often feels.

In our relationship, the usual division of labor and power have been reversed. David has played the role of faculty wife, caring for our son, Gabriel, and doing the kind of secretarial work for me that male professors are always thanking their wives for in the acknowledgment section of their books. Most of the time, I am able to display gratitude for David's help on a more regular basis and to encourage him in his own work, but I have also been spoiled by the bargain prices he offers on his services; like my male counterparts, I've gotten into the habit of depending on certain unpaid labors from him. So, back at home, when I discover that the tape on which I am expecting to base my paper for the women's health conference hasn't come out, a paper that must be ready to present in a week, I break out in a merciless fury.

"Why did you give me that microphone in the first place? I've never used that silly thing before! How was I to know it needed its own battery? Aren't you the one who always handles that stuff? Now what am I going to do? I can't replicate the conversation I just had with Marta! I may as well forget about going to the conference. And my paper is one of the plenaries. Thanks to you, I won't be able to go!"

David's head sinks. "I'm sorry," he says. But I go on, repeating the litany of my complaints, even though I know I'll be able to piece my paper together from notes and memories. After a while he gets angry enough to say, "Well, next time, you get the tape recorder set up."

"That's very easy to say now, isn't it?"

"Look, if you don't like the way I do things, maybe I should just leave."

"You really love to press the anxiety button by threatening to leave just when I'm counting on you to take care of Gabriel. That's so cruel!"

In the afternoon the two of us go to our Yoga class, where we pretend not to recognize one another and occupy different parts of the room as though we were strangers.

Sometimes anthropology comes too close to home.

A few days later we return to Marta's house with a functioning tape recorder. David goes off to look at computers, and I stay with Marta and Eddy. Our conversation is not so intense this time because of Eddy's interruptions. At one point Marta takes Eddy in her arms and holds him tight. "I try to remember to do this at least once a day," she says. But later, he gets wilder, and trying to get her attention, he punches her in the belly. "I'll be right back," she says and goes into the bathroom with Eddy. I think I can hear her hitting him. Lisandra is back from her high school and comes in to entertain me. No, I can't believe she'd hit Eddy, her one and only. Would she?

Marta returns with Eddy and I can't read any clues in his face or hers. From the closet she pulls out her photo album, and we slowly turn the pages, looking at the pictures of her as a student, eyes gleaming with promise. Eddy points to a picture of Marta and says, "Stupid!" Marta calmly says to him, "Don't say that. Say chicken." Eddy points to the picture again and says, "Stupid!" Marta takes a deep breath and repeats, "Say chicken, Eddy, okay?" Her eyes look like they're starting to water. Finally, Eddy whispers "Chicken" and Marta says, "*Gracias,* that's better, Eddy."

Eddy soon tires of the pictures and rushes out to the living room to watch the cartoons on television. Lisandra, always good-natured, excuses herself and follows after him. Glad to be alone with me again, Marta returns to her closet and pulls out a stack of neatly folded, sparkling clean towels. "These are my towels," she says. "I don't let Saúl or my brother Polo use them. Polo has pimples and I don't want him staining my towels."

The Marta pulls out a big plastic bag. It is full of letters, the love letters Saúl wrote to her from Minnesota, North Dakota, and Michigan in the two years of their romance. She reads from two of them: one letter is about his struggle to find work after deciding to leave Minnesota; the other is about how they should deal with the problem of getting married by the Catholic Church, given his family's conversion to Protestantism (but later, as Marta explains, it turns out that his grandmother had baptized him and there was no problem at all). He'd start his letters with Amor mío ("My love"), punctuating them constantly with those words. He wrote very lyrically and in correct Spanish. When he went to ask Marta's father if he would let her marry him, Saúl announced, "I have a great weight upon my heart," and her father said, "Forget the poetry and get to the point."

Saúl saved all her letters just like she saved all of his. But her letters are gone. Destroyed by her own hands. Why, I ask, unable to hide the disappointment in my voice. Marta says she just decided, one day, to tear them all up. She told Saúl she was going to do it. And all he said was, "Well, if that's what you want to do . . ."

Back in a small town in Mexico, in the front room where her *abuelitos* sleep, Marta's wedding dress hangs from a nail in the wall. The dress remembers her body. Remembers how she danced before she said goodbye. Waits for her.

Routes to Identity
Life History Dialogues on Race and Adoption

Sandra Patton-Imani

In the United States, our efforts to know who we are depend significantly on cultural constructions about our roots, our ideas about connections we have with our ancestors. But how do we understand who we are when we are adopted? Who are you when your mother is not your "real" mother? In this mind-bending life history exploration, Sandra Patton-Imani enters into a series of dialogues with Lynn, a woman whose adopted parents differ from her birth parents in race, class, religion, and ethnicity.

Patton-Imani shows how the adoptee's special situation both complicates and illuminates the problematic cultural and social structural routes to our seemingly fixed but actually precarious and shifting senses of who we are. She weaves her conversations with Lynn and her interpretations of the unfolding dialogues with the parallel story of her own changing sense of identity as an adoptee. Taken together, these themes illuminate adoptees' struggles to establish and confirm a sense of identity. This life history also illuminates the cultural and social structural dimensions of the ongoing attempts we all make to understand who we are.

This essay was written for this volume and draws on material Sandra Patton-Imani develops further in her book BirthMarks: Transracial Adoption in Contemporary America (New York: New York University Press, 2000). This reworked material is used by permission of the publisher.

In 1994, Lynn, a twenty-nine-year-old biracial adoptee, and I, a twenty-nine-year-old white adoptee, were sitting at the dining room table in my apartment in Adelphi, Maryland, talking about adoption and identity. To the naked eye we were just two women sitting across the table from each other with a tape recorder between us. But we weren't really the only people in the room. Although at that time neither of us had much sense of who our birth parents were, their ghostly presence surrounded us, infusing our life stories with haunting questions. Lynn told me a story about the mysteries of her family tree.

> It's hard being adopted, in many ways. . . . I mean, when I was in fourth grade – this is something that stays with me today because my father is getting into it again – we had to do family trees. And I refused. And the teacher said, "Well, go home and do the assignment at home." And I remember being – I mean, there are very few moments I remember being upset about school because I loved school, but I was upset about this homework assignment. And my mom said to me, "Well, we're your family now." And I said, "But that's not my real family." [with anger] I mean, I had this definite idea [that] to have a family tree you had to know – I mean, I had an idea of *roots* – that you had to be able to trace it *biologically*. I mean, I knew that even at whatever age you are in fourth grade, at age nine. And I got so – I never did the assignment. And I don't know if the teacher decided that she just wasn't going to like deal with this, because obviously, I was just being so obstinate. And there was no way, ever, I was going to do this assignment.

Lynn's story about roots and family trees implies the question, What makes us who we are? Lynn articulates one of the most fundamental and deeply felt issues adoptees face: How do we, lacking knowledge of our birth families, claim a history, a heritage, and an ancestry in a social context that largely defines "real" kinship through bloodlines? Who are our ancestors? How is it that the ghosts of our original families feel so real? Through what avenues might we claim the histories we seek? How might knowledge of our ancestors inform our own identities? For American transracial adoptees like Lynn, these questions are further complicated by beliefs about the racial differences between her adoptive parents, who are white, and herself, who is black. She has struggled with questions of history, culture, and the meaning of race in her continual process of identity construction and maintenance.

Identity was the central issue that emerged in the ethnographic interviews I conducted with Lynn and twenty-one other transracial adoptees – African American and multiracial adults who were adopted and raised by white parents. As an adoptee, I have spent my life struggling with issues of who I am in relation to my family, my birth family, my unknown ancestors, and the messages I receive from social interactions and media representations regarding the roots of my "true" self. Adoptees, including those I interviewed formally, those I know personally, and the countless people I have spoken with more casually, can typically recite the most dominant public narrative concerning adoption and identity – namely, that searching for and being reunited with our birth parents (more often mothers) is the only way we can know who we "really" are. Some embrace this view, while others are more critical. While narratives of search and reunion typically lean toward the nature side of the nature-nurture divide, other public discourses stress the importance of culture and environment, particularly in the controversy over transracial adoption. However, little attention is accorded either to the interactions between biology and culture or to the possibility that other social forces, such as public policy and social institutions, fundamentally shape the lives we lead. Adoptees' selves are often represented in public discourse as an embodiment of the nature-versus-nurture tensions at the core of Western assumptions about identity.

Adoption has emerged in recent decades as a common topic in such media as news coverage, political rhetoric, television talk shows, made-for-TV movies, and films. What do non-adopted viewers find compelling about adoption narratives? Why is the issue of transracial adoption so interesting to the vast number of people whose lives are not affected by it? What is it about search-and-reunion stories that draws such interest? In my view, transracial adoption – and adoption more generally – have become so prevalent in public discourse at this historical moment because adoption narratives speak to the ambiguities of identity, race, and family that characterize the lives of so many people living in the United States at the beginning of the twenty-first century. Anthropologist James Clifford asserts: "Allegory prompts us to say of any cultural description not 'this represents, or symbolizes, that' but rather, 'this is a (morally charged) story about that.'"[1] Adoption narratives can be usefully considered as sociopolitical allegories of identity. As sociologist Katarina Wegar argues:

> The emancipatory discourse of self-discovery [in adoption search narratives] reflects a broader cultural preoccupation with the search for identity or the individual's moral right to embark upon this quest. Ideological or not, the pursuit of "finding oneself" has become a moral phenomenon in modern social life, as the morality of self-actualization both shapes and is shaped by the "institutions of modernity." One reason that search narratives in today's public and expert discourse appear to be increasingly intelligible is that the moral vocabulary drawn upon by search activists – that is, the ethic of self-

discovery – has become not only acceptable but perhaps even normative to the way Americans perceive the quest for identity.[2]

Adoptees' lives separate the categories of biology and culture that are typically used as organizational frames in considering questions of identity, thereby making evident the role of social structure in shaping selves. We are not defined solely through our genetic heritage; nor are we exclusively shaped by our culture and environment. Rather, like everyone navigating life in the complex, globalized, socially stratified contemporary United States, adoptees construct and reconstruct their identities through their biological "roots," through the various cultural meaning systems they encounter, and through their interactions with public policies and social institutions. Perspectives that discuss the ambiguities, ambivalences, and complexities of the question of adoption and roots are rarely heard in public discourse. In this essay I offer a complex, exploratory counternarrative – an alternative story of identity – to the public view that adoptive identities are defined by our birth ties, whether these are cast as biological or cultural. My counternarrative considers the social construction of identity and race at multiple levels: biological, cultural, and structural. More importantly, I focus on the complexities of identity formation in the border zones between such neatly divided categories of understanding.

I have constructed this essay as a dialogue on identity between two adoptees, one biracial and one white. Both were born in 1965, relinquished for adoption by their birth mothers, and adopted by white middle-class families on the West Coast. At the time these dialogues took place, each adoptee was pursuing a doctoral degree at a large state university on the East Coast. Both have chosen race as a central focus of research and teaching. Lynn Praeger is the transracial adoptee whose life story I focus on, and I am the white adoptee with whom she engaged in dialogue. Lynn was one of twenty-two transracial adoptees I interviewed as part of a larger research project. She, like a few others, emerged as a key informant, and one whose views on adoption were often similar to my own. Lynn and I established an ongoing dialogue on race, adoption, and identity that has, thus far, spanned the course of four and a half years. Although I focus on the words of just one person I spoke with, I draw on the understandings of identity, race, gender, family, culture, and social structure that I gained in ethnographic interviews with all twenty-two of the adult African American and multiracial adoptees who were raised in white families.

The alternative story of identity and race that emerges from these dialogues suggests a sociopolitical allegory that moves beyond the question of roots. Sociologist John Gabriel suggests: "Cross-cultural fertilization provides an important source of ethnic identity rather than simply hanging on to and reproducing old ethnic divisions. The analysis of 'routes' rather than roots becomes a more effective way of understanding new ethnic configurations."[3] Moving from roots to routes shifts our understanding of identity formation from an exclusive focus on biology and culture as signifiers of race and identity to metaphors of roads, paths, intersections, borders, bridges, boundaries, and diasporic histories. Such images may be used to link individual lives to institutional and structural forces in societies that move us along the routes through which we become who we are. As Paul Gilroy puts it, we are all "rooted in and routed through" society's power-infused social structures.[4] The routes of identities include the race, gender, ethnicity, and class histories of our birth and adoptive families, as well as our parents' multiple relationships to the social institutions regulating the social reproduction of families. In this framework the genealogy of individuals moves beyond the inclusion of ancestors to encompass the multiple paths through which people make meaning in their lives. I begin with a discussion of search narratives, continue with a consideration of race, ethnicity, and culture, and conclude with an exploration of the role of social institutions in shaping adoptive lives.

In recent years, ethnographers, feminists, and other cultural studies scholars have emphasized the contextual and relational character of identity. With regard to ethnographic method, increasing attention has focused on the ethnographer's presence as a force in shaping the self-narratives of the people being interviewed. As anthropologist Renato Rosaldo explains, "The study of differences, formerly defined in opposition to an invisible (ethnographic, authorial) 'self,' now becomes the play of similarities and differences relative to socially explicit identities. How do 'they' see 'us'? Who are 'we' looking at 'them'? Social analysis thus becomes a relational form of understanding in which both parties actively engage in 'the interpretation of cultures.'"[5] The interviews I conducted were indeed contextual, relational, interactive moments of identity construction and definition. Not only did I provide an occasion for self-reflection and the articulation of self for those I interviewed, but my identity as an adoptee gave them a listener and questioner who was an "insider." The sense of validation was powerful for me as well, as each of us experienced a fairly unique dialogue in which another person "gets it" – that is, an "inside" view of adoption. There are certainly profound differences among the people I spoke with, but some foundational assumptions seemed present in almost every encounter. We are all people whose lives carry the stigma of having been "given up" or "relinquished" or "abandoned." We all have the experience of kinship in which the biological understanding of family is separated from cultural, emotional, and experiential understandings. We all have a sense that our identities are not "natural" but rather contingent and constructed. We know that we could easily have grown up in other families and thus that we could have been entirely different from the selves we now know. Not only are we aware that we might have grown up as members of our birth families, but we also know that we could have easily been adopted into families other than the ones that did adopt us. The possibilities for who we might have become are vast and unknown.

This essay is an experimental ethnography. I am not a detached observer; I am part of the story being told. And although I have struggled with how much of myself I feel comfortable revealing – unlike Lynn, I am not anonymous – I must ultimately include my story in the larger narrative if I am to honestly present what I have learned from this research. Who I am – as an adoptee, as a white woman, as an interdisciplinary feminist ethnographer – shaped the life stories my informants told. Their stories have shaped my sense of self as well. In fact, my views on adoptions, searches, reunions, and families have changed significantly since I began this research. Thus, the story I present here is by necessity a partial, momentary snapshot of the interactions between myself and one of the transracial adoptees I interviewed.

Searching for Roots

Questions concerning roots and history are central to Lynn's sense of being in the world. She and her younger sister were born in 1965 and 1966 to a white woman who had had an extramarital affair with a black man. For a short period of time they lived with their birth mother and her white husband, and then they lived in a succession of foster homes and an orphanage. They were adopted by white parents, when they were six and seven years old, into a family with three birth children and two other children who had been adopted transracially. They grew up in a predominantly white area on the West Coast. Lynn currently lives on the East Coast. Here she continues her discussion of family trees:

> And my father, over the last couple years – well, my father, they traced their family – my adoptive father and his family – back to the Revolutionary War, when like his great-great-great-grandfather was given land, actually, up near Harpers Ferry, which was really *strange*. There's actually quite a few Praegers in this area and in the Ohio basin. They were farmers. So like when we were growing up there were always like all these family pictures, like all on the wall. And I remember just looking at these and thinking, "These aren't my people." I mean, I very consciously knew these were not my relatives. The last couple of years my father has gotten this computer program that is for – that you can use to help trace your family tree. And the Praegers – because it's a relatively small – they have like a whole newsletter of people who are Praegers that is out of Ohio, but it goes to other people. Like the only other person who – Praeger – who moved to our area ended up being like a fifth cousin to my dad. I mean, it was really bizarre. I mean, there's not a lot of Praegers around. And so my dad – I remember a couple summers ago – was like, "Lynn, come look at this really cool family tree program." He was really excited. And I didn't have the heart to say to him at age twenty-seven, twenty-six, "You know, Dad, that's not my family." And he said, "Look, I'm going to put your name in." And he didn't even write "adopted" on it. He just drew the lines without thinking about adoption, or maybe he put it in some other section, but I never saw it. Because this computer program – it's really amazing. It'll print out your whole family tree if you put the names in. It's wonderful. But I remember thinking, "Gosh, I would really like to know my family history." And that's been something that like these family trees drive me nuts! I'm sitting there talking to Terence last night, and he wants me to help him trace his family tree. Because Terence is like on this Africa kick, and so wants to see if he can trace himself all the way back. So when he was talking about it I started thinking again, you know, about family trees, and that maybe – my sister and I for the last four years have gone back and forth – well, I've gone back and forth – about doing a search. But it's hard. Those are really hard things – kind of assumptions we make about family.

As Lynn makes evident in recounting the genealogical quests of her father and her (at that time) fiancé, the question of roots resonates beyond the lives of adoptees. Indeed, since Alex Haley's *Roots* was published and televised in the 1970s, researching genealogies has become a fairly common endeavor in the United States. Cultural studies scholar Julia Watson explains:

> Genealogy is an abiding passion and a big industry in the United States. It establishes the family's collective biography as a rooted network that has legitimately and verifiably inhabited the past. Tracing one's ancestors is a hedge against mortality in an increasingly mobile, global world. Genealogy specifies origin. Its fundamental assumption is categorical: Humans are defined by who and where we are "from" – in terms such as stock, blood, class, race. Books of genealogy refer to the "pedigree," the validated evidence documenting ancestral identity, transactions, and events. (emphasis added)[6]

Rooted, legitimately, origin, stock, blood, class, race, ancestral identity – the idea that identity is largely determined through our familial bloodlines is, indeed, a prevailing sociopolitical allegory that underlies social understandings and political discourse concerning relationships among self, family, community, culture, race, nationality, ancestry, and social inequality. Lynn articulates one of the central points of contention for transracial adoptees in grappling with questions of family history. The history of her white adoptive family reveals that they owned land "up near Harpers Ferry, which was really strange." For her, this was strange because Harpers Ferry was the site of a slave rebellion in the nineteenth century. This knowledge makes evident for her the divergent histories of her birth and adoptive families and points out that her own familial histories reflect the institutional racism embedded in the histories of whites and blacks in the United States. The racial differences and the lack of biological connections between Lynn and her adoptive family's ancestors preclude her accepting their forebears as her own. As she states, such knowledge makes her think, "Gosh, I would really like to know my family history." The sense of being a person without a family history can be overwhelming. As she demonstrates, for adoptees this longing for a family history often sparks a desire to search for birth relatives. Not all adoptees feel compelled to resolve this yearning for familial – and indeed racial – roots. Searching for their birth parents is a necessity for some, but others find resolution by claiming their adoptive family's history as their own or by immersing themselves in the history and cultures of blacks in Africa and the diaspora.

Reunions between adoptees and birth parents have become standard media narratives. On television, adoptees' struggles with a sense of mystery or confusion about identity, family, and history typically lead to searches for a "real self" that people assume will be revealed in reunions with birth families. The search is, perhaps, the most compelling aspect of adoption narratives. Stories of search and reunion have become common media scripts. Anthropologist Judith Modell comments: "Dramatized on television and reported in newspapers, reunions between long-lost kin resonate to Western literary and religious traditions. The sight of a child embracing a parent she has never known stirs the imagination, and also compels a reconsideration of love, parenthood, and relationship."[7] The search is often the fulcrum in the life histories of adoptees – in both fictive and actual lives. Anyone familiar with daytime television talk shows or made-for-TV movies could recite the typical search narrative. It is often scripted as an adoptee's identity quest – a search for the "true" self through access to forbidden knowledge, to a previously unknown origin narrative, to a family history, to a genetic and/or medical history, and often, foremost, to the birth parents (more often the birth mother). One of the primary tenets of the culture of the search community that both adoptees and birth parents often become part of while on their quests is that a reunion is the only way adoptees can heal their "primal wounds" and come to know their "real" selves. Indeed, in much of the search literature and television discourse, searching is discussed in ways that suggest it functions as a sort of rite of passage for adoptees, a rebirth through the rewriting of the origin narrative. This discourse is fueled by the tremendous loss that most adoptees feel, but it is infused with the power of biological and genetic explanations of the "nature" of identity.

Sociologist and adoptee Katarina Wegar's study of the adoption search movement in the contemporary United States found that popular search rhetoric, academic studies drawn on by search activists, and media representations of reunions among birth families focused strongly on biological sources of identity formation. In psychological research on the issue, adoptees were often represented as "genealogically bewildered" and driven by nature to search for their biological origins. Psychology functions here as a normalizing discourse, asserting that adoptees who profess not to feel the need to search are repressing their true selves; searching is thus represented as an expression of a universal human need.[8] While the desire to search for one's birth parents – and particularly for one's birth mother – is often keenly felt among adoptees, I spoke with a number of people who did not believe that searching was the only way they could know who they were.

Lynn was one of the people I spoke with who had ambivalent feelings about searching, and this was a point of connection between us from the first time we met. I first interviewed her several times in 1994; from that point we rarely saw each other, but we touched base periodically either by phone or through a common friend. The most recent interview I conducted with Lynn, in 1998, was structured as a dialogue focusing on the developments that had occurred in our lives since we last talked. Here we discuss an encounter I had at a birth parent/adoptee support group in which I was directly confronted with the ideology of biological origins that infuses the search movement.

— SANDI: I went to one [support group] that was for, um, mostly birth mothers, but also adoptees were welcome. And it was one of the most horrible experiences of my life! [laughs]

— LYNN: Of your life.

— SANDI: They jumped on me. They totally attacked me. And this woman was talking about how she wanted to find her birth son and everything and she said, "Well, if he's like me he'd be this way. If he's like his birth father he'd be this way." Going on and on about this. And I said, "Well, you know, he might be like his adopted parents, too." And just kind of added that perspective. And I said, "You know, I haven't found my birth parents, but I do know that I'm an awful lot like my adoptive father." And you know, there's some validity in that. And they just jumped on me like crazy. They were like, "You're deluded! You're only saying that because you've never found your birth parents, and if you did you would see that you're really not like your adoptive father, and . . ." I just could not believe it.

— LYNN: They're the people who . . . It's interesting that they have somehow bought into this that somehow you're gonna be unchanged by this environment you're in. That's wild!

— SANDI: It blew me away. Just blew me away.

Lynn and I share a resistance to the idea that biology fully defines our identities. Although a great deal of search rhetoric draws on this perspective, she and I both engage a system of meaning that places at least as much emphasis on culture as on biology.

Tensions between nature and nurture and between biology and culture are frequently present in discourse concerning adoptees. I employ the concept of social construction as a perspective that encompasses both culture and biology. To argue that identity is socially constructed is to see individual selves developing through complex interactions among biologically and genetically embodied people, cultural meaning systems, material circumstances, social institutions, public policies, and socioeconomic politics. With regard to the specific tension – generally present for adoptees – between heredity and environment, I accept recent scientific perspectives that emphasize the interdependence of these two categories and point out that the separation of the two is conceptual rather than practical. Indeed, in my view, the existence and use of these categories as separate forces shaping individuals reflects Western dualistic frames of organizing the world. I am not arguing that these are not *real* forces, though, since the widespread, unquestioning belief in and use of these two ways of explaining identity makes them real in their effects.

Genetics is one system of meaning available for explaining who we are, but let us be clear that none of us – adoptees and non-adopted people alike – knows our actual DNA structure. Rather, we infer these genetic maps from our phenotypic characteristics and by how such traits are similar to and different from those of our family members. Thus it is the cultural discourse of genetics, perhaps as much as our actual DNA, that gives meaning to our identities. The social weight of this meaning system is apparent in the life stories of adoptees who, in many cases, have no familial genetic touchstone by which to guide their construction of such narratives of family and self.

Media narratives often portray reunions as joyous, unproblematic events, but few televised versions go beyond the dramatic first meeting. In the lives of adoptees, reunion experiences range from life-affirming to disturbing. The primary difference from media narratives, however, is that in the lives of adoptees the reunion isn't the end of the story; it's just the beginning of what is often a profound redefinition of self.

Lynn and I were both born in 1965, and thus we were children in the 1970s when Alex Haley's *Roots* ignited widespread interest in genealogical research. I remember experiencing the miniseries, and later the book, in a very powerful way. It touched in me a longing – similar to Lynn's – for family history, particularly when I too was required to create a family tree for a school project. I remember sitting on the floor of my bedroom, wondering what it would be like to have a "real" family history. I was in fifth grade and had recently been introduced – by my teacher, who was also adopted – to the then-emergent idea that adoptees could search for birth parents. At the time it seemed to me the only way to claim a family history, and thus to find my "real" identity.

— SANDI: I want to go back to the family tree thing. Fourth grade? Was that the year *Roots*, the television series, was on?

— LYNN: I think so.

— SANDI: Because that comes up in the literature in the stories of transracial adoptees. And it also – I mean, I have similar experiences around those issues. Because in a way, it's like, okay, I can reconcile that I'm not biologically related to my family, but we are related by love and by law. But, you know, I didn't even *know* the people that came before me. So how can they be my family? And I actually – I ended up resolving it, I think, pretty well for myself. It ended up happening after my father died, when I was twenty-two, because I had to kind of renegotiate what those ties were going to mean. The metaphor that makes sense of it for me is a grafted tree.

— LYNN: Hmm.

— SANDI: If you take, you know, a peach tree and you graft it onto an apple tree, it's still a peach, but it's being nourished by the roots of an apple tree.

— LYNN: That's a very good analogy. I like that!

— SANDI: It really helped me! Because it's like all of a sudden I went, I *do* have some kind of claim on that history, because my parents are products of that history and, you know, who they are has grown through that.

— LYNN: Well, you know, I think I've never been forced to do that. Sometimes I like – my sister and I both – and I certainly think that this comes from being adopted and wrenched from a family. But I have dreams about her dying. She'll have the same types of dreams. It's weird. And I am just devastated because she is truly like my *tie*, like my *blood* in ways that I don't even. . . . Like people see us and they're amazed at how close we are. Like she's like my best friend. Which Terence is, like, "She can't be your best friend. She's your sister" [mocking him]. You know? He actually doesn't think that wives and husbands can be best friends. He has these notions that family aren't friends. It's weird. But we are best friends, *really*. And sometimes I think about if I lost her I would, in many ways, be forced to reconcile these things. Whereas now, she's there and I don't have to really push it too much. It's strange. I can't quite describe it. But she has the same types of anxiety dreams that I do. Which makes sense.

— SANDI: I cannot *imagine* having a birth relative. It's totally beyond my comprehension what it would be like to look into the eyes of someone that I'm related to biologically.

— LYNN: Well, you know when my brother had his first – when he had his son – I couldn't understand what he was talking about, because I've taken it for granted having a blood relative. When he and his wife had this child, who's now four, he kept going, "This is my blood. This is part of me." And we're like, "Chris, chill out. We all know it." But it became such a point, like a pivotal point in his life, that he had this blood relative. And what's interesting is after his son was born he searched for his mother.

— SANDI: My sister is searching right now.

— LYNN: Oh, really.

— SANDI: And she had to have kids for that reason. I mean, other reasons too, but that was a really important thing for her – was having biological ties.

— LYNN: Actually, when I was in high school I had a friend who found her – when I was eighteen years old I had a friend who found her mother. So I've always known people who have searched and found their parents. The one thing that has always kept me from doing it is it's incredibly unromantic. You know, she found her mother and her mother had four sons, and her dad was an alcoholic and had just gotten out of prison. And you know, her and her mother established some type of friendship, but it's not like this rosy thing that's gonna, "Oh, I'm gonna find this person and they're gonna be really rich and they're gonna be really wonderful, and they're gonna be so happy to have me back in their life!" That doesn't happen!

— SANDI: I don't have that feeling either.

While many adoptees feel compelled to search for their origins, others, like Lynn and I, do not. Neither perspective is right or wrong; rather, I offer this story as a counter to the dominant public view that adoptees are driven to search for their birth families, particularly their birth mothers. The public narrative has been limited in its representation of adoptive and birth families and identities; the actual stories complicate that view. Indeed, most of the life stories I heard were more complex, nuanced, and ambivalent than those presented in the media. The construction of meaning in human lives rarely fits neatly into the space of a television show or film.

Social Constructions of Race and Identity

Questions of family, race, and identity have been of fundamental importance in public dialogues concerning transracial adoption since it first emerged as a controversial issue in the early 1970s. This heated public debate has focused on the transmission of African American cultural identity to black and multiracial children adopted into white middle-class families.[9] The central question regarding the appropriateness of this social practice is whether or not white parents are capable of teaching their children African American culture and history and providing them with the skills they need to survive in this racially unequal society. Concerns over the transmission of identity have shaped public opinion and social policies regarding racial matching between children and parents for more than three decades.

Different approaches exist for studying racial identity. Perhaps the most widely known is the psychological research conducted by Robert T. Carter, William Cross, Janet Helms, and T. A. Parham, which tracks the development of racial identity through a four-stage model. Although some of my informants narrated their identity progression through similar stages, what is more striking to me is the depth and diversity within the developmental stages. I engage, instead, a life history approach that focuses on the insider's view – the ways in which people experience themselves in relation to family, community, culture, and society. This perspective provides a useful framework for considering the multiplicity of individual identities through an exploration of the various systems of cultural meaning they draw on in navigating their lives.

The concept of culture is often engaged as a category that describes groups of people. In this view, individuals either belong or do not belong to particular groups; they are either members or outsiders. I utilize a definition of culture as a system of meaning that individuals draw on to make sense of their worlds. This framework assumes that people construct their identities and navigate their lives through a variety of cultural meaning systems. In this view, not only do we all juggle a repertoire of cultural systems, but we engage various cultures in different ways and to different degrees. A number of cultural anthropologists have engaged this person-centered approach to ethnography, in which, as anthropologist John L. Caughey explains, "We see that we need to attend to the fact that it is not only modern communities but modern individuals that are multicultural. That is, contemporary Americans are likely to think about themselves and their worlds in terms of several different cultural models and also to play multiple social roles which are associated with and require operating with diverse and often contradictory systems of meanings."[10] This approach is particularly relevant in considering the identities of transracial adoptees, whose lives have been structured in ways that invite the engagement of multiple systems of cultural meaning. Renato Rosaldo affirms an approach to culture and identity that explores multiplicity and hybridity: "Creative processes of transculturation center themselves along literal and figurative borders where the 'person' is crisscrossed by multiple identities."[11]

With a few exceptions, most of the transracial adoptees I interviewed actively sought out African American cultures and communities in their struggles for self-understanding and social survival. The issues for most of them have involved which cultural meaning systems regarding race they had access to. This is a structural as well as a cultural consideration. Adoptees living in predominantly white communities rarely had access to insider views of black culture, and many of them reported drawing their views of African Americans from television.

Lynn, like most of the people I interviewed, found her parents' socialization around issues of race to be inadequate. It is important to contextualize their familial experiences within a broader societal framework. In public discussions of transracial adoption the question of culture is too often addressed solely at the individual and familial level, whereas access to and awareness of black culture is also a structural issue. Lynn's parents, like most white people who grew up and were educated in the 1950s and 1960s, lived in predominantly segregated communities and went to schools in which little attention, if any, was given to African American history or culture.

Indeed, in the 1970s, when Lynn and her siblings were growing up, the area they lived in was still profoundly segregated. When schools were desegregated by busing, the class differences between Lynn and the black children who were new to her school seemed so stark that she felt less comfortable with them than with whites with whom she had already established friendships. By the time she reached college she knew who Sojourner Truth, Harriet Tubman, and Frederick Douglas were – as she put it, she knew the "biggies" – but beyond this she had little knowledge of black culture or history. However, having been raised in a middle-class white family and community, she was well versed in white culture and history. It was not until she went to college that she began to explore African American history and culture and to question the way she had been raised, as she explains:

> I had decided to do a Black Studies minor, but continued to take like all these classes in Black Studies. Because I thought, "At least I better get educated, so I know what this is about." I took an Intro to the Black Woman, or whatever – uh, Black Women in America – with this professor that was wonderful. And so I started reading all that literature. And it just didn't add up in my head, that somehow someone had missed my education. Why didn't I know this stuff before? Why was I denied access to the black community before? So, of course, I blamed my parents.

Lynn describes this time in her life as her "radical black phase," a time when she questioned the racial assumptions she had been raised with, immersed herself in African American culture and history, and became part of her school's black community. Her immersion in black cultures was part of a search for an identity. It was often upon leaving home that the transracial adoptees I interviewed first began to grapple with the social and personal meanings of being black in the contemporary United States, and Lynn's story illustrates the power of self-discovery and transformation that is often involved in such a quest. Here she discusses her second semester in college, which she spent in Paris. Just before leaving school for the semester, she began dating a South African man.

— LYNN: And I had a black friend, like my [with emphasis] *first black friend*, who I'm still friends with.

— SANDI: God, you gave me chills. I mean, to be a sophomore in college, or whatever, and to have your first black friend is really – that's really powerful.

— LYNN: As a freshman in college. Yes. So Amanda Williams, who I'm still friends with, and who still drives me insane – but we were actually roommates when we were in Paris together. And she gave me some James Baldwin to read. So I read that and I thought about it. And she let me read like part of her journal. She kept a journal and she wrote poetry, and really a lot of it was about what it was like being black on an all-white campus, or being black on this tour. I mean it was really interesting. She's a really bright woman. She's working on her doctorate in chemical engineering. I mean, she's very smart. So I was reading this stuff, and started thinking, "Huh." And then I thought I should read some stuff about South Africa if I'm going to date this guy, so I started to buy books. I started to read books about Nelson Mandela being on Robben Island. And that started me thinking, "Why are white people doing this to black people?" And then I came back and went back to school. And Louis and I lived together. And Louis – it was interesting, too, because he was of mixed-race heritage. They call it "colored" in South Africa. But he was half Indian. His family had – they were Malay, and from New Delhi. And then his father was Sutu, so African. So within their own family they had this dichotomy between races, which in South Africa, as you can imagine, was really strong. So Louis was the most self-righteous black person I had ever met in my life. He just really really believed he was black, and he looked Indian. So people always said, "Oh, you're Indian." And he always said, "No, I'm African." And that completely, like changed my frame of mind. And he was – considered himself a Marxist, to top it off. So he's like espousing Marxist ideology all the time. This is the guy I got engaged to. And you know we had an awful marriage, but it completely transformed my identity. I mean, most of my friends at the university were Africans, so on some level they did not make that color differentiation. You know, that color stratification within the black community. Because Africa, the continent is made up of all sorts of people. And so we moved – I mean, we had friends who were South Africans and from Nigeria and Ethiopia. So we had this group of African people – and Liberia – who we're buddies with. And they were pretty radical. And then we started to – we used to go down to African Heritage House. I used to go down with him, and then I started going to the meetings. And then they would have sisters meetings, and so I would go to those. And I started taking – I remember, I'm so embarrassed I ever said this. I took this Intro to the Black Novel class in the Black Studies Department. It was the first semester I got back to school after being in Europe. And the teacher said, "Why are you here?" And everybody else had to go around and say – and I said, "Well, I'm here because I want to learn some-thing about my cultural identity." Which, you know, in that context was probably a little – they were probably like, "What the hell is she talking about?" Because they didn't know where I was coming from. You know, I started to read, you know, black writers for the first time. I mean, I knew who Harriet Tubman was and my mother gave me a book on Sojourner – I knew who Sojourner Truth was 'cause my mom gave me a book on her. They were like these isolated – I knew who Frederick Douglas was. I mean, I knew the biggies. . . . So I started, you know, Ralph Ellison. And reading this stuff that I didn't even know existed, and reading black po-etry. And it was really powerful.

— SANDI: I bet.

— LYNN: And so then I became – not to like my white family so much. And it became really hard for me to reconcile being – getting radicalized with this white, upper-class elite – which my family had become by that point.

This is how Lynn constructs her roots. She explores the routes of black culture as they intersect the various pathways she walks. During her "radi-cal black phase" she explored and claimed an insider view of black cul-tures, and since then she has also come to embrace the mainstream white cultural meaning systems she was raised with.

Although the experiences of the adoptees I interviewed varied widely, patterns emerged regarding their constructions of racial identity and their levels of comfort with issues of race. Racial identity was a profound issue for all of them, but the degree of struggle associated with this aspect of their lives varied depending on the racial attitudes of their parents, the racial makeup of their communities and schools, and the presence or ab-sence of African American adults in their lives. Adoptees from families that lived in racially integrated communities with parents whose advice and understanding regarding racism was systemic (that is, who moved the issue to a higher plane than that of individual behavior and attitudes) fared better than those whose parents explained racism as the ignorance of individual people. For the former, race and identity were still issues to be dealt with, but the level of struggle seemed more akin to the identity struggles many adoptees in same-race families experience. Transracial adoptees' struggles were more profound in families that lived in segre-gated white enclaves in which parents avoided the subjects of race and racism. One of the other important factors for those I interviewed was having other African Americans in their lives, particularly adults who were available for mentoring and support.

While tensions between biology and culture in the construction of self were evident in the adoptees' identity narratives, one overriding factor was present in every origin story I heard: the power of public policies and social institutions in constructing their lives as members of the families they were placed in. It was striking how aware most of them were of the public policy issues involved in the regulation of transracial adoptions; indeed, a number of them mentioned having researched the topic for school projects. Adoptees cannot help but be aware of the state's role in constructing who we are when the tales of our beginnings typically involve elements like "the home study" and being picked up at the agency rather than coming home from the hospital. For transracial adoptees, the apparent differences in commonly identified "racial characteristics" between their families and themselves led to common social interactions that pointed out these disjunctures and served to regularly remind them of the constructedness of their families and identities. Renato Rosaldo explains:

> More often than we usually care to think, our everyday lives are crisscrossed by border zones, pockets, and eruptions of all kinds. Social borders frequently become salient around such lines as sexual orientation, gender, class, race, ethnicity, nationality, age, politics, dress, food, or taste. Along with "our" supposedly transparent cultural selves, such borderlands should be regarded not as analytically empty transitional zones but as sites of creative cultural production that require investigation.[12]

Transracial adoptees can rarely "pass" as non-adopted people; their presence in white families often serves as a marker of familial border crossings.

Structuring Families and Race

Transracial adoption is represented in public discourse as a question of culture, focusing on how black children raised in white families will acquire survival skills and a positive sense of African American cultural identity. Yet, as Mary Helen Washington argued in her 1997 American Studies Association presidential address, "personal cross-cultural experiences only become comprehensible and liberatory when they are connected to a relevant institutional history."[13] The issues of "culture" that face transracially adoptive families and that characterize the public debate have been created and configured through such social structures as the child welfare system, the labor market, the widespread segregation of housing and education, and the criminal justice system, among others. As cultural studies scholars Sidonie Smith and Julia Watson explain, interacting with social institutions engenders engagement with "their already provided narratives of identity, their already mapped-out subject positions."[14] These social institutions operate in accordance with particular narratives about gender, race, family, and identity that both draw on and enact cultural assumptions regarding what kinds of families and citizens should be reinforced and reproduced.

The lives of adoptees demonstrate the complexities involved in the concept of the social construction of identity. "Social construction" is often taken to refer to the cultural or nurture side of the nature-nurture tension, but that assumption usually disregards the role of social structure in shaping and constructing individual identities. This is particularly important when considering the social construction of race. As the work of multiracial feminists has emphasized, considering the sources of diversity and difference solely in cultural terms obscures the history of oppression and inequality that various racial-ethnic groups have endured. Systemic racism and exclusionary public policies have, for example, led to different forms of family structure among African Americans, Latinos, Native Americans, and Asian Americans. Different racial-ethnic groups have been assaulted and oppressed by the state in various and unique ways, and thus cultural responses to social inequality – survival skills – have varied as well. Different relationships to social institutions such as the labor market, the social welfare system, and public education have, over time, led to different patterns of family formation among various racial-ethnic groups.

The state has historically reinforced some family forms while discouraging others, and this has been manifested in public policies and social attitudes that treat women differently based on their race and the race of their children. Maxine Baca Zinn explains the importance of viewing families as products of social structure, not only of culture: "Although Western feminist thought takes great care to underscore race and class differences, it still marginalizes racial-ethnic families as special 'cultural' cases. In other words, when it comes to thinking about family patterns, diversity is treated as if it were an intrinsic property of groups that are 'different,' rather than as being the product of forces that affect all families, but affect them in different ways."[15] Birth families are separated for countless reasons, including issues of economics, gender, or race. Social workers construct adoptive families according to the policies and practices of adoption agencies, which reflect social assumptions about what makes a good family. Indeed, the history of the U.S. public adoption system following World War II demonstrates that black and white unwed mothers were treated differently in relation to the "market" demand for healthy white infants for infertile middle-class white couples. Historian Rickie Solinger's study of single pregnancy prior to the legalization of abortion found that psychologists regularly counseled unwed white women that the only psychologically healthy and mature decision would be to relinquish their children; conversely, single black women were typically informed that there were no available adoptive homes for their babies and were urged to keep them.[16] Until reforms in the late 1960s and 1970s, the U.S. adoption system functioned to meet the "needs" of middle-class white infertile heterosexual couples for healthy white infants, and largely disregarded the needs of children of color for adoptive families. While the practice of transracial adoption that became more prevalent in the mid- and late 1960s represents a new focus on the placement of black children, it still operates within a framework that focuses on the needs of white prospective adoptive families.

Lynn discusses her origins:

> But it's hard, I mean, I think about it, you know, it's starting to stress me out more as I think about motherhood. And I never thought it would, but the more I think about having a kid, I think, "Well, am I just going to give it up and make them do a family tree that begins with me?!" Is that what their family life will be? Do I do a search? Do I find, like, this mother who couldn't cope [with having two biracial children]? And I doubt . . You know, she has a white kid. [After she relinquished Lynn and her sister to foster care, she gave birth to a white son whom she kept.] She chose to lead a certain type of life. You know, sometimes I think about, I remember this really came to me when I was like probably a sophomore in college and I was taking like a history – a black history class. And we got to the sixties, and one of the things the teacher really wanted to talk about was kind of the interracial relation-

ships that were going on. And I'm really a product of that. It was 1965; a lot of experimenting was going on. And so I'm a product of a very specific time too that sheds light on who I am. Whereas I look at like biracial kids now, and I think that their relationship to society is a little different. Oftentimes, there's not this kind of – I mean there is a little bit – but less of a stigma of having like a white parent and a black parent. I mean, you see that a lot more on the West Coast.

Lynn consciously locates herself as a product of the experimentation with interracial relationships that occurred in the 1960s. She mentions the "choice" her birth mother made to relinquish her two biracial daughters for adoption. However, this matter of "choice" is more complex than it appears. How was this "choice" circumscribed by ideological and structural forces in society? This was a white woman, married to a white man, who, as a result of an extended extramarital relationship, gave birth to two biracial daughters. We don't know what her options actually were. We don't know what happened to the birth father. We do know that in 1965 the employment prospects for a single white woman raising two children were not auspicious. We know that finding housing in the midwestern city they lived in, as a white woman with two biracial children, would have been difficult. We also know that a white woman who had "crossed the color line" would have been profoundly stigmatized by the white community in the 1960s. To what extent was her "decision" coerced? One of the most painful aspects of this story for Lynn is that after relinquishing her two daughters, her mother gave birth to and kept a white son. For Lynn this makes clear how profoundly her birth mother's "choice" was shaped by the prevailing race and gender norms of the time. The genealogy of her identity includes the social circumstances that led to her birth parents' decision to relinquish their children, the policies and practices of the child welfare system that placed them first in a black, working-poor foster home and then in an orphanage, and the social circumstances and public institutions that led to their adoption by white middle-class parents who raised them in a predominantly white community.

The issue of origins follows most adoptees throughout their lives; the stories they are told about their births and beginnings often change, depending on the inclinations of parents and social workers, discoveries of hidden identity documents, and/or finding or being found by birth parents. Thus our origin stories are told and retold, constructed and reconstructed as we continue to come-into-being. Adoptees often cite the lack of a birth story as one of the core issues in their struggles over identity and as a prime motivation for initiating a search for birth parents. Tales of being born – of physical birth – are often lacking for adoptees who don't know their birth parents, but the lack of factual birth narratives does not mean they have no origin stories.

Adoptees's origins seem, at times, more discursive than physical; many of our narratives begin with an anonymous infant written into being by a social worker in a secret file – the "sealed records" – that we are forbidden to see. The omniscient creator in our stories is the social worker as an agent of the state; she is the only person granted the power of legitimacy – the power to make the weighty decisions regarding who these anonymous infants will become and what families will transform them from illegitimate citizens to legitimate ones. She is the only person in possession of the complete stories of birth and origin; she is the state's guardian of knowledge, the keeper of our truths.

In the following excerpt from our most recent dialogue, Lynn and I discuss our birth ties. It is striking how integral adoption agencies and social workers are to this dialogue on our origins; they are the institutional mediators of our families and identities.

— LYNN: Suzanne [Lynn's sister] and I have begun to talk a little bit of my dad, in fact. My parents never talk with me about adoption issues, which I always find very interesting. They always talk to Suzanne. I don't know if it's because of her social work background that they feel like she has more of a handle on it or something and I'm just like this . . . ? I don't know what they think. They offered to actually hire a private detective for us to find our birth parents.

— SANDI: Do you want to?

— LYNN: Well, Suzanne and I have talked about it. And I kind of feel the urge as I get older more to find it. I mean, for me it's mostly [that] I've had actually some cervical health issues. They found pre-cancer cells on my cervix and so I'm, now I'm kind of getting more anxious about those types of issues than I had before. And so my sister and I have, you know, I finally told my sister, sure. But I'm not sure I wanna meet anybody. I mean . . . beyond . . .

— SANDI: It's really a trip. [laughs]

— LYNN: I mean, that's . . . for me it's just kind of knowing that that person is there. Like, who they are. Kind of what their biographical facts. Get the facts! I'm just, like, my life is so incredibly insane being a step-mother and being a wife and my family that I . . . It's hard for me to think about kind of meeting. But if this woman gave us up there must have been some very specific reasons. She has not put a search in our files, a request. My sister has checked our files periodically. Like she checks it every now and then just to see and she hasn't ever done that. So, that kind of to me is an indication.

— SANDI: She may not know she can do that, though.

— LYNN: Right. She may not know.

— SANDI: I didn't even know.

— LYNN: Right.

— SANDI: That's how it happened to me. I was interviewing social workers in California for my dissertation and I was kind of following a trail of connections through agencies and I ended up where I was adopted. So, I, like, told the social worker, you know, as I sat down to interview her and she was all into it. She went, "Oh, my goodness. You've signed one of our waivers, haven't you?" And I was like, "What? What are you talking about?"

— LYNN: Uh huh.

— SANDI: So, she said, "Well, you know, in California if you sign a waiver [of] rights of confidentiality and both parties have done that then they can match you up." So, they can't go searching for you . . .

— LYNN: Right. But like you're both . . .

— SANDI: But if you're both in there. So, I was like, "Well I really want medical information and stuff, and so could I have that?" And whatever else on the paper and I did not even, I didn't even really think about it. I just kind of did it. Thinking, you know, it'll sit in the files.

— LYNN: Yeah.

— SANDI: You know? And, as I walked out I kind of thought to myself, god, wouldn't it be something if she was searching for me?

— LYNN: Yeah.

— SANDI: 'Cause I – I didn't feel like I needed to search. So, you know, the dissertation was some kind of search.

— LYNN: Mm hmm.

— SANDI: Only a couple of weeks later I got a letter saying she had been searching for me for . . . well, she had signed the letter in 1990.

— LYNN: Wow.

— SANDI: The waiver. She'd actually been searching for me for like thirteen years.

— LYNN: Mm!

— SANDI: Since I turned eighteen.

— LYNN: Hmm. Well, that's a very exciting . . .

— SANDI: Yeah.

— LYNN: . . . What's become a bigger issue now is having children. And my parents can . . . are appalled that my sister and I don't have kids yet. And my dad keeps saying, "You have these great genes. How come you're not gonna pass them on?" But, in fact, I was thinking . . . have been thinking ever since this cervical issue came up because now I have to wait until all these Pap smears come back clean over like a year or two-year period. But it's . . . it then becomes like what kind of legacy. It's like, are Suzanne and I it? Like, are we kind of the end of the road? Or do you decide to have kids and then start up all, like, do you decide then to test on your genes for a generation, or . . . For my brother that was why he had kids . . . Chris. Because he always felt like he was so alone in the world. And that by having a child he in fact, finally, had a real family, even though he had an adopted family. By having the son, and then having his wife divorce him was the most . . . even though it was almost 100% his fault. . . . I hate to side with my sister-in-law [laughs] because now she's really, really mean to him and I disagree . . . but . . . He was not a very good husband at all. But his son is the most important thing in his life. Partly because of that kind of history and family and blood.

— SANDI: I remember you talked about when he was first born, that Chris was like, "He's mine!"

— LYNN: Yeah.

— SANDI: "He's my blood!" [laughs] You know!

— LYNN: Yeah. And so . . . and he still has that kind of attitude about it.

— SANDI: Well, you know, we've talked before. There was a section where we were talking about, you were talking about your tie with Suzanne. . . . And how that blood tie is really profound.

— LYNN: Mm hmm.

— SANDI: And I was saying, "You know, I cannot relate at all. I cannot imagine looking into the eyes of somebody that I'm related to." And when that did finally happen for me I really . . . I was right before. I couldn't imagine it. I . . . you know, it was like . . .

— LYNN: Yeah.

— SANDI: I feel like I got a little bit of a clue about what other people experience in a very unconscious way and I realized how different it is to be adopted . . .

— LYNN: Mm hmm.

— SANDI: . . . as I, like, I mean, I look just like her (my birth mother). And especially with my eyes . . . are exactly like her. They're the same color. And to look her in the eye is just mind boggling to me. Like, I'll look at her . . . or just . . . I came from her body? You know, it's just beyond comprehension to me. It still makes no sense in a way.

— LYNN: Yeah.

— SANDI: You know? It's really a strange thing and it really . . . I think you can go on and pretend when you're white and you're adopted by a white family. You can often pretend that you're "normal," you know?

— LYNN: Yes, you can.

— SANDI: But inside you don't feel that . . . usually . . .

— LYNN: Or the people are always saying, "You look just like your mother." And not knowing that you're adopted.

— SANDI: Right. Right. But this really made me go . . . Okay. There's stuff people just take for granted that I just don't even get, still. You know?

— LYNN: You know there's a lot about – it's interesting – about being adopted and, like, even when you tell people, even today . . . I don't tell very many people. It's interesting.

In this conversation, Lynn and I touch on some of the profound ways that adoptees experience a sense of difference from other people. I find that people are fascinated by the fact that I have met my birth mother and developed a relationship with her. It goes beyond mere curiosity; at times I feel like I'm being viewed as a social experiment. I often have the sense that my story provides listeners with a sense of vicarious adventure in the realm of identity. This often collides with my own sense of existential vertigo around these issues. Lynn too has expressed that people are often either fascinated or put off by the facts and stories of her adoption.

The question I was asked most frequently by both the adoptees and the social workers I interviewed was whether or not I had searched for my birth parents (there was often an implicit "yet" attached to the inquiry). I explained that I hadn't and that at that time in my life I didn't feel compelled to search. Unlike many of the people I talked with, I am quite resistant to the idea that I can't know who I "really" am until I know my birth parents. For those who continued to probe I shared that there had been times, particularly during my teen years, when I had felt that need, but that, as curious as I've always been, the drive had dissipated in my early twenties. I never ruled out the possibility that I might, at some time in the future, embark on such a quest.

In January 1996, while concluding my interviews in California, I found myself, through a series of connections between area agencies, sitting in the lobby of the agency through which I was adopted, waiting to interview a social worker. I couldn't help thinking: "I came from here. This is the place where it was determined who I was to become. And somewhere in this building is the file holding my sealed adoption records – my identity papers, those magical, ominous keys to the story of my birth, my beginnings, my possibilities, the original shadows of a self I might have become." I've never talked to an adoptee whose records were sealed for whom this mythical, elusive file does not stir both longing and fear. What narratives of truth might those government forms and clinical observations reveal?

The stories opened by the information in my adoption file were both familiar and foreign narratives about my birth, my birth parents, and their families. This file felt, at times, like a Pandora's box of new "family" ties. I was suddenly overwhelmed with new "relatives" – how do I refer to my birth father's sister, my birth mother's stepfather, my three new "half birth" siblings? What do "blood" ties mean when they are divorced from ties of emotional, familial, and cultural meaning? The stories they told me about themselves, their families, and their ancestors didn't fit into any organizational frameworks in my head. This wasn't simply new information about my family; it was a fundamentally new kind of information, a new cultural category of meaning – biological kinship – about which I had no experiential or tangible knowledge. What does it, can it, should it mean to a thirty-one-year-old woman who was raised as a WASP-ish Lutheran and now leans toward Eastern thought to learn she is biologically half Jewish? What is my ethnicity when I'm Jewish by birth but haven't been raised with the cultural knowledge telling me what that means? The shadow identity that has haunted me – a self I might have been – now has a name. How does Sandra Patton incorporate a spectral self named Nicole Goldberg?!

The vigorous flow of life stories that baptized me into these families wreaked havoc on my sense of family history and identity. I didn't – and in some senses still don't – know how to incorporate their family histories into my own life story. What might it mean to my current self that I would have been half Jewish in an alternative life?

We make sense of our lives not only through familial and cultural narratives we collect from our families, our communities, and the media but also through our interactions with social institutions. My own experience makes evident the power of a governmental agency and its application of hegemonic definitions of family, ethnicity, gender, and class. The one-page, handwritten sheet of information my parents were given about my birth parents and their families provided such information as the height, weight, hair and eye color, skin tone, age ranges (teens), occupations, and ethnicities of my birth parents, as well as the occupations, ages, and brief medical histories of their families. However, this documentation of my birth family's history does not match the story told in my case file. Most of the information is accurate, but the inconsistencies are revealing. Anything that may have indicated a "deviance" from the "mainstream" white nuclear family ideal prevalent in 1965 was either left out or changed. The most glaring omission concerns ethnicity. I was told that one birth parent was Irish, Scottish, and English and the other was German and Polish. The information that my birth father is Jewish was left out. My birth mother was told that because I was a white infant I would be placed immediately, yet I remained in foster care for almost four months before I was adopted. My reading of this is that the agency probably spent the almost four months I stayed in foster care trying to match me with a Jewish family – it was standard practice during that time to make close ethnic and religious matches when possible. By the time I was a few months old it was evident that with my red hair and fair skin I didn't "look Jewish," so I was matched with my adoptive parents, who were Irish, English, and Scottish, and German and Swedish. In 1965, when adoption records were supposed to be irrevocably sealed, I assume my case worker thought no one would ever detect the omission. Information that might have indicated that my birth parents' families deviated from mainstream middle-class gender identities was changed as well. My birth mother's mother was listed as a housewife. The case file reveals that she was a waitress and a seasonal cannery worker. Even the minor disability of my birth father – one arm was slightly deformed at birth – was left out. I was quite literally "whitewashed" and "rewritten" – symbolically born anew – through the selective discourse of the social welfare system.

Our life stories make evident the slippery quality of identity. Here Lynn and I discuss the fact that we both found out as adults that one of our birth parents was Jewish.

— SANDI: You're half Jewish biologically, right?

— LYNN: Mm hmm.

— SANDI: What does that mean to you?

— LYNN: Not much. [laughs] I hate to say it. I mean, it's not much. I don't . . . I keep thinking . . . it's interesting, though, because I've completely avoided going to the Holocaust museum. Terence and I don't live, like, that far from it.

— SANDI: Oh, wow.

— LYNN: I mean, I know that I just know . . . I can't emotionally deal with that 'cause I feel like there's some connection to that. On the other hand, I don't go around telling very many people I'm Jewish because most people would be like, "Yeah, whatever." I mean, I guess it would be different if it was an active parent in my life. But the fact that it's this kind of disconnection . . . I mean, in theory I'm Jewish because my mother was. It passes through the woman.

— SANDI: Oh, yeah. See, for me it's my father. So I'm not even technically . . .

— LYNN: Yeah. So technically I am. But it's not what's interesting. I don't know if I told you, I was obsessed with the Holocaust.

— SANDI: Oh, really?

— LYNN: And, like, Israel when I was in high school. I would read all this stuff on the . . .

— SANDI: Did you know that then?

— LYNN: No! And I would read like all this . . . I was obsessed with it. It was weird. I read all of these books on the Holocaust.

— SANDI: I actually, I read a fair amount too, now that I think about it.

— LYNN: Yeah.

— SANDI: Um . . . The Hiding Place.

— LYNN: And all these kind of, yeah, narratives about growth and . . .

— SANDI: Yeah.

— LYNN: So I went through kind of this phase about it, but it's not as much as an adult. And I guess I just don't . . . it's not when I go to synagogue with my girlfriend that I feel like at home there. I don't. My family was raised a Unitarian and that's where I feel at home. And then if we're talking about a religious place where you go to . . . that's where I'm comfortable. So, no. It doesn't mean that much to me. I don't think it means to my sister either.

— SANDI: When did you find out?

— LYNN: When she dug around in our files.

— SANDI: Oh.

— LYNN: 'Cause it was listed on the file. So, you know how she . . . best of all stories [laughs] . . . even to going and getting our file. Gets fired over that. Yeah.

— SANDI: Wow. I mean, I'm kinda of the same way. When I first found out it was like, whoa! And I thought about it and I just don't even, I don't even know how to get my head around it.

— LYNN: Yeah, I know.

— SANDI: You know. It's like, I do feel like I have a different sense of the history of the Holocaust now. 'Cause I know that there were people that I am biologically related to that were killed.

— LYNN: Sure. Yeah.

— SANDI: You know. So . . . it's just a . . . I went with a friend right after I found this out to Rosh Hashanah services. And I was sitting there and I was looking around and the music was beautiful and everything was really beautiful. And people were so moved and really into it. And the looks on their faces were like what I see when I go to, or what I feel sometimes when I go to, like, Christmas service or something.

— LYNN: Right.

— SANDI: It's that familiar, comforting old thing and not that I'm even religious. But it's that familiar, comforting thing. And I can't relate. And I find that – I mean, I've said, and people that know me well agree with this – it would have made more sense to me to find out I was black.

— LYNN: Yeah.

— SANDI: You know what I mean?

— LYNN: Completely, yes.

— SANDI: Because I know about that.

— LYNN: Yeah.

— SANDI: I mean, I know about Jewish culture to a certain extent. I have a lot of friends, but I don't have the feeling of identification there. Whereas with African American culture I do feel an identification and I feel a part of it in my own way. I don't feel that way with Jewish culture. I feel like a complete outsider.

— LYNN: A total alien. Like it's such, it's so removed from who I am. I mean, it's a beautiful culture and I'm sure if someone knew they were Jewish and they were saying those things there that, you know, you have this . . . It's that same notion that this is a birth parent or biological parent. There's that kind of disjuncture there. That you know that there is this other set of people who are blood related to you . . . but . . .

— SANDI: Right. Yeah.

— LYNN: It's not like this everyday reality for me, I guess.

— SANDI: Yeah.

— LYNN: I mean, since I know who they are; they're in my space . . . that we interact. Or, and to be honest, I can't – I keep coming back to this – I really can't imagine meeting a birth parent. Going through all of this and having, like, learning this. It just seems like one of those really bizarre and disjointed experiences.

The disjuncture between the lives we've lived and the other possible lives we might have lived raise provocative questions about how identities are shaped by biology, cultural meaning systems, and social institutions and policies. As James Clifford writes: "Ethnography is actively situated *between* powerful systems of meaning. It poses its questions at the boundaries of civilizations, cultures, classes, races, and genders" (emphasis in source).[17] The gaps between who we are and who we might have been are a rich site to explore in attempting to understand how individuals in the contemporary United States construct meaningful lives for themselves through the available systems of meaning, in their sociopolitical contexts.

Conclusion

The problematics of being and meaning are not solely the province of adoptees. The shifting narratives of self that adoptees may fashion throughout their lives speak beyond the specificities of familial experiences. Their lives point out the contingency of identity, the tenuousness of coherence, the fictional character of all human life stories. Adoptees are not the only people asking "Who am I really?" They are not alone in receiving conflicting stories about who we are and how we should be. It is not only adoptees who must construct a sense of self through partial familial "truths" and convoluted cultural "lies."

We all write and rewrite ourselves into being as we continually construct and refine our life stories throughout the course of our lives. Yet, as the identities of adoptees make apparent, the scripts we are given are not solely our own. As Smith and Watson explain, "On a daily basis, then, personal narrators assume the role of the bricoleur who takes up bits and pieces of the identities and narrative forms available and, by disjoining and joining them in excessive ways, creates a history of the subject at a precise point in time and space" (emphasis in source).[18] We make sense of our lives not only through familial and cultural narratives we collect from our families, our communities, and the media but also through our interactions with social institutions. As cultural studies scholar Wahneema Lubiano explains: "I am interested in under what circumstances, for whom, and to do what in the world the political subject is constructed. In other words, *the state thinks the subject too.* Thus, to some extent, what we think of ourselves in relation to the world, what we imagine ourselves to be in relation to the world, is also, under most circumstances, at least partially a state project" (emphasis added).[19] The identities of adoptees are constructed and shaped through a broad range of discursive sources, including the politics of family, race, and poverty; social policies regulating governmental aid; public policies governing child welfare and adoption; the practices of adoption agencies; available cultural meaning systems; media narratives; the social relations they are part of in their communities; and the enculturation they receive in their families.

Consideration of how the lives of adoptees have been constructed through social institutions and the policies that govern them provokes a retooling of our understandings of race, family, and identity as socially constructed. Attending to the forces of social structure in the shaping of people's lives broadens and enhances approaches that only consider culture and biology; such attention displaces frameworks that obscure the role of power in the development and maintenance of families and identities of various races and ethnicities.

Although people who were not adopted cannot point so easily to the role of the state in determining who they are, I would argue that lives and identities are continually shaped and constructed in interaction with myriad social institutions in subtle ways that our cultural assumptions about individuality typically prevent us from seeing. Definitions of race and ethnicity, along with gender, class, disability, and sexual orientation, are inscribed in and enforced through such social institutions as the educational system, the social welfare system, and the labor market, and they are regulated through such politically charged policies as immigration laws, welfare legislation, and affirmative action measures. As Renato Rosaldo explains: "All of us inhabit an interdependent . . . world marked by borrowing and lending across porous national and cultural boundaries that are saturated with inequality, power, and domination."[20] All of us living in the contemporary United States must navigate such racial terrain as multiply defined, multicultural people. Perhaps we can draw on the experiences of transracial adoptees in charting the routes of our identities.

Notes

Introduction

1. For more on biculturalism see, for example, David C. Pollock and Ruth E. Van Reken, *Third Culture Kids: The Experience of Growing Up among Worlds* (Yarmouth ME: Intercultural Press, 2001); and Claudine C. O'Hearn, *Half and Half: Writers on Growing Up Biracial and Bicultural* (New York: Pantheon Press, 1998).

Chapter 1. Individuals and Their Cultures

1. On ethnographic practice see Robert Emerson, *Contemporary Field Research* (Prospect Heights IL: Waveland, 2001); and James Clifford, "Spatial Practices: Fieldwork, Travel, and the Disciplining of Anthropology," in his *Routes: Travel and Translation in the Late Twentieth Century* (Cambridge: Harvard University Press, 1997), 52–91.

2. On cultural complexity see Ulf Hannerz, *Cultural Complexity: Studies in the Social Organization of Meaning* (New York: Columbia University Press, 1992).

3. For reviews of life history research see Gelya Frank, "The Story of the Life History," *American Anthropologist* 97, no. 1 (1995): 145–48; and Lawrence C. Watson and Maria-Barbara Watson-Franke, *Interpreting Life Histories* (New Brunswick NJ: Rutgers University Press, 1985).

4. Within the culture of ethnography, the individual one interviews has traditionally been referred to as one's "informant." Many ethnographers now avoid this term due to its objectifying and othering connotations. Here I will generally use the terms "research participant," "research partner," or occasionally "subject" to refer to the person to be interviewed.

5. For one take on person-centered ethnography see Robert I. Levy and Douglas W. Hollan, "Person-Centered Interviewing and Observation," in *Handbook of Methods in Cultural Anthropology*, ed. H. Russell Bernard (Walnut Creek CA: AltaMira, 1998), 333–64.

6. For important takes on individual multiculturalism see Ward H. Goodenough, *Culture, Language, and Society* (Menlo Park CA: Benjamin Cummings, 1981); Anthony F. C. Wallace, *Culture and Personality* (New York: Random House, 1970); and Peter Caws, "Identity: Cultural, Transcultural, and Multicultural," in *Multiculturalism: A Critical Reader*, ed. David Theor Goldberg (Cambridge: Blackwell, 1994), 371–81.

7. For approaches to cultural traditions see Michael Agar, *Language Shock* (New York: William Morrow, 1994); Charlotte Linde, *Life Stories* (New York: Oxford University Press, 1993); Bradd Shore, *Culture in Mind* (New York: Oxford University Press, 1996); and Chris McCollum, "Relatedness and Self Definition: Two Dominant Themes in Middle Class Americans Life Stories," *Ethos* 30, nos. 1–2 (2002): 113–39.

8. One way of approaching the relationship between an individual and a cultural tradition is to borrow a framework that British Cultural Studies scholars have used for thinking about the relationship between an individual and a form of media – that is, does the person have a "dominant," "negotiated," or "oppositional" relationship to a given tradition? See John Finke, "British Cultural Studies and Television," in *Channels of Discourse, Reassembled*, ed. Robert Allen (Chapel Hill: University of North Carolina Press, 1992), 284–326.

Chapter 2. Methods in Life History Research

1. Barbara Myerhoff, *Number Our Days* (New York: Simon and Schuster, 1978), 18.

2. Jacques Maquet, *Introduction to Aesthetic Anthropology* (Reading MA: Addison Wesley, 1971), 2.

3. On ethical issues in interviews and fieldwork see James Spradley, *The Ethnographic Interview* (New York: Holt, Rinehart and Winston, 1979); Margaret D. LeCompte, Jean J. Schensul, Margaret R. Weeks, and Merrill Singer, *Researcher Roles and Research Partnerships* (Walnut Creek CA: Altamira Press, 1999); and Elizabeth Murphy and Robert Dingwall, "The Ethics of Interviewing," in *Handbook of Ethnography*, ed. Paul Atkinson, Amanda Coffey, Sarah Delamont, John Loffland, and Lyn Loffland (Thousand Oaks CA: Sage, 2001), 339–51.

4. For more on ethics see Barbara W. Sommer and Mary Kay Quinlan, *The Oral History Manual* (Walnut Creek CA: Altamira, 2002).

5. On cultural interviewing see Spradley *The Ethnographic Interview*, 55–68; Grant McCracken, *The Long Interview* (Newbury Park CA: Sage, 1988); and Sommer and Quinlan, *The Oral History Manual*.

6. For a discussion of using photography, video, and hypermedia in ethnography see Sarah Pink, *Doing Visual Ethnography* (Thousand Oaks CA: Sage, 2001).

7. On observational fieldwork see Robert Emerson, Rachel Fretz, and Linda Shaw, *Writing Ethnographic Fieldnotes* (Chicago: University of Chicago, 1995), 66–107.

8. In addition to the manual forms of sorting notes that are recommended in many books on ethnographic method, several computer software programs for sorting qualitative research materials are available, including ETHNOGRAPH. Information on ETHNOGRAPH can be reviewed online at www.Qualis Research.

com. See also Nigel Fielding, "Computer Applications in Qualitative Research," in Atkinson et al., *Handbook of Ethnography*, 453–67.

Chapter 3. Individual Identities, Multiple Cultures

1. For a review of categories of difference and their intersection see Lynn Weber, *Understanding Race, Class, Gender, and Sexuality* (New York: McGraw Hill, 2001). On personal narratives dealing with oppression and resistance, see, for example, Gwendolyn Etter-Lewis and Michele Foster, eds., *Unrelated Kin: Race and Gender in Women's Personal Narratives* (New York: Routledge, 1996).

2. Joshua C. Woodfork, "Same Story, Different Domain: An Ethnographic Study of the Chat Room Experiences of Bisexual/Gay Biracial Young Men" (paper presented at the Constructing Cyberculture(s) Conference, University of Maryland, College Park, April 6, 2001).

3. For his work on breakdowns and rich points see Michael Agar's *Language Shock* and his *Speaking of Ethnography* (Newbury Park CA: Sage, 1988).

4. On identification exercises for actors, many of which are applicable to explorations in life history, see Uta Hagen, *A Challenge for the Actor* (New York: Scribner, 1991).

Chapter 4. Negotiating Cultures and Values

1. See Paul Pederson, *The Five Stages of Culture Shock* (Westport CT: Greenwood Press, 1995).

2. George and Louise Spindler, *The American Cultural Dialogue and Its Transmission* (New York: Falmer Press, 1991).

3. Lila Shah, "Being Indian in America: My Ethnic Roots and Me," in *Becoming American, Becoming Ethnic*, ed. Thomas Dublin (Philadelphia: Temple University Press, 1996), 211–12.

4. John L. Caughey, "Gina as Steven: The Social and Cultural Dimensions of a Media Relationship," *Visual Anthropology Review* 10, no. 1 (1994): 126–35.

5. Sudhir Kakkar, *Shamans, Mystics, and Doctors* (New York: Knopf, 1982), 9.

6. For a detailed discussion of this case see Caughey, "Gina as Steven."

7. On the cultural dimensions of dreams, media use, and internal dialogues see John L. Caughey, *Imaginary Social Worlds: A Cultural Approach* (Lincoln: University of Nebraska Press, 1984); and Dorothy Holland, William Lachicotte Jr., Debra Skinner, and Carole Cain, *Identity and Agency in Cultural Worlds* (Cambridge: Harvard University Press, 1999), especially chapters 3 and 11.

Chapter 5. Writing Multiple Cultures in Life History

1. Vincent Crapanzano, *Tuhami: Portrait of a Moroccan* (Berkeley CA: University of California Press, 1980).

2. On issues involved in showing ethnographic accounts to informants see Caroline B. Brettel, ed., *When They Read What We Write: The Politics of Ethnography* (Westport CT: Bergin and Garvey, 1993).

3. For a scary account of deception in life history, including attention to what the ethnographer wants to believe, see Bruce Jackson, "The Perfect Informant," in *The World Observed: Reflections on the Fieldwork Process*, ed. Bruce Jackson and Edward D. Ives (Chicago: University of Chicago Press, 1996), 206–26.

4. On making the story of our own experience useful to life history see Ruth Behar, *The Vulnerable Observer* (Boston: Beacon Press, 1996).

5. See, for example, Ivor F. Goodson, "The Story So Far: Personal Knowledge and the Political," in *Life History and Narrative*, ed. J. Amos Hatch and Richard Wisniewski (Washington DC: Falmer Press, 1995); and compare Lyn Weber's argument for balancing research on the societal level with attention to the micro level as developed in her *Understanding Race, Class, Gender, and Sexuality* (Boston: McGraw Hill, 2001).

Reading 3. Needle and Thread

1. Shmuel preferred the term *Jewish* to *Yiddish* in referring to his native language in order to emphasize its status as a bona fide language and not, as some supposed, a mere dialect.

2. All right; so.

3. The one who sings passages of the liturgy in synagogue services.

4. Synagogue.

5. Peasants or farmers; in this context, ignoramuses.

6. Homes for the elderly.

7. Platform from which the Torah is read.

8. Non-Jewish boy.

Reading 5. "That Really Happened"

1. Quotes from reenactors cited in this essay are drawn from the personal interviews I conducted with them as well as from e-mails written by reenactors and sent to various reenactor newsgroups, which I followed for several years. They are also drawn from reenactors' written responses to a nine-page survey on reenacting that I mailed to more than five hundred twentieth-century war reenactors in the United States.

Reading 6. A Chameleon-Like Approach

1. Epigraph. Ruth Behar, *The Vulnerable Observer: Anthropology That Breaks Your Heart*

(Boston: Beacon Press, 1996), 13. Behar insists that the ethnographer place himor herself as part of the subject.

2. Joshua C. Woodfork, "Journal: Semester at an HBCU" (spring 1996).

3. Naomi Zack, *Race and Mixed Race* (Philadelphia: Temple University Press, 1993).

4. Zack, *Race and Mixed Race*; Naomi Zack, ed. *American Mixed Race: The Culture of Microdiversity* (Lanham MD: Littlefield & Rowman, 1995); Lise Funderburg, *Black, White, Other: Biracial Americans Talk about Race and Identity* (New York: William Morrow and Co., 1994); Maria P. P. Root, ed., *Racially Mixed in America* (Newbury Park CA: Sage, 1992; Root, ed., *The Multiracial Experience* (Thousand Oaks CA: Sage, 1996). Other works include Carol Camper, ed., *Miscegenation Blues: Voices of Mixed Race Women* (Toronto: Sister Vision Press, 1994), and the following memoirs: Gregory Howard Williams, *Life on the Color Line* (New York: Dutton, 1995); James McBride, *The Color of Water* (New York: Riverhead Books, 1996); and Scott Minerbrook, *Divided to the Vein* (New York: Harcourt Brace, 1996). This scholarship/autobiography worked to overturn the myth of the "tragic mulatto" and raised new questions about racial identity. Much has been published in the last few years. For a more detailed overview, see Joshua C. Woodfork, "Shifting Whiteness: A Life History Approach to U.S. White Parents of 'Biracial' or 'Black' Children" (Ph.D. diss., University of Maryland, 2005), chapter 2.

5. Epigraph. Funderburg, *Black, White, Other*, 378.

6. Epigraph. Patricia J. Williams, *The Alchemy of Race and Rights* (Cambridge: Harvard University Press, 1991), 226–27.

7. Epigraph. Martha Minow, *Not Only for Myself: Identity, Politics, and the Law* (New York: The Free Press, 1997), 39.

8. Ania Loomba, *Colonialism/Postcolonialism* (London: Routledge, 1998), 173.

9. John L. Caughey, this volume. See especially chapters 4 and 5.

10. Behar, *The Vulnerable Observer*, 13.

Reading 7. The Sound of It Stayed in My Ears

1. Mari Evans, "And the Old Women Gathered (The Gospel Singers)," in *It's a Woman's World: Century of Women's Voices in Poetry*, ed. Neil Philip (New York: Dutton, 2000), 78.

2. Here and throughout this essay I use pseudonyms to respect the interviewees' concern for privacy. In some cases, the women and their families have achieved prominence in their communities and are uncomfortable identifying themselves as former domestics.

3. Anansee is a spider who is small and always crafty. This small insect always creates the resources it needs to survive. Anansee stories are always the model for

small, insignificant people who continuously create something good out of the problems of life. See W. Bruce Willis, *The Adinkra Dictionary: A Visual Primer on the Language of Adinkra* (Washington DC: The Pyramid Complex, 1998), 76–77.

4. Nell Irving Painter, *We Were Always Free: The Maddens of Culpepper County, Virginia: A 200-Year Family History* (New York: Vintage Press), ix–x.

5. Florette Henri, *Black Migration: Movement North, 1990–1920* (Garden City NY: Anchor Books, 1975), x.

6. Zora Neale Hurston. *Their Eyes Were Watching God* (Urbana: University of Illinois Press, 1978), 31–32.

7. Jacqueline Jones, *Labor of Love, Labor of Sorrow* (New York: Basic Books, 1985), 158; Gloria Hull, *Color, Sex and Poetry: Three Women Writers of the Harlem Renaissance* (Bloomington: Indiana University Press, 1987), 3–4.

8. Henri, *Black Migration*, vii–xi.

9. Sara Lawrence Lightfoot, *Balm in Gilead* (Reading MA: Addison-Wesley, 1988), xix.

10. Elizabeth Clark-Lewis, *Living In, Living Out: African American Domestics in Washington, D.C., 1910–1940* (Washington DC: Smithsonian Institution Press, 1994) (hardback); see also *Living In, Living Out: African American Domestics and the Great Migration* (New York: Kodansha Press, 1996).

11. Compare with Stephanie J. Shaw, *What a Woman Ought to Be and to Do* (Chicago: University of Chicago Press, 1997), xi; and Rosalyn Terborg-Penn, *African American Women in the Struggle for the Vote, 1850–1920* (Bloomington: Indiana University Press, 1998), 159.

12. Robin D. G. Kelley, "We Are Not What We Seem: Rethinking Black Working Class Opposition in the Jim Crow South," *Journal of American History* 80 (June 1993): 75–112; David R. Roediger, *The Wages of Whiteness* (New York: Verso, 1991), vii–viii; Charles Dickens, "Washington: The City of Magnificent Intentions," in *American Notes for General Circulation* (Avon: Penguin Press, 1975), 163, 168–69, 177.

13. Alyce Gullattee, "Psychiatric Factors to Consider in Research on the Black Woman," *Journal of Afro-American Issues* 2 (summer 1974): 199–203.

14. Daniel E. Sutherland, *Americans and Their Servants* (Baton Rouge: Louisiana State University Press, 1981), 128.

15. Robin D. G. Kelley, *Race Rebels* (New York: Free Press, 1996), 35–53; Gloria Wade Gayles, *Pushed Back to Strength* (Boston: Beacon Press, 1993), 4; Richard Wright, *Twelve Million Black Voices* (1941; New York: Thunder's Mouth Press, 1988), 10; Zora Neale Hurston, *Mules and Men* (1935; New York: Harper and Row, 1990), 2; Clark-Lewis, *Living In, Living Out*, 41–44. Peculiarly, although the women interviewed for this study recalled their training, they had difficulty articulating the methodology of their "fool Miss Ann" training. Harold Garfinkel explores this difficulty in *Studies in Ethnomethodology* (Englewood Cliffs NJ: Prentice Hall, 1967), 9, 38.

16. Painter, *We Were Always Free*, ix.

17. Paul Lawrence Dunbar, "We Wear the Mask," in *The Complete Works of Paul Lawrence Dunbar*, ed. W. D. Howells (New York: Dodd, Mead, 1922), 71.

18. Kelley, *Race Rebels*, 32, 51–52.

19. Jacquelyn Grant, "Black Women and the Church," in *All the Women Are White, All the Blacks Are Men, but Some of Us Are Brave* (New York: The Feminist Press, 1982), 141, 144.

20. Mary F. Berry, "Repression of Blacks in the South, 1890–1945," in *The Age of Segregation: Race Relations in the South, 1890–1945*, ed. Robert Hawks (Jackson: University Press of Mississippi, 1978), 28–45; Rayford W. Logan, *Betrayal of the Negro* (New York: Collier Books, 1965), 11–12; Henri, *Black Migration*, 51.

Reading 9. Routes to Identity

1. James Clifford, introduction, in *Writing Culture: The Poetics and Politics of Ethnography*, ed. James Clifford and George Marcus (Berkeley: University of California Press, 1986), 100.

2. Katarina Wegar, *Adoption, Identity, and Kinship* (New Haven: Yale University Press, 1997).

3. John Gabriel, *Whitewashed: Racialized Politics and the Media* (London: Routledge, 1998), 1–2.

4. Paul Gilroy, *The Black Atlantic: Modernity and Double Consciousness* (Cambridge: Harvard University Press, 1993).

5. Renato Rosaldo, *Culture and Truth* (Boston: Beacon Press, 1993), 206–7.

6. Julie Watson, "Ordering the Family: Genealogy as Autobiographical Pedigree," in *Getting a Life: Everyday Uses of Autobiography*, ed. Sidone Smith and Julia Watson (Minneapolis: University of Minnesota Press, 1996), 297.

7. Judith Modell, *Kinship with Strangers: Adoption and Interpretations of Kinship in American Culture* (Berkeley: University of California Press, 1994), 144.

8. Wegar, *Adoption, Identity, and Kinship*, 136.

9. These categories of social identity are particularly problematic in the context of transracial adoption. Many of the children of color placed in white families are considered "mixed race" but are defined as black in U.S. society.

10. John L. Caughey, "Gina as Steven: The Social and Cultural Dimensions of a Media Relationship," *Visual Anthropology Review* 10, no. 1 (1994): 129.

11. Rosaldo, *Culture and Truth*, 216.

12. Rosaldo, *Culture and Truth*, 207–8.

13. Mary Helen Washington, "Disturbing the Peace: What Happens to American Studies If You Put African American Studies at the Center," *American Quarterly* 50, no. 1 (1997): 13.

14. Smith and Watson, *Getting a Life*, 11.

15. Maxine Baca Zinn, "Feminist Rethinking from Racial-Ethnic Families," in *Women of Color in U.S. Society*, ed. Maxine Baca Zinn and Bonnie Thornton Dill (Philadelphia: Temple University Press, 1994), 305.

16. Rickie Solinger, *Wake Up, Little Suzie: Single Pregnancy and Race before Roe vs. Wade* (New York: Routledge, 2000).

17. Clifford, *Writing Cultures*, 2.

18. Smith and Watson, *Getting a Life*, 14.

19. Wahneema Lubiano, "Like Being Mugged by a Metaphor: Multiculturalism and State Narratives," in *Mapping Multiculturalism*, ed. Avery Gordon and Christopher Newfield (Minneapolis: University of Minnesota Press, 1996), 65–66.

20. Rosaldo, *Culture and Truth*, 217.

Suggestions for Further Reading

This list of resources is a selection of recent and classic work in life history that presents methodological suggestions and examples of cultural studies of individuals written in a relatively clear, nontechnical format. It is subdivided into the following categories: "Issues in Life History and Culture Theory" includes general works that address the connections between individuals and culture and that deal with issues of interpreting individual lives from a cultural perspective; "Methods in Life History Research" includes strategies for interviewing and participant observation; "Self-Ethnography and Reflexive Culture Studies" includes work on turning life history research back on ourselves, the authors and researchers; "Literary Journalism" includes work in this neighboring genre, which is particularly pertinent to life history research; and "Examples of Life History" includes a selection of traditional and contemporary cultural studies of individual lives, including ethnographies that pay particular attention to individual experience. Further readings are available through the bibliographies in these works and in academic journals such as *Ethos*, *Journal of Narrative and Life History*, *Journal of Contemporary Ethnography*, *Qualitative Inquiry*, and, for literary journalism, *Creative Nonfiction*, and, for documentary portraits, *Double Take*.

Issues in Life History and Culture Theory

Agar, Michael. *Language Shock*. New York: William Morrow, 1994. Informally written interpretation of research in language and culture. Particularly helpful on working with "breakdowns" and "rich points," areas in which the traditions of the researcher and the informant are usefully different.

Berger, Peter. "The Problem of Multiple Realities: Alfred Schutz and Robert Musil." In *Phenomenology and Sociology*, ed. Thomas Luckmann, 343–67. New York: Penguin, 1978. Essay on negotiating multiple cultures drawing on the phenomenology of Alfred Schutz and *The Man without Qualities*, a novel by Robert Musil. Important on the issue of the multiple, imaginal worlds into which all individuals regularly migrate.

Frank, Gelya. "Life History." In *Encyclopedia of Cultural Anthropology*, ed. D. Levinson and M. Ember, 2:705–8. New York: Holt, 1996. Useful overview of the field.

Gergen, Kenneth J. *The Saturated Self: Dilemmas of Identity in Contemporary Life*. New York: Basic Books, 1992. Exploration of the ways in which the contemporary self is saturated by alternative and competing systems of meaning.

Goodenough, Ward H. *Culture, Language, and Society.* Menlo Park CA: Benjamin Cummings, 1981. General review of cultures as knowledge systems. Chapter 6, "Culture, Individual and Society," is a foundational discussion of the ways in which individuals are typically multicultural.

Holland, Dorothy, William Lachicotte, Debra Skinner, and Carole Cain. *Identity and Agency in Cultural Worlds.* Cambridge: Harvard University Press, 1998. Important discussion of identities as systems of cultural self-understanding and issues in their ethnographic investigation.

Langness, L. L., and Gelya Frank. *Lives: An Anthropological Approach to Biography.* Novato CA: Chandler and Sharp, 1981. Review of the history of life history and the methods, ethics, and issues involved.

Linde, Charlotte. *Life Stories: The Creation of Coherence.* New York: Oxford University Press, 1993. Important study of life stories as constructed narratives we are obligated to maintain and present in accounting for who we are. Discusses the role of coherence systems (or cultural traditions) in shaping how people make sense of their past.

Lindholm, Charles. *Culture and Identity: The History, Theory, and Practice of Psychological Anthropology.* New York: McGraw Hill, 2001. This account of psychological anthropology provides cross-cultural, comparative perspectives on the ways in which culture influences human lives. Chapter 8 provides an important exploration of hybridity and the decentered self.

Mathews, Gordon. *What Makes Life Worth Living? How Japanese and Americans Make Sense of Their Worlds.* Berkeley: University of California Press, 1996. Addresses the fundamental issue of how people find importance and meaning in their lives. Also interesting in comparing a series of pairs of similarly situated individuals (such as urban female lawyers) in two very different cultures, U.S. and Japanese.

Shore, Bradd. *Culture in Mind: Cognition, Culture, and the Problem of Meaning.* New York: Oxford University Press, 1996. Comprehensive review of contemporary culture theory that looks carefully at the role of cultural models in individual thought and experience.

Smith, Sidone, and Julia Watson, eds. *Getting a Life: Everyday Uses of Autobiography.* Minneapolis: University of Minnesota Press, 1996. Anthology of readings on the many contemporary uses of autobiographical storytelling, including self-disclosure narratives in media such as TV talk shows.

Weber, Lyn. *Understanding Race, Class, Gender, and Sexuality.* New York: McGraw Hill, 2001. Offers a clear and useful framework for considering how the intersecting issues of race, class, gender, and sexuality affect individual lives.

Methods in Life History Research

Cole, Ardra, and J. Gary Knowles, eds. *Lives in Context: The Art of Life History Research.* Walnut Creek CA: AltaMira, 2001. A useful guide to life history research that emphasizes reflexive issues, empathy, and artistic approaches. Includes selections from novice researchers reflecting on the challenges they faced in their life history projects.

Coles, Robert. *The Documentary Tradition*. New York: Oxford University Press, 1997. Reflections on the philosophical, literary, and moral issues involved in doing documentary research.

Emerson, Robert, Rachel Fretz, and Linda Shaw. *Writing Ethnographic Fieldnotes*. Chicago: University of Chicago Press, 1995. Broader than the title suggests, this is a guide to qualitative research and its encodement into writing. It is particularly strong on participant observation as a way of getting at "members' meanings."

Gluck, Sandra, and Daphne Patai, eds. *Women's Words: The feminist Practice of Oral History*. New York: Routledge, 1991. A series of essays on using feminist perspectives in oral history, ethnography, and life history. Anderson and Jack's essay on interviewing is particularly helpful.

LeCompte, Margaret, Jean J. Schensul, Margaret R. Weeks, and Merrill Singer. *Researcher Roles and Research Partnerships* (Walnut Creek CA: AltaMira, 1999). Part of a seven-volume series on ethnographic methods, this book discusses the kinds of multiple cultural obligations and roles that field research imposes on the ethnographer as he or she negotiates different social worlds. Also provides a discussion of ethics including federal regulations and university Institutional Review Board (IRB) guidelines.

Sommer, Barbara W., and Mary Kay Quinlan. *The Oral History Manual*. Walnut Creek CA: AltaMira, 2002. This systematic guide to oral history research includes helpful chapters on ethical issues and interviewing.

Spradley, James. *The Ethnographic Interview*. New York: Holt, Rinehart and Winston, 1979. Still one of the best guides to the kind of cultural interviewing suggested here. Oriented to beginning students who are interviewing a single individual about a particular cultural tradition, it includes very clear practical suggestions on interviewing, ethics, note keeping, and writing.

Watson, Lawrence C., and Maria-Barbara Watson-Franke. *Interpreting Life Histories*. New Brunswick NJ: Rutgers University Press, 1985. A classic overview of life history research and interpretation with particular emphasis on attending to insider meanings. Includes guidelines for investigating the multiple social and cultural contexts of a life and offers suggestions for using hermeneutics, phenomenology, and existentialism in life history interpretation.

Self-Ethnography and Reflexive Culture Studies

Barrington, Judith. *Writing the Memoir: From Truth to Art*. Portland: Eighth Mountain Press, 1997). This how-to guide on writing memoir offers a variety of suggestions that are useful for the reflexive dimensions of life history research.

Behar, Ruth. *The Vulnerable Observer*. Boston: Beacon Press, 1996. In chapter 1, the title essay, Behar provides a very good overview of issues in reflexive ethnography. She argues that ethnography is always partly a product of the intellectual and emotional orientations we bring to our research, and she persuasively suggests reasons for reflecting on and reporting aspects of this in a life history portrait.

Bromley, David G., and Lewis F. Carter, eds. *Toward Reflexive Ethnography: Participating, Observing, Narrating*. Oxford: Elsevier Science, 2001. Ten personal accounts of fieldwork by ethnographers working with religious groups marginal to the American mainstream. Includes attention to personal reactions to events and the impact of the research on the ethnographer as a person.

Caughey, John L. "How to Teach Self Ethnography." In *Strategies for Teaching Anthropology*, ed. Patricia Rice and David McCurdy, 174–80. Upper Saddle River NJ: Prentice Hall, 2002. Argues for the importance of using self-ethnography in cultural studies and describes methods for doing so.

Davies, Charlotte Aull. *Reflexive Ethnography: A Guide to Researching Selves and Others*. New York: Routledge, 1999. Proposes a model of fieldwork that steers between postmodern and traditional forms of ethnography, seeking to develop an approach that uses a self-reflexive perspective while still oriented to researching the constructions of the subject.

Marcus, George. "On Ideologies of Reflexivity in Contemporary Efforts to Remake the Human Sciences." In *Ethnography through Thick and Thin*, 181–202. Princeton: Princeton University Press, 1998. Drawing on the work of Bourdieu and Haraway, Marcus offers a critical evaluation of reflexive work in feminism and anthropology.

Markham, Annette N. *Life On Line: Researching Real Experience in Virtual Space*. Walnut Creek CA: AltaMira, 1998. This study of online interactions is both an interesting example of reflexive ethnography and a set of arguments for doing it.

O'Hearn, Claudine Chiawe, ed. *Half and Half: Writers on Growing Up Biracial and Bicultural*. New York: Pantheon, 1998. A collection of nineteen autobiographical essays by bicultural and/or biracial individuals on the difficulties of negotiating such backgrounds. The essays regularly complicate the book's premise by suggesting that the authors are "multi-" rather than merely "bi-" cultural.

Ruby, Jay, and Barbara Myerhoff, eds. *A Crack in the Mirror: Reflexive Perspectives in Anthropology*. Philadelphia: University of Pennsylvania Press, 1982. A series of classic essays by anthropologists such as Victor Turner, Barbara Myerhoff, Dan Rose, and Paul Rabinow on the reflexive dimensions of anthropology.

Literary Journalism

Agar, Michael. "Literary Journalism as Ethnography." In *Representations in Ethnography*, ed. John Van Maanen, 112–29. Thousand Oaks CA: Sage, 1995. An ethnographer's assessment of literary journalism and its attempt to use literary devices such as scenes, character development, plot, authorial presence, and interior monologue to describe actual lives. Raises the question of the extent to which the authors are willing to bend empirical truth to the service of artistic values.

Agee, James, and Walker Evans. *Let Us Now Praise Famous Men: Three Tenant Families*. Boston: Houghton Mifflin, 1941. Classic, powerful, and beautifully written portrait of the individuals in three southern tenant families during the depression. Presented as an experiment in the literary "description of the actual," the book includes a searching meditation on the moral problems of this kind of study and a sensitive account of Agee's connection with those whom he and Walker Evans studied.

Conover, Ted. *Newjack: Guarding Sing Sing*. New York: Random House, 2000. An effective and disturbing account of prison life and the role of the prison guard within this world. Denied journalistic access to prisons, Conover was accepted as a corrections office trainee, went through the training program, and became a guard at New York's Sing Sing prison. An excellent example of using a reflexive, first-person, participant-observation narrative to open up a window on a closed social world.

Fadiman, Anne. *The Spirit Catches You and You Fall Down*. New York: Noonday Press, 1997. Explores the lives and interactions of individuals caught up in a clash between the medical beliefs of Hmong immigrants and those of American medical practitioners in California.

Franklin, J. *Writing for Story*. New York, Plume, 1994. Manual on the craft of writing literary journalism by a two-time Pulitzer Prize winner.

Harrington, Walt. *At the Heart of It: Ordinary People, Extraordinary Lives*. Columbia: University of Missouri Press, 1996. Portraits of individual American lives.

————. *Intimate Journalism: The Art and Craft of Reporting Everyday Life*. Thousand Oaks CA: Sage, 1997. Fifteen examples of literary journalism from a range of contemporary practitioners. Each article is followed by an afterword in which the author discusses how he or she investigated, conceptualized, and wrote the account.

————. "What Journalism Can Offer Ethnography." *Qualitative Inquiry* 9, no. 1 (2003): 90–104. Clear and useful argument for the importance of bringing certain journalistic values and practices into life history.

Maclean, Norman. *Young Men and Fire*. Chicago: University of Chicago Press, 1992. Beautifully written account of the author's quest to understand the 1949 Mann Gulch fire in Montana, which took the lives of twelve smoke jumpers. His investigation, which works on scientific, literary, and philosophical levels, includes biographical explorations of several of the key figures and how their orientations and attitudes contributed to the unfolding of the tragedy and its subsequent interpretation.

Root, Robert L., and Michael Steinberg. *The Fourth Genre: Contemporary Writers of/on Creative Nonfiction*. 2nd ed. New York: Longman, 2002. This useful anthology considers personal essays, memoir, academic cultural criticism, and literary journalism. Part 1 offers examples, and part 2 discusses the craft of writing nonfiction.

Sims, Norman, and Mark Kramer. *Literary Journalism: A New Collection of the Best American Nonfiction*. New York: Ballantine, 1995. An anthology of work by fifteen contemporary literary journalists, including John Mcphee, Tracy Kidder, Susan Orlean, and Ted Conover.

Wolfe, Tom, ed. *The New Journalism* (New York: Harper and Row, 1973). American Studies PhD and novelist Tom Wolfe, who wrote an extravagant series of literary journalistic accounts, also edited this still interesting collection of early literary journalism, which includes essays by Hunter Thompson, Joan Didion, and Terry Southern. The introduction discusses ways of adapting literary techniques such as scene-by-scene construction, dialogue, and point of view in journalistic and life history writing.

Examples of Life History

Angrosino, Michael V. *Opportunity House: Ethnographic Stories of Mental Retardation*. Walnut Creek CA: AltaMira, 1998. This study includes the experimental use of fiction in telling the life stories of inhabitants of a residence for mentally retarded adults.

Bateson, Mary Catherine. *Composing a Life*. New York: Penguin, 1989. Discusses the issues of composing and improvising one's life in the shifting multiple cultural contexts of contemporary American life and illustrates with five women's lives.

Brown, Karen McCarthy. *Mama Lola: A Voudou Priestess in Brooklyn*. Berkeley: University of California Press, 1991. Vivid experimental account of the friendship between the ethnographer-author and Alourdes, a voudou priestess from Haiti who is practicing her craft in New York City.

Caughey, John L. "Gina as Steven: The Social and Cultural Dimensions of a Media Relationship." *Visual Anthropology Review* 10, no. 1 (1994): 126–35. Explores how an individual's media consumption can be connected to her multiple cultural traditions through a study of the psychotherapist Gina's interest in the martial arts actor Steven Segal.

Clark-Lewis, Elizabeth. *Living In, Living Out: African American Domestics in Washington, D.C., 1910–1940*. Washington DC: Smithsonian Institution Press, 1994. Drawing on interviews with eighty-one African American women who migrated from the culture of the rural South to take up roles as domestic servants in the households of wealthy white families in Washington DC, this study provides moving portraits of individual women and their struggles to increase their autonomy and freedom.

Desjarlais, Robert. *Shelter Blues: Sanity and Selfhood among the Homeless*. Philadelphia: University of Pennsylvania Press, 1997. Ethnographic study of homeless and mentally ill individuals associated with a Boston shelter. Gives close attention to individual experience.

Frank, Gelya. *Venus on Wheels: Two Decades of Dialogue on Disability, Biography, and Being Female in America*. Berkeley: University of California Press, 2000. Brings a sophisticated, cultural approach to the study of disability in the lives of the subject and the author.

Freidenberg, Judith. *Growing Old in El Barrio*. New York: New York University Press, 2000. Combining attention to social context and personal experience, Freidenberg uses life history to explore patterns of aging experienced by Latina women in Harlem.

Harper, Douglas. *Good Company*. Chicago: University of Chicago Press, 1982. An intensive life history of Carl, a freight-train-riding hobo who educates the sociologist-author on the ways of the road.

Lipsitz, George. *A Life in the Struggle: Ivory Perry and the Culture of Opposition*. Philadelphia: Temple University Press, 1988. This life history of Ivory Perry, an African American activist who participated in the civil rights movement and other cultural change efforts, provides an example of the mind-set of a grassroots activist. It is also interesting for the effort Lipsitz makes to verify Perry's stories through documentary sources.

Myerhoff, Barbara. *Number Our Days*. New York: Simon and Schuster, 1978. Beautifully written portrait of the lives of elderly Jewish immigrants in Venice, California. Includes vivid portraits of these individuals and the ways they balance their cultural traditions.

O'Brien, Sharon. *The Family Silver: A Memoir of Depression and Inheritance*. Chicago: University of Chicago Press, 2004. A portrait of individual family lives, a memoir, and an effective and compelling cultural exploration of depression in an Irish American family.

Patton, Sandra. *Birth Marks: Transracial Adoption in Contemporary America*. New York: New York University Press, 2000. Drawing on interviews with twenty-one African American or biracial individuals who were adopted by and grew up in white families, this study uses life history to carefully explore fundamental questions about race and the cultural construction of American identities.

Rogovin, Milton, and Michael Frisch. *Portraits in Steel*. Ithaca NY: Cornell University

Press, 1993. An important example of collaboration between a photographer and an oral historian. The book combines Frisch's oral history interviews with Rogovin's photographs of a dozen individuals, picturing them in work roles and family roles, who once worked in the steel mills of Buffalo, New York.

Sacks, Oliver. *An Anthropologist on Mars: Seven Paradoxical Tales.* New York: Knopf, 1995. Portraits of seven individuals with neuropsychological deficits and the paradoxes of their social lives.

Turner, Sugar, and Tracy Ehlers. *Sugar's Life in the Hood: The Story of a Former Welfare Mother.* Austin: University of Texas, 2000. Account of the life history collaboration of an African American welfare mother and a white middle-class academic researcher.

Weber, Lyn, and Heather Dillaway. *Understanding Race, Class, Gender, and Sexuality: Case Studies.* New York: McGraw-Hill, 2002. Offers eight case studies of individuals in social situations where issues of difference intersect.

Wolcott, Harry F. *Sneaky Kid and Its Aftermath.* Walnut Creek CA: AltaMira, 2002. Account of the life history the author wrote about a mentally disturbed school dropout, the intimate relationship they shared, the violence that followed, and the legal and ethical aftermath.

Contributors

Ruth Behar is a professor of anthropology at the University of Michigan in Ann Arbor and author of *The Vulnerable Observer* and *Translated Woman*.

John L. Caughey is a professor of American studies at the University of Maryland, College Park, and the author of *Imaginary Social Worlds*.

Elizabeth Clark-Lewis is a professor of public history at Howard University and author of *Living In, Living Out*.

Douglas Harper is a professor of sociology at Duquesne University and author of *Good Company*.

Melissa Landsman is working in Las Vegas and considering graduate school in English literature.

Barbara Myerhoff was a professor of anthropology at the University of California in Los Angeles. She is the author of *Number Our Days*.

Sandra Patton-Imani is an assistant professor of culture and society at Drake University and author of *Birth Marks*.

Lila Shah is working in advertising. She wrote her contribution to this volume as an undergraduate at SUNY Binghamton.

Jenny Thompson is a public historian and an independent scholar who has taught history and American studies at the University of Maryland and Roosevelt University in Chicago. She is the author of *War Games: Inside the World of Twentieth-Century War Reenactors*.

Joshua C. Woodfork is an assistant professor of American studies at Skidmore College.

Index